Language and the African America

How do children acquire African American English? How do they develop the specific language patterns of their communities? Drawing on spontaneous speech samples and data from structured elicitation tasks, this book explains the developmental trends in the children's language. It examines topics such as the development of tense–aspect marking, negation, and question formation, and addresses the link between intonational patterns and meaning. Lisa J. Green shows the impact that community input has on children's development of variation in the production of certain constructions such as possessive *–s*, third person singular verbal *–s*, and forms of copula and auxiliary *BE*. She discusses the implications that the linguistic description has for practical applications, such as developing instructional materials for children in the early stages of their education.

Lisa J. Green is Professor of Linguistics and the founding Director of the Center for the Study of African American Language at the University of Massachusetts. Her previous publications include *African American English: A Linguistic Introduction* (Cambridge, 2002).

Language and the African American Child

Lisa J. Green

CAMBRIDGE UNIVERSITY PRESS
Cambridge, New York, Melbourne, Madrid, Cape Town, Singapore,
São Paulo, Delhi, Dubai, Tokyo, Mexico City

Cambridge University Press
The Edinburgh Building, Cambridge CB2 8RU, UK

Published in the United States of America by
Cambridge University Press, New York

www.cambridge.org
Information on this title: www.cambridge.org/9780521618175

First published 2011

Printed in the United Kingdom at the University Press, Cambridge

A catalog record for this publication is available from the British Library

Library of Congress Cataloging in Publication data
Green, Lisa J., 1963–
    Language and the African American child / Lisa J. Green.
        p.   cm.
    Includes bibliographical references and index.
    ISBN 978-0-521-85309-5 (hardback) – ISBN 978-0-521-61817-5 (paperback)
    1. Black English–Phonology.   2. English language–Dialects–United States.
    3. Sociolinguistics–United States.   I. Title.
    PE3102.N42.G74 2010
    427'.97308996073–dc22
    2010035583

ISBN 978-0-521-85309-5 Hardback
ISBN 978-0-521-61817-5 Paperback

In memory of my father

Charles Joseph Green

1926–2006

Contents

Figures

Tables

Foreword

When a pre-eminent scholar in theoretical linguistics turns her hand to the topic of child language, one can expect novel insights and expository innovation. Lisa J. Green has brought her incomparable knowledge of African American English to bear upon conversations with black children. Many of these exchanges have emerged from her seminal experimental work, but, with a touch of genius, she elucidates the intricate grammatical tapestry behind ordinary conversations. She preserves our sense of real children as she exposes how they bring together elliptical discourse, intonation, and subtle semantic implications when they just answer an ordinary question or make a heartfelt assertion.

Thus she is able to illustrate the most tantalizing features of AAE with careful situation-grounded discussions: aspect, tense, negation, and question formation. Her explorations of and sensitivity to verbatim and elliptical meanings constitute an advance in acquisition research as well. We learn a great deal from this kind of microscopic dissection of real conversations that cannot be gleaned from statistical summaries of naturalistic data or cross-sectional experimental work. Children's own explanations reveal much more about their grammars than first language researchers have thus far realized.

The result is a linguistic tour de force at once making the reader eager to meet these children and eager to understand the structure behind the language they use. Her work here is informed by her earlier landmark book on African American English, but in a sense this book is a good prelude to that one. A number of sophisticated theoretical ideas about the theory of concord, question formation, and tense are skillfully embedded in her observations about what children do.

Green also takes an important leap into the world of practical application, a world so complicated and interwoven with social attitudes that most researchers shy away in uncertainty. She advocates the D.I.R.E.C.T. Model, which has the major goal of teaching students to use the English variety of the marketplace, that is, MAE, alongside their own native variety by capturing the nuances in the mainstream dialect that they are accustomed to expressing in their native variety.

It has been my belief for a quarter century that understanding AAE is part of what it should mean to be an American citizen. In Canada, a bilingual country (as in many other such countries), all children are obliged to learn French as well as English, even though some parts of Canada are thousands of miles from where French is spoken. In America 20 million people, found in every state, speak varieties of AAE. It is often at the advanced edge of the direction of the mainstream dialect. For instance, mainstream English has lost most of its inflections – we no longer say "thou singest," and it is only a matter of time before the last inflection on the third person disappears (he runs => he run), but this step has already been taken in AAE. (See Roeper (2007) for discussion.) In addition, popular songs and TV incorporate many expressions of AAE. Nevertheless the most sophisticated aspects of AAE are more challenging and need to be treated with the care and rigor of teaching a foreign language, though of course it is much closer than a real foreign language. Therefore, I think all American citizens should be taught the contrasts and differences between dialects and I believe that a one- or two-month high school course could accomplish this very well. Thus one can argue that some version of the D.I.R.E.C.T. program should be in everyone's curriculum.

The ultimate goal should be to fight language prejudice as we fight race prejudice. While teaching the "cash" language or "standard" English should be advocated, we need to be aware that actually eliminating all traces of dialect or origin is very difficult to do. I, for instance, say /rum/ for /room/ and /ruf/ for /roof/ reflecting my middlewest upbringing. Thirty years in Massachusetts has not changed this, nor do I wish to change it. If we use tiny pronunciation differences as a basis of judgment, even if it is linked to a visceral response, there is no way to educate everyone so carefully that these telltale signs do not arise. The only approach is to educate people not to be judgmental and prejudiced against them. I would much rather see a society where we each wear these dialect features as a badge of individuality rather than a source of social differentiation. It is not reasonable to expect that education in different dialects can eliminate dialect-traces even when people ostensibly are able to "code-switch."

Programs such as D.I.R.E.C.T. can be naturally paired with other efforts to articulate the legitimacy of AAE in pedagogical language policy and classroom teacher programs. One example is the Diagnostic Evaluation of Language Variation, which has been developed by Harry Seymour, Jill de Villiers and me, with Lisa J. Green's work in the background.

The test seeks to identify important kinds of language disorders beyond the usual realm of inflection – where dialect often interferes – for instance in the realm of quantification. Children with disorders do not understand that a sentence such as *who bought what* refers to sets of *whos* and *whats*, not just one *who* and one *what*. This deficit has nothing to do with a particular dialect and is currently being studied in languages all over Europe. Thus we have to avoid having dialect stand in the way of identifying other linguistic problems that are far deeper than dialect differences. An analogy may help: differences in vision lead to the prescription of individually crafted glasses. Color-blindness or astigmatism is a problem of a different order which needs a different approach.

And finally Green addresses the question of code-switching with an observation of fundamental importance: it is not clear how much of the MAE dialect and AAE dialect can be considered part of one big English grammar where dialect variations can be represented in a single grammar (see Green and Roeper (2007)). Thus in many respects the special features of auxiliaries (*be, done, BIN*) can all occupy a position in the word order of a sentence. For instance, a sentence that I heard at the airport from an airline person ran "I could have done BIN checked you in already"; that is compatible with MAE, which gets most but not all of the same meaning with the expression "I could have checked you in already" but the "done BIN" emphasizes that it would have happened significantly earlier. It should be noted that the use of this dialect-laden sentence did not disqualify him from his job nor impair our communication.

Let me make a foray into the substance of a couple of Green's concerns. As an able teacher, she brings a light touch to guiding the reader through the options that a child has, for instance, in using negative concord. The negative system has a number of subtleties to integrate for the AAE dialect child as it does for the MAE dialect child. Often differences look to be parallel: *some* => *any* after negation in mainstream English, but *some* => *none* in AAE:

(a)   Mainstream and African American English: I have some
(b)   MAE: I don't have any
(c)   AAE: I don't have none.

But the acquisition path for negation in both MAE and AAE is much more complex – leading beyond even the examples that Green discusses. Neither kind of acquisition happens instantly but the deviations in the acquisition path can be quite intricate. Consider Labov's famous example from teenagers:

"it ain't no cat can't get in no chicken coop"

First in the example above the meaning that many MAE speakers obtain is: every cat can get in the chicken coop, but for (one sub-dialect of) AAE it means: no cat can get in any chicken coop where negative concord crosses a sentence boundary [S1 ain't no cat [S2 (that) can't get in ...]].

Negative concord does not cross the sentence boundary in MAE dialect, hence it is easily misunderstood. It resembles the case where Green finds that children allow negation across a noun phrase boundary:

he didn't see the dog with no hair

which is taken by MAE dialect speakers to mean that the dog has no hair, but some of the children allow the negative meaning to cross into the noun phrase and therefore understand the second *no* as just an echo of the first, without a semantic shift: didn't see the dog with hair.

This looks like a simple contrast, but the MAE dialect is not consistent on this point because the MAE dialect seems to allow exceptions just like AAE, but elsewhere:

(a)   he didn't feed his dog because someone told him to
(b)   he didn't feed his dog because <u>anyone</u> told him to

where (a) is ambiguous about whether he did or did not feed his dog, and (b) means he didn't feed his dog. The *anyone* responds to the higher <u>negation</u> in the first sentence since we cannot say:

*he fed his dog because anyone told him to

although its meaning is not simply negative. The important point is that here the negation is crossing a sentence boundary in MAE, so now the MAE dialect appears to be inconsistent where AAE is consistent.

This dialect question seen across the country is still more complex. In Iowa it is acceptable to say:

anybody can't do that

where it means 'nobody can do that'. Here the usual rule that a verbal negative can mark a nominal negative, but not the reverse, does not hold.

The mature speaker of these dialects ultimately gets it all right, but linguistic theory has not yet found a natural way to state exactly how and when these boundaries are respected for adults, nor do we have more than a rudimentary grasp of the acquisition path for children. The challenge is most clearly seen in the AAE examples, but in many respects goes to the heart of the concept of "barriers" in linguistic theory.

As she explores the pragmatic and human background of these exchanges, Green zeroes in on how questions in the AAE dialect deviate from mainstream English:

(a) why you don't like it
(b) they have some Playstations
(c) what else we gon do

Everything seems to be the same, but there is no inversion of subject and verb. However, she notes that the intonation of subject–verb inversion in mainstream English questions is carried over to uninverted structures, and then notes that the final intonational section fails to rise in AAE as it does in mainstream English for (b). We are left with an important mystery: how exactly does this novel form of question intonation work? How do children get it so quickly? Does it convey a meaning unlike any meaning in mainstream English? We might go further and ask: is there perhaps a presupposition present that resembles the difference between tag question and a non-tag question in mainstream English:

Can you go outside
You can go outside, can't you

Yet, although with a different acquisition path, AAE also has tag-questions. So now we might ask: is there a unique kind of question being asked here? It is certainly not unique in its information structure – its relation to truth or falsity in the world – but it might be unique in the interpersonal assumptions that it carries about what knowledge the hearer shares.

This delivers us to the question that lies behind our intuitive sense of dialect: something unusual is actually conveyed in the subtle structure of one dialect that is not easily translated into another dialect. Some of that impression is due to our awareness of social context. Other aspects of it reflect an awareness of real, but subtle, differences in meaning not directly obtainable in another dialect. Thus the habitual *be* carries the notion of habituality in a way that is different from adding the adverb habitually to the end of a sentence. That is what we intuitively seek to appreciate, and that is why we need Lisa J. Green's work and its pedagogical extensions to understand it.

One virtue of Green's book is that we come to grasp how much of theoretical linguistics remains in its infancy – much is still in the form of descriptions whose role in theory and acquisition remains a challenge. The informality of style found in this book, coupled with rigorous knowledge and a light conversational approach, makes it engaging in a way that should inspire students and scholars to explore these questions. They are questions that can be explored by both PhD students and middle-schoolers alike. This book, along with work by Maya Honda and Wayne O'Neil (2007), as well as a popular book of mine (Roeper 2007), seeks to make us all engaged in linguistics, just as other forms of social progress require knowledgeable commitments and efforts from us all.

Tom Roeper

Preface

First and foremost descriptions of language used by 3-, 4-, and 5-year-old developing African American English (AAE)-speaking children give us some insight into their general patterns and norms of language use. Descriptions such as those in this book serve as a starting point for presenting child AAE as the native variety of some children that they acquire and develop systematically in stages. Owing to ever-present discussions about race, ethnicity, and education, questions about language use and child AAE are often raised in the context of the quest to overcome barriers to academic success. To what extent do differences between AAE and mainstream American English (MAE) impede academic success? This is an important question and considerable focus has been placed on different angles from which the topic is addressed. It is my hope that the information in this book will have practical application in a number of areas and disciplines related to linguistics and that it might be useful not only in showing how the language of 3-, 4-, and 5-year-old developing AAE-speaking children differs from that of their peers from other speech communities but also how it is similar to their peers' language. In trying to learn more about developing-child AAE, it is important to describe it in its own right; however, given what we know about inherent variability in adult AAE, we raise the question about developmental patterns of variation in child AAE, also.

This book can be used in linguistics and general education courses that address properties of developmental and adult AAE and in general courses about early language use in different speech communities. It can also be used in courses designed to introduce teachers, early childhood specialists, and speech pathologists to language patterns in the speech of some African American children.

The language samples and linguistic description are geared toward illustrating what is meant by systematic language use and patterns in development. In addition the data collected from scenarios and elicitation tasks should also be useful in discussions about the developmental paths child AAE speakers take in using certain constructions.

I started this project on child AAE when I was a member of the faculty in the Linguistics Department at The University of Texas at Austin, and the faculty, students, and staff helped me in significant ways. The late Carlota Smith gave me valuable feedback on scenarios and elicitation tasks, especially those relating to tense and aspect. Graduate students Qiuana Lopez, Rebecca Quigley, Nikki Seifert, Jessica White-Sustaíta, and Kendra Williams helped with transcriptions, data analysis, and story creation and sketches. What was most rewarding for me was that they also became interested enough in the child data to engage in their own research projects on various topics such as tense–aspect properties of past marking and question formation. I gratefully acknowledge the assistance of Shadetra Rouwtt, an undergraduate at The University of Texas Austin. I have also received assistance from faculty, students, and staff in the Department of Linguistics at the University of Massachusetts Amherst. Graduate students Tracy Conner, Noah Constant, and Helen Stickney assisted with the data. Minta Elsman's work on the index was indispensable. Dinah Gorelik's assistance and organization were right on time. I am very grateful for Barbara Pearson's help along the way. It was also my good fortune to be able to talk with Tom Roeper about many different issues related to child language and to receive very useful feedback from the reviewers. I understand that many issues in developing child AAE are still unfolding, and I am grateful for all of the feedback that is so very crucial in helping me to take these beginning steps. I am so fortunate to have benefited from Andre Jones's talent and willingness to work on the illustrations for this project. I also wish to thank Sarah Green and Andrew Winnard at Cambridge University Press, for their help in the process of moving this project along. Part of the research for this project was funded by National Science Foundation grant BCS-0003158 and research support from the University of Massachusetts. I also express my thanks to Matt Davies, Out of House Publishing Solutions, for his assistance and patience in answering my questions. I am very grateful for being on the receiving end of Lorraine Slipper's copy-editing services. I am eternally grateful to Mrs. Carolyn Simon and the staff and parents at the Jeff Davis Parish child development centers. I am especially grateful to the many children whose voices are represented in this book.

My family has always been and continues to be a source of strength for me. My mother, Ramona Green, still has the gift of encouraging me. She is great! My niece, Haley, has played such an important role in my life in her own special way. I was certain that she would stop calling me as she got older and found more interesting things to occupy her time, but at eleven, she still calls me just about every day, as she has done since she was five years old. I appreciate all that my husband Vincent Jackson does for me. Sometimes I think he can do everything.

Note on the text

Throughout this book mainstream American English (MAE) glosses or African American English (AAE) sentence correspondences are indicated in single quotes (″).

1 Child AAE: an introductory overview of the data and context

LJG: Now I'm gonna read a story and you are gonna have to tell it
*   back to me. You think you can do it?*
Dawn: Yes mam.
LJG: I know you can. You can do everything.
Dawn: I'm smart.

Developing African American English (AAE)-speaking children are no exception. Like other children who are acquiring language, they show ingenuity as they are acquiring AAE. Early on they show signs of using specialized words to indicate that an event is located in the distant past and that an event occurs regularly. They also make subtle distinctions in the meaning and use of *is* and *be* that are not made by speakers of other varieties of American English. That is, they make a distinction between the following two sentences that is often missed by speakers of other varieties of American English:

- He is eating chocolate.
- He be eating chocolate.

In addition they acquire *had* + VERB (e.g., *had jumped*) sequences early on and use them in simple past contexts, and they do not seem to confuse that *had* with the past perfect *had* that is acquired later. They are mastering a complex system and learning to make subtle differences between words and constructions that may or may not be made in other varieties of American English.

I would like to state what may or may not be obvious at the outset. It has become the norm, for reasons I will address in Chapter 2, to characterize AAE as being maximally different from mainstream American English (MAE), and by association child AAE is viewed in the same light. There are some stark contrasts between the two varieties, subtle differences and similarities, and considerable overlap, all of which will be reflected in the data presented in this book. Indeed some language patterns that will be addressed in the chapters of this book certainly occur in the speech of children from other language, dialect, and socioeconomic backgrounds.

More research has been conducted on AAE than on any other variety of American English; however, research on developmental patterns in child AAE makes up a small percentage of that body of literature. I believe that one of the major reasons that developmental AAE or the acquisition of AAE was not a major focus of the linguistic research on AAE in the 1960s, during the first significant wave of work on the variety, is that a goal of the pioneering research was to show that AAE was logical and not a reflection of cultural deficit or linguistic deficiency. Specifically, the aim, then, was to show that AAE was rule-governed, and speakers who had already acquired it were adhering to rules in using the language system. A second reason that developmental AAE was not a major topic in the first wave of AAE research was that given the approach to the study of the variety, it was important to focus on the group that appeared to represent the "most vernacular" form or, in a sense, the most developed form of AAE that was least influenced by the standard or MAE. That group seemed to be adolescents, teens, and adults – not young children.

However, starting in the 1970s, questions about the development and use of AAE by children began to be addressed, especially in relation to patterns and variation that had already been observed in adolescent and adult AAE. Much of that early research, although limited, was primarily in the domain of communication sciences and disorders, and the trend has continued such that a majority of research on developmental patterns in child AAE is from the perspective of that discipline. The contributions made by researchers A. Fay Vaughn-Cooke and Ida Stockman were groundbreaking, especially in the area of frameworks for analyzing developing AAE-speaking children's language, and continue to serve as the foundation and impetus for work on child AAE, especially in the area of semantic categories and morphological forms (e.g., Stockman and Vaughn-Cooke 1982). The history of interest in child AAE in communication sciences and disorders is due, in part, to the questions about the line of demarcation between legitimate dialectal patterns and disorders. Not understanding where the line should be drawn can lead to misclassification of normally developing AAE speakers as having speech and language disorders because their language reflects properties that are not the norm for standard varieties of American English. On the other hand, speakers may be misclassified as not having disorders in the development of AAE when they actually do because without clear descriptions of AAE patterns, it is possible to lump all speech patterns that are not in line with the standard variety into the AAE category, without recognizing that not all patterns may qualify as AAE. Researchers in communication sciences and disorders are faced with the task of developing tools that can fairly assess language of children acquiring AAE, tools that do not automatically identify it as pathological (Stockman 2007; Vaughn-Cooke 2007). Along these same lines, researchers in communication sciences have to think in general about assessment tools that can be used for MAE, AAE, and speakers of other varieties of English alike, without penalizing any group of speakers for using language that is consistent with patterns of their speech communities. Some significant strides have been made in this domain, especially with the development of the Diagnostic Evaluation of Language Variation Screening and Norm-Referenced tests (DELV) (Seymour, Roeper, and J. de Villiers, with contributions by P. A. de Villiers 2003). The DELV is significant in that it is not an assessment tool only for AAE-speaking children; it can be used as a diagnostic test for all American English speakers, MAE-speaking as well as non-MAE-speaking. A major advantage is that the assessment tool will not overidentify non-MAE-speaking children as having speech disorders because, unlike some of its predecessors, its focus is on commonalities shared among English speakers, not their differences. That focus alone is an innovative approach, but there are other features of the DELV that distinguish it from other assessment tools. For instance, it is based on research in the areas of universal grammar, descriptions of patterns in AAE and in other dialects within theoretical linguistics frameworks, and specific language impairment cross-linguistically (Seymour, Roeper, and J. de Villiers, with contributions by P. A. de Villiers 2005).

Research on child AAE, from the 1970s to the present, can be divided into six major categories:

1. Studies on morphological forms (e.g., Steffensen 1974; Stokes 1976; Cole 1980; Kovac 1980; Wyatt 1991, 1996; Oetting and McDonald 2001)

2. Meaning and use of words and phrases (e.g., Stockman and Vaughn-Cooke 1986, 1992; Ross, Oetting, and Stapleton 2004; Horton-Ikard and Weismar 2007)

3. Comprehension and development (e.g., Craig, Washington, and Thompson-Porter (1998); Jackson (1998); Jackson and Green (2005); Horton-Ikard and Weisman (2005); de Villiers and Johnson (2007))

4. Syntax and semantics (or linguistic structure and meaning associated with structure) (e.g., Stokes 1976; Benedicto, Abdulkarim, Garrett, Johnson, and Seymour 1998; Coles-White 2004; Green and Roeper 2007; de Villiers, de Villiers, and Roeper in press)

5. Assessment (e.g., Seymour, Bland-Stewart, and Green 1998, Seymour 2004; Pruitt and Oetting 2009; Stockman 2010)

6. Literacy (e.g., Charity, Scarborough, and Griffin 2004; Connor and Craig 2006; Craig and Washington 2006)

The sources above do not take the place of a bibliography on child AAE, but they do serve as a sample of the type of work that has been done in this area over the years. The research is separated into discrete categories; however, it is possible to cross list the references, such that the sources may be associated with more than one area. For instance, there is a separate assessment category, but the research in most of these areas has some type of assessment component. Take, for example, research by Oetting (and colleagues) represented in the categories, which also discusses AAE in the context of comparison of some morphological features in AAE to those used by children with specific language impairment. Research in these areas under-scores the importance of shining the light on the types of problems that could arise in the absence of normative data on developing child AAE and on the consequences of using developmental MAE as the yardstick for the language of developing AAE speakers. Seymour, Bland-Stewart, and Green (1998) highlight the importance of con-sidering non-contrastive features, or those that are shared between AAE and MAE, in assessment of disorders in AAE, especially given that the differences were greater in the use of non-contrastive fea-tures between normally developing AAE and AAE with disorders than the differences in the use of contrastive features, or those asso-ciated with AAE, between the two groups.

Some of the earliest studies on child AAE were on morpho-logical forms that included suffixes such as plural (–s) and its forms, possessive (–'s), and tense and agreement (third person singular –s) marking and the extent to which they appear in the speech of devel-oping AAE speakers (e.g., Steffensen 1974; Stokes 1976; Cole 1980; Kovac 1980). The production of such forms has continued to be an area of research in the study of child AAE. In her work on the copula in the speech of 3-, 4-, and 5-year-olds, Kovac (1980) found that due to the interconnection between developmental and sociodialectal proc-esses, it was virtually impossible to determine the different effects of these processes on variation in the occurrence of forms of the copula. That is, children could start off producing sentences with-out the overt copula *be* (i.e. zero copula *be*, Ø) forms such as in *The truck Ø in the driveway* ('The truck is in the driveway') due to devel-opmental properties, but may also produce such sentences because they are the norm in the language they are developing. The chal-lenge according to Kovac was to sort out which factors influenced such language patterns. Extending findings from prior research, Wyatt (1991, 1996) noted that variable copula forms were governed by pragmatic constraints as well as by other linguistic factors. To some extent, Horton-Ikard and Weismar (2005) address the question about factors in the development of child AAE. One of the goals of the study is to evaluate the "non-standard" features in the speech of 2.5-year-old and 3.5-year-old toddlers from AAE backgrounds as a means of trying to determine whether the features were due to normal developmental issues and whether there were indicators of dialect-specific influences. They conclude that not all non-standard features in toddlers from AAE backgrounds can be characterized as general development; some appear to be AAE-influenced.

Some of the more current research on child AAE in the area of syntax and semantics is relevant for assessment, too, but the work also pays considerable attention to the acquisition path (e.g., Coles-White 2004; Green and Roeper 2007; de Villiers, de Villiers, and Roeper in press). One of the advantages of that research is that it begins to bring child AAE in line with developmental research on other languages and naturally provides more concrete support for the long-standing claim that AAE is systematic. The research provides data for comparison with general acquisition developmental patterns that have been reported in the literature, and it begins to raise questions about the nature of variation in child AAE and the general principles of language that can be used to account for it. For instance, de Villiers, de Villiers, and Roeper (in press) compare AAE- and MAE-speaking children's interpretations of *wh*-questions such as *How did the woman learn what to bake?* What they found was that AAE-speaking children were less likely than MAE-speaking children to answer the *what* in such questions and more likely to answer the *how*. They attribute AAE-speaking children's success in correctly answering these complex questions to a particular strategy of forming certain types of questions in AAE. The claim is that because these children are developing a variety in which a certain type of strategy for asking questions (to be addressed in Chapter 6) is allowed, they are able to use that strategy in answering complex *wh*-questions. In another study, Green and Roeper (2007) raised questions about AAE-speaking children's development of tense and aspect properties in comparison with cross-linguistic generalizations about past tense.

While sociolinguistic variation has been the dominant theme of research on adolescent and adult AAE, it has not always been taken into consideration in the study of the development of AAE-speaking children's overall system, but there are some noteworthy exceptions. Kovac (1980) and Wyatt (1991, 1996), for example, who have reported on variation, considered children's variable production of the copula and frequency rate of production in relation to that of adults.

The characterization of AAE as a variable system has important implications for the study of the acquisition of AAE. To what extent is variation part of the early acquisition process or development? In addition, as noted in Seymour (2004), questions about variation and relation to dialect influence as well as disorders should be addressed. In more recent discussions about the effect of language on the academic success of African American school-age children, the question about variation and variable linguistic forms is at the forefront, and it would be worthwhile to link the acquisition of variable dialect-specific forms to the language of school-age children. It is not uncommon to link the variable use of AAE by school-age children to the influence of MAE used in the school environment. Consider the well-known example of the auxiliary *be* ('s) below, in which AAE speakers may or may not include it in some contexts:

1.   (a) Sue's playing ball today.
     (b) Sue Ø playing ball today.

In (1a) the auxiliary *be* is in its contracted form ('s), and in (1b) it is in its zero form or not pronounced, indicated by "Ø". Both sentences could be produced by speakers of AAE, and according to some analyses, the probability of producing one or the other depends on linguistic as well as extra-linguistic or social factors. However, a speaker who uses two copular forms variably, that is, who uses (1b) in some contexts and then (1a) in others, may be said to be exhibiting an instance of dialect-shifting from AAE to MAE in using (1a). Dialect-shifting continues to be addressed in relation to issues regarding AAE speakers' academic success and use of classroom English. In fact, it is somewhat of a hot topic in work on literacy and AAE. Charity, Scarborough, and Griffin (2004) reported a correlation between familiarity with MAE and better reading achievement.

In their book of work on child AAE, which is based on a large database and long-term data collection of AAE language samples, Craig and Washington (2006) maintain that there is a direct correlation between knowledge of MAE and reading achievement; thus, AAE-speaking children who are able to dialect-shift (or "code-switch" in their terms) have a higher rate of success than those who cannot. They go on to note the following: "Students with better language skills acquire dialect-shifting abilities as part of early schooling" (p. 99). If dialect-shifting boosts reading skills and, in the long term, academic success, then it is beneficial to understand the process and how children acquire skill in it. What does it mean to dialect-shift, and how is it determined when a child is indeed dialect-shifting? The crucial question here is to what extent is it possible to distinguish variable use of AAE "features" (e.g., as illustrated in (1a, b)) from dialect-shifting or to determine whether variable use of AAE is dialect-shifting. Craig and Washington's view on this topic is not clear, but if it is the case that there are academic advantages to dialect-shifting, then it is necessary to determine what that process entails and how to create environments for it so that all AAE-speaking children have the opportunity to be dialect-shifters and benefit from strengthened reading skills. If dialect-shifting is a strategy that will foster the skill in use of different language varieties by native AAE speakers and play a positive role in sustaining children's early confidence, then it is still worth pursuing theoretical and practical issues related to it. In the wave of reports on the African American achievement gaps in reading such as those published by the National Assessment of

Educational Progress, it is useful to research strategies that might help to reduce the gap, although it is clear that dialect-shifting will only be relevant to that part of the achievement disparity that is due to barriers emanating from differences between classroom American English or MAE and AAE. Similar educational issues are beginning to be addressed in research in the area of AAE and literacy.

The children in the study on which the data for this book are based are 3-, 4-, and 5-year-old participants who were enrolled in an early childhood development program in a parish seat in southwest Louisiana. They were from three neighboring towns in the parish, including the parish seat, and met certain needs criteria to participate in the program. Most of the children in the program were born in the area and have lived there all of their lives; however, a few participants were born in other regional areas. The distance between the two towns that are farthest from each other, one ten miles south of the parish seat and the other about ten miles west of the parish seat, is twenty miles. The population of the two towns is approximately 3,000 to 3,500, and the population of the parish seat is about 12,000. About 150 children enroll in the program each year. The developing AAE-speaking children in the study are African American and the Southwest Louisiana vernacular English-speaking (SwLVE) children are Anglo American. The number one subject selection criterion was community, so children who were members of the AAE-speaking community (and had lived there all of their lives) were automatically assumed to be members of the AAE-speaking group.

The social, political, economic, and racial history of the South has left certain marks on the linguistic patterns. Like many other small towns and areas in the southern United States, the towns in southwest Louisiana where I have focused my research are still very much divided such that African Americans live in one area and Anglo Americans in another, although the situation is changing in some pockets or sections of the towns and residents are not confined to either community. These areas may be divided by railroad tracks, streets, or some other boundary marker, imaginary or real.

Such division makes it relatively easy to refer to the AAE-speaking community. While African American and Anglo American children attend the same schools now, that was not always the case, and integration has not erased all of the divisions that were established early on, although there is significant interaction between the groups.

It is true that given the historical contact between African Americans and Anglo Americans in the southern United States, the groups share linguistic patterns. In fact, the developing AAE-and SwLVE-speaking children share some patterns that may be uniquely associated with AAE in other areas of the United States and not with non-AAE in other regions. For instance, children from both groups expressed the existence of some object by using what has been referred to as expletive *it* followed by a form of *have*.[1] The example in (2a) was produced by a developing AAE-speaking child, and in (2b) by a developing SwLVE-speaking child:

2.   (a) It have a bowling ball in there, too. (Barry, 5, M, AAE)
            'There is a bowling ball in there, too'
     (b) It had a green crawfish in my yard. (Sami, 4;7, F, SwLVE)
            'There was a green crawfish in my yard'

Also, African Americans and Anglo Americans in southwest Louisiana share patterns that are not shared by speakers in other areas in the southern United States, or in northern Louisiana for that matter. For instance, African Americans and Anglo Americans in southwest Louisiana use "yes/yeah" (affirmative) and "no" (negative) tags, as in (3):

3.   (a) affirmative tag: Go before they close the store, yeah.
            'Do go before they close the store'
     (b) negative tag: Don't try to drive that car, no.
            'Do not try to drive that car'

These constructions are referred to as tags here because either an affirmative ("yeah") or negative ("no") response is tagged onto the end of the sentence.

Throughout the book, children are identified by the following information: a pseudonym, age in years and months, sex, and speech community. For instance, "Rayna, 4;8, F, AAE" refers to a developing AAE-speaking female who was four years and eight months at the time of data collection, and "Sami, 4;7, F, SwLVE" refers to a developing SwLVE-speaking female who was four years and seven months a the time of data collection (see Appendix A). In some cases, data were collected from children at multiple times, which is reflected in the different ages reported for them.

These children also include in their speech some of the older and more conservative constructions and lexical items that are found in the speech of adults in their communities. For instance, children in the study often used *icebox* for *refrigerator*, so in retelling the *Good Dog, Carl* narrative, which will be discussed in Chapter 4, children described the scene in which the dog goes to the refrigerator in the following way:

4. (a) He open the icebox and got some food. (Xavier, 5;9, M, AAE)

    (b) He was lookin in icebox. (Jeffrey, 5;7, M, AAE)

Of course, there are some differences in varieties used by these groups of speakers in the AAE-speaking communities and the SwLVE-speaking communities. Work such as that by Oetting, Cantrelle, and Horohov (1999) and Oetting and Garrity (2006) also points to differences between AAE and Anglo American child speech in communities in southeastern Louisiana.

Who are the developing AAE-speaking children, and what linguistic criteria must they meet to be labeled as such? Researchers have employed various strategies such as listener judgment, type-based counts, and token-based counts, which are based on features reported for adult and adolescent AAE speakers, to determine whether children are AAE speakers (Oetting and McDonald 2001). It is undeniable that there is merit in using these approaches as selection criteria for AAE-speaking children. However, given the limited research on what developmental AAE looks like, the extent to which the same type of feature inventory used for school-age children and adults should be used to identify developing AAE speakers is not clear. The problem is that even in child AAE studies that use type- and token-based counts of features of AAE, there is no discussion about whether or not features identified and counted in child AAE exhibit developmental patterns or not or appear as they do in adult AAE, a point that will be addressed in Chapter 2 and referenced throughout this book. Work such as that in Horton-Ikard and Weismar (2005) begins to address this point head on, but it is not clear whether the discussion should only be about general development or specific patterns in the development of AAE. I find that, in some ways, beginning with type- and token-based counts and relying solely on them can be circular. That is, the aim is to study the properties of child AAE, while at the same time certain properties associated with AAE are used to identify a child as an AAE speaker before it is clear what those properties should look like in child language. I am not denigrating those approaches, as they have been used in insightful research on AAE; however, I do believe that they have some limitations. Along these same lines, I can see that it may appear to be necessary to fall back on those methods given questions about reliability and concrete criteria used to decide to include a child in a study as an AAE speaker. It is also necessary to work toward descriptions of child and developing AAE.

In this book, I use community as a starting point, and it makes sense to do so given the "traditional" separation that has been perpetuated in the geographical regions of the communities of speakers under discussion. While readers will recognize that the patterns I discuss do occur in AAE feature lists, my aim is not to use them to confirm that the children are developing the patterns of their communities or to prove that the child should be characterized as a developing AAE speaker. The aim is to show where the children are in development. I assume that children who grow up in the community will develop the language patterns of the community – of course at different levels due to a number of factors. That is, children in the AAE-speaking community also show signs of being at different places on the AAE continuum.

It is the goal of this book to address some of the questions in the body of research on child AAE in light of data from developing AAE-speaking children in communities in southwestern Louisiana and to bring to the forefront new issues for future research. Although the problem of the African American achievement gap has already been raised in this introductory discussion, the work presented here is not intended to address that issue head on, but I do hope that the data and description presented in this book will have some relevance for the topic. I have taken a basic step by presenting what I refer to as the D.I.R.E.C.T. Model to suggest a way in which linguistic description can have practical application.

Data from both spontaneous and elicited speech, collected to address questions about production and comprehension, are included to give a broader picture of developing AAE. Data collection began in 2003, and it is ongoing. All of the language samples in the database were collected by me during spontaneous speech sessions and elicitation tasks. On some occasions two children were interacting during spontaneous speech and play sessions, and on other occasions I interacted alone with one child. Toys and books were used during spontaneous speech sessions. I worked with one child at a time during elicitation tasks. In talking to the children during spontaneous speech sessions and elicitation tasks, my goal was to be as natural as possible, using a type of "teacher talk" including what some will associate with MAE in some situations and with AAE in others. The children's teachers knew that the children would be participating in literacy-related activities with me, and they often encouraged the children to "talk a lot," but they never coached them on what type of linguistic variety to use.

An advantage of a large database spanning a period of years is that it becomes possible to observe general patterns of production for some constructions, although as clearly pointed out by Stromswold

(1998), it might be necessary to record data for a substantial period of time in order to collect sufficient tokens of a construction that will provide information about its acquisition. Likewise Demuth (1998) also addresses some limitations of spontaneous production data. For instance, she notes that it is quite difficult to determine why a particular construction does not occur in a sample. On the other hand, she goes on to assert that the presence of a particular construction in a speech sample does not necessarily attest that it is productive. It is obvious that the claims that I will be able to make about the acquisition of constructions in AAE will be limited because my data are restricted to 3- to 5-year-olds from a certain geographical area, with a focus on 4- and 5- year-olds. It was established that in some cases 3-year-olds were not able to handle some of the comprehension tasks, and in those cases emphasis was placed more on selecting 4- and 5-year-olds from the classrooms. Thus there are more samples from the older group just because they were selected to participate more often. What is clear is that the 3-year-olds do produce some of the AAE patterns in their spontaneous speech that are discussed here. To get more detailed information about comprehension, it is necessary to devise more sophisticated elicitation and comprehension tasks that can really shed light on whether 3-year-olds do or do not comprehend certain constructions or whether they simply cannot handle the elicitation tasks. As will be pointed out in connection with some of the aspectual marker data, it seems to be clear that 3-year-olds do not have a handle on them. In some cases the spontaneous speech productions serve to raise questions about actual constructions in developing AAE, and in others claims about constructions in child AAE are further supported by production data based on elicitation tasks.

The data on the pages of this book reflect some patterns in the development of AAE that I have been able to look at systematically, but other patterns from the lexicon, phonetics and phonology, and syntax and semantics of AAE that will not be discussed have been observed in the children's language. Perhaps some of these other features are more closely linked to AAE grammar than to the grammars of other varieties of American English, and they might be sufficient to certify that children who use them are indeed learning the language of the AAE-speaking community of which they are part. I will briefly note some of them here and underscore the point that they should be taken up in further research.

Children use lexical items that are common in AAE-speaking communities, as shown in the examples in (5):

5.   Lexicon
      (a) He turned on some little music. (Nia, 5;4, F, AAE)
      (b) ... like they was playing dress up, looking all cute.
      (c) Hey, wha's up? (Barry, 5, M, AAE)

In the example in (5a), *little* seems to have its common use as a marker indicating appreciation for an action or entity (in this case music) or acknowledgment that the action or entity is noteworthy. It is not a diminutive. The lexical item *all* in (5b) is used by the same speaker in (5a) to emphasize the "cute" appearance. The common greeting in (5c) was used to initiate a make-believe phone conversation with a peer.

The examples in (6) highlight properties associated with the sound patterns in some AAE-speaking communities:

6.   Phonetics and Phonology[2]
      (a) This cain [can't] open. (Barry, 5, M, AAE)
      (b) ... me and K__ be acking [acting] crazy at her house ...
          (Donovan, 5, M, AAE)
      (c) Barry: Can I use this phone?
          Rashandra: Yeah. Sho [sure]. (5, F, AAE)
      (d) Tha's [that's] fuh [for] huh [her]. (Rashanna, 4, F, AAE)
      (e) Why? You scaed [scared]? (Lela, 3, F, AAE)
      (f) Pit [put] the back down. Got back seat, back do [door].
          (Tyron, 4, M, AAE)
      (g) I'm finna [fixing to] call my daddy. (Bethany, 3, F, AAE)
      (h) I saw a monkey head. (Deon, 3;10, M, AAE)

(i) LJG: That's called a retainer. So my teeth won't move.

Dawn: My teeth moving? (5;9, F, AAE)

LJG: Yeah. That's good, 'cause you a big girl.

Dawn: My teeth moving.

LJG: Yeah. 'Cause you a big girl.

Dawn: You not a big girl?

In (6a) the negative cain 'can't' is pronounced without the contracted *n't*. The word ends with a nasalized vowel, not a *t* sound. The word *acking* 'acting' (6b) is pronounced with the common consonant cluster reduction or omission of the second of two consonants in the *ct* sequence in AAE that generally occurs at the end of the word. In *acting*, the consonant cluster reduction or omission of the *t*, which is reflected by retention of only the part of the *ct* cluster that makes a "k" sound, takes place in the medial word position, before –*ing*. In adult AAE, when the word *acting* refers to having fun or misbehaving, it can occur with the reduced cluster and be pronounced as in (6b) (Green 2002). The examples in (6c, d, e, f) *sho* 'sure,' *fuh* 'for,' *huh* 'her,' *scaed* 'scared,' and *do* 'door' are *r*-vocalization cases in which the "r" following vowels is not pronounced. The *r*-vocalization occurs at the end of the syllable (or word) in each case except in *scared*, in which *r*-vocalization occurs in the middle of the word. The vowel in *put* (6f) is pronounced the same as the vowel in *hit*. Given my observations, this pronunciation of *put* occurs in child AAE and not in adult AAE in the regional area under consideration.

The examples in (6g) and (6h) also reflect sound patterns that are used in the AAE-speaking communities in the children's geographical region. While AAE and non-AAE speakers in this regional area use some version(s) of "fixing to" to mean 'getting ready to,' the pronunciation *finna* in (6g) (and some other variations, e.g., *fitna*) seems to be more closely associated with the AAE-speaking communities. In general, and in the case of (6h), the first vowel in *monkey* is pronounced the same as the first vowel in *bone*. The final line in (6i) is intended to reflect a case that shows that developing AAE-speaking children also acquire the intonational patterns associated with questions (that genuinely request yes/no answers) in their AAE-speaking communities. Given my explanation about the retainer, Dawn concluded that her teeth were moving. Her analysis, then, was that if her teeth were moving because she was a big girl, shouldn't mine be allowed to move – if indeed I was a big girl. It is not clear how to capture the intonational patterns that have been said to set off adult AAE from other varieties of English, and there is even less research on prosody and child AAE. I will return to intonational patterns in questions in child AAE in Chapter 6, where yes–no and *wh*-questions are addressed.

Finally, a few patterns from syntax/semantics that are not addressed further in this text are noted here.

7.   Syntax (and Morphosyntax) and Semantics
      (a) What they have up in there? (Donavan, 5, M, AAE)
      (b) I seen B__ to the store. (Rashanna, 4, F, AAE)
      (c) LJG: Have you ever gone to a birthday party?
           Dawn: Yes mam … a girl birthday to my cousin. (5;9, F, AAE)
      (d) Gi [give] my phone. (Tyron, 4, M, AAE)
      (e) I'ma have to read a book? (Nia, 5;4, F, AAE)

In (7a, b, c) the focus is on prepositions. As in (7a), the preposition compound *up in* is used interchangeably with *in*, and the preposition *to* is used to introduce a location (7b, c), and is not used in the context of a direction, such as "went to the store." The prepositional phrases in (7b, c) can be understood as 'at the store' and 'at my cousin's house,' respectively. Possessives such as *my cousin* will be discussed in Chapter 7. In AAE some verbs may occur with either one or two nouns to complete their meaning. For instance, *give* and *bring* are two verbs that can optionally occur with just one noun, as in (7d) *Gi my phone* (cf. 'Give me my phone'). The direct object (*my phone*), but not the indirect object (*me*), is included. The contracted form *I'ma* 'I am going to' is used in (7e).

One point that has become very clear as a result of my work with developing AAE child speakers is that they are very confident in their use of language and other literacy-related abilities. For instance, as Darrell (5;3, M, AAE) progressed through one of the comprehension tasks, he noted: "I know these, hunh?" Declarations of being smart, such as that of Dawn presented at the beginning of this chapter, are very common among the children in my study. They were also enthusiastic about completing tasks, such as telling stories, listening to stories, and responding. They were often up for whatever the challenge might have been and asked questions such as "I'ma have to read a book?" (Nia, 5;4, F, AAE) ('Am I going to have to read a book?').

Some of the patterns of language use that I address throughout this book can be generalized to groups of AAE-speaking children throughout the United States, and others may be found in the speech of particular populations of AAE-speaking children. The bulk of the data is from developing AAE-speaking children (and their non-AAE-speaking peers) in three towns in southwest Louisiana. It has been noted that AAE in the southern United States and that spoken in the northern United States differ in a number of ways. In spite of those differences, which have not been systematically or specifically addressed in the literature, there are overwhelming similarities. It should be possible to be able to generalize at least some of the patterns identified here across populations of AAE speakers in different regions of the USA, although it is useful to keep in mind the questions that Wolfram (2007) raises about sociolinguistic myths and claims about core features of AAE and a uniform language variety across the United States.

The major focus of this book is on linguistic descriptions of patterns and, to some extent, variation in language use by 3-, 4-, and 5-year-old developing AAE-speaking children. Chapter 2 sets the foundation for the discussion in this book by laying out issues that arise given previous and current characterizations of AAE. It raises questions about different ways of characterizing and defining AAE, such as by reference to features in lists and to different components, such as the general English and the African American components. A broad characterization of AAE based on areas of the grammar, such as syntax, semantics, and phonology, is given, and the patterns- and systems-based approach to AAE that will be followed throughout this book is introduced. Finally, that chapter highlights questions about variation in the description of child AAE, some of which are picked up in Chapter 7. Most of the linguistic description of the data is presented in Chapters 3 through 6. Spontaneous speech samples are given throughout this book, and elicitation tasks are reported specifically in Chapters 3 through 6. Chapters 3 and 4 focus on the production and comprehension of constructions that refer to the time and other properties of events. In particular, constructions that reflect the way children mark notions such as non-past, habitual, and past are presented. One observation that is made in Chapter 3 about non-past marking as well as in Chapter 4 about past marking is that children, at least in some environments, show a preference for preverbal markers. Negation is the topic of Chapter 5, in which children's early monoclausal concord structures are quite similar to those that have been reported in the literature for children acquiring other varieties such as MAE and Bristol English. Data are also considered in light of inquiries about the extent to which developing AAE-speaking children allow negative concord to cross syntactic boundaries, that is, whether they allow two negative elements that are separated from each other by a syntactic boundary such as a phrase to be related to each other in an agreement relation. Children's production of questions is taken up in Chapter 6, and the occurrence of auxiliaries in yes–no and *wh*-questions is discussed. Do the occurrence and position of auxiliaries in questions suggest stages in development and/ or the acquisition of variable question patterns? As it turns out, the type of auxiliary inversion that is evident in some questions may also occur in negative structures. To that end, negation is also linked to this chapter. In general, these chapters are geared toward sentence structure and meaning; however, reference is made to pragmatics and intonational contours that also play a major role in the interpretation of sentences. In reconsidering variation in the form and use of constructions in child AAE, I introduce variable-shifting in Chapter 7 and suggest that it differs from dialect-shifting. Along these lines, variation may exist on different levels and may not always involve shifting from one dialect or code to another, depending on which variables are intrinsic to the AAE grammar. The goal of Chapter 8 is to take a step toward showing how linguistic description might be extended to practical application in educational settings. Some of the issues in the study of child AAE that are raised in Chapter 2 in light of claims about links between academic achievement and language use of African American school-age children resurface in this chapter. Also, the patterns in child language are considered within what I refer to as the D.I.R.E.C.T. Model, which can be used in educational settings in which some emphasis is placed on teaching accurate MAE correspondences to AAE structures in environments of variable- and dialect-shifting. Questions are raised about issues regarding the link between academic success and language use in the classroom and dialect-shifting, which is beginning to receive widespread attention in the area of classroom instruction.

2 Characterizing AAE: feature lists, dual components, and patterns and systems

LJG: <directed to the duck puppet about Zeke's excellent performance on the elicitation and comprehension tasks>
Watch Z__. He knows how to get these answers. So watch how quiet he is and watch how he pays attention.
Zeke: We finna – we fin – I finna pass this test.[1]

INTRODUCTION

What is AAE? The answers to this question or the definition can vary depending on perspective. For instance, the focus can be placed on the speakers, such that AAE can be characterized as a way of talking by groups of African Americans. Also, AAE has been even more narrowly defined as the "vernacular" form used by African American youth and young adults who are part of the popular culture. Such characterizations do not provide much insight into the AAE linguistic system itself, nor do they say much about the patterns used as part of the linguistic system, although they do link AAE to groups of African Americans and to social use of language. In the description in this book the focus will be on the AAE linguistic system and ways to capture developmental patterns. Three methods of characterizing AAE that are concerned with properties of the linguistic system itself are used in the literature and each captures certain intuitions about the linguistic variety. Also, each method places emphasis on a different property of the linguistic variety. For reference, I will use the following labels for the models of methods of characterizing AAE: feature lists, dual components, and patterns and systems. The method of portraying AAE that is more in line with the approach in this book is the patterns and systems characterization.

2.1 FEATURE LISTS AND DENSITY MEASURES: HOW AAE DIFFERS FROM MAE

The tradition of characterizing adult AAE in such a way to show how it differs maximally from MAE remains strong. The approach is to list a line of features that are in opposition to what is acceptable in standard American English, and it goes back to early studies in AAE when, in the beginning stages, researchers were trying to explain what actually constitutes AAE. One common list is in Wolfram and Fasold (1974), in which AAE is addressed along with other American English social dialects. Of course, the earlier feature lists are based on observations of adolescent and adult language, but the lists have also been extended to child AAE. For instance, in categorizing AAE according to what they have observed in the speech of children in the pre-kindergarten through fifth grade age groups, Craig and Washington (2006) give a list of morphosyntactic features, some of which are also commonly associated with adolescent and adult AAE. Craig and Washington's introduction links the features in the list to standard American English: "The morpho-syntactic feature system includes the variations from SAE [Standard American English] that involve free and bound morphemes, and word order" (p. 35). Thus AAE is characterized in terms of the way it differs from MAE; the "features" in the list are not associated with MAE. The 24 features Craig and Washington isolate are reproduced here:

1. Features Suggested in the Literature
   (1) Ain't
   (2) Appositive pronoun
   (3) Completive *done*
   (4) Double marking
   (5) Double copula/auxiliary/modal
   (6) Existential *it*
   (7) *Fitna/sposeta/bouta*
   (8) Preterite *had*
   (9) Indefinite article

(10) Invariant *be*

(11) Multiple negation

(12) Regularized reflexive pronoun

(13) Remote past *been*

(14) Subject–verb agreement variations

(15) Undifferentiated pronoun case

(16) Zero article

(17) Zero copula

(18) Zero *–ing*

(19) Zero modal auxiliary

(20) Zero past tense

(21) Zero plural

(22) Zero possessive

(23) Zero preposition

(24) Zero *to*

In their discussion of developing AAE-speaking 2.5- and 3.5-year-olds, Horton-Ikard and Weismar (2005) also include a list that includes features from lists published earlier. The list consists of grammatical and phonological features, and they include just a few features that are not on the list in (1) (e.g., *go* copula, *gonna/gone* semiauxiliary). At least three major advantages of the list in (1) (and others) should be noted. One advantage is that the list can be used for comparative purposes to show the overlap of reported features of child AAE and adult AAE. Secondly, the list can serve as a quick reference for practitioners, such as speech pathologists and educators, who may have questions about whether patterns in African American children's language are commonly associated with AAE, which may be the language of the child's speech community, or whether they point to some anomaly in the child's grammar. Simply put, if a pattern in the child's speech is found on the list, then it can be further investigated to determine whether it is a pattern of AAE, not a disorder. Thirdly, these features can serve as a general summary of the morphosyntactic and syntactic differences between AAE and MAE, and, more generally, the list can be used to highlight features of AAE in comparison with features of other varieties of English. Certainly the list has merits, but I suspect that one of the reasons that properties of AAE continue to be promulgated in lists is that they follow the tradition established in early research of listing features of AAE.

A number of questions about the conceptualization of child AAE are raised, especially about the patterns of development along the lines of each feature, when the feature list approach is taken in characterization of child AAE. Many of the features in (1) are also on lists for adult AAE, so there should be a way to account for developmental patterns that might be associated with a particular feature in child AAE, if there are any. For instance, do completive *done* (#13) and invariant *be* (#10) in the list in (1) have the same meaning they would have in lists based on adolescent and adult AAE? Perhaps the point of the list in (1) is to convey that, in some ways, child AAE is indistinguishable from adult AAE. Another question that arises in reference to the feature list in (1) is related to the status of the "zero" features in #16 through #24. Are the "zero" characterizations intended to capture the property that, at this stage of AAE, certain morphemes, such as the copula and genitive (or possessive) –'s, are categorically non-overt, or does the "zero" status apply only to certain environments? A third question, which is somewhat linked to the developmental issue, is about the extent to which the features on the list can be understood as clustering in certain ways or related to each other, at least with respect to developmental properties. For instance, a number of the features represent properties associated with marking time and talking about the way events are carried out, such as those highlighted in (2):

2.   Features Related to the Tense–aspect System
    (a) #17 zero copula
    (b) #20 zero past tense
    (c) #8 preterite *had*
    (d) #13 remote past *been*

(e) #3 completive *done*

(f) #7 *fitna/sposeta/bouta*

(g) #10 invariant *be*

Do features such as those in (2) suggest something about the development of systems in child AAE, and can they be organized in a way to provide some insight into general patterns of development in properties of the tense–aspect system in child AAE?

It is not difficult to see how reference to a handy tool such as a feature list leads to the possibility of counting the number of features or calculating the frequency of occurrence of certain features in an AAE speaker's language samples to make some determination about his or her level of dialect use or about whether the speaker uses the requisite number of features to be classified as an AAE speaker. There is a well-established tradition of quantitative approaches in studying adolescent and adult AAE, especially in research on the extent to which a feature varies in production. For instance, many quantitative studies on the copula (and auxiliary *be*) have been conducted to show that the environment of the *be* form and other factors conspire in determining the likelihood that *be* will occur in its overt form (e.g., *I am here.*) versus in its non-overt form (e.g., *He Ø here.*) (Labov 1969; Wolfram 1974; Baugh 1980; Rickford 1998; Walker 2000). Similar studies have been extended to the occurrence of the copula in child AAE (e.g., Kovac 1980; Wyatt 1991, 1996). The quantitative studies are used to answer a number of questions about the occurrence of certain features in linguistic environments and about use of features by groups of speakers based on factors such as age and sex.

The approach in Craig and Washington (2006) falls under the quantitative analysis category. They use a method of calculating features to draw conclusions about how much dialect occurs in a child's speech or how extensive the feature use is, where extensive seems to be a measure of quantity and not of nature of feature use. By dividing the number of features a child produces by the number of words in

Table 2.1 *DDM of morphosyntactic features (adapted from Craig and Washington 2006, p. 20)*

Grade	MorDDMs
Pre-K	0.11
K	0.09
1st	0.05
2nd	0.04
3rd	0.035
4th	0.04
5th	0.04

the child's language sample, they arrive at the dialect density measure (DDM), which is taken as an indication of the rate of children's production of AAE features. The DDM is a quantitative measure that is not geared toward providing information about the rules and principles governing the use and occurrence of particular features, the developmental patterns in production, or systems of feature types that are manifested in developmental stages. Craig and Washington note that even in light of some obvious shortcomings of the rate measure and the limitations on what it can actually tell about language use, correlations have been shown to exist between lower DDM rates and academic success, such as reading performance. The authors also add that by charting the DDM, they were able to show that AAE-speaking children in their study moved from AAE to mainstream English as they went through school. The measures from Craig and Washington (2004), and also reported in their 2006 book, are intended to show a decrease in DDM as children's school grades increase. They give the figures in Table 2.1 for DDM of morphosyntactic features.

According to the authors, the generalization is that children replace AAE features with corresponding features of MAE as they get older.

It is clear that the DDM is about rate of production of features. However, given the reports on the decrease in DDM from pre-kindergarten to fifth grade, it is natural to ask whether the measures and trends also lead to some other general observations or raise insightful questions about children's linguistic development of AAE. Is there a correlation between decrease in rate of features and development of certain systems of use in AAE? For instance, although children go through the stage in which the number of morphosyntactic features per number of words decreases, is there any evidence of developmental patterns in the children's grammar such that the features come to be used more selectively and in more defined linguistic environments that are compatible with adolescent and adult AAE? Going back to (1), we can speculate that at least some of the features, or their uses, are basically limited to child AAE. If the DDM decrease is due to development of AAE by weeding out patterns that are more closely associated with child AAE, then to characterize the situation as replacement of AAE by MAE may not be accurate. In other words, the suggestion I am putting forward here is that other alternatives are available as an explanation for what happens during the period of DDM decrease. Also, I want to make clear the point that Craig and Washington's explanation surely has merit, but it may not be the complete picture. As considerable emphasis is likely to be placed on the DDM decrease in school, it would be useful to have all of the information that might contribute to it.

Another important question that needs to be answered in discussions about DDM and what goes into its calculation is whether certain criteria are followed in selecting constructions that are taken as instantiations of a feature. For example, one feature that stands out in AAE is zero copula, Feature #17 on the list in (1). While this feature is robust in AAE, there are clearly some environments in which it is not generally applied. It does not typically occur with first person singular or third person neuter pronouns, so the sentences in (3a, b) are not taken to be acceptable constructions in adult AAE. (Note that the asterisk (*) indicates an unacceptable sentence in adult AAE.)

3. (a) *I happy. ('I'm happy' is the acceptable construction in adult AAE.)

   (b) *It nice. ('It's nice' is the acceptable construction in adult AAE.)

What is not clear from the DDM point of view is whether all instantiations of zero copula, including those that do not conform to restrictions on adult AAE, in a child's language sample are included or whether only zero copula constructions that meet certain specifications are counted. My specific question regarding copular constructions, for instance, is whether a decrease in developmental patterns in child AAE copular constructions also counts as a decrease in DDM. If so, that is clearly misleading, given that DDM is a measure of dialect density. That is to ask the following rhetorical question: If child AAE speakers start off producing sentences such as those in (3) but get rid of them as they continue to develop AAE copular patterns, does it then appear that the children's AAE dialect density is decreasing when in actuality the child could be maturing with respect to the production of AAE copular constructions? Put another way, if young children stop using sentences such as those in (3), then is the instance of decrease in AAE patterns due to exposure to the language of the school, or is it a developmental trend in the acquisition of AAE? Without answering that question, it is not clear that the decrease in DDM as grade increases necessarily makes any sort of claim about the decrease in use of AAE, especially given the important acquisition questions to be answered. In actuality, they could also be maturing in the use of AAE. Another case in point is Feature #5 double copula/auxiliary/modal, which refers to the use of two auxiliary elements, as indicated in the examples from Craig and Washington (2006, p. 121):

4. (a) I'm is the boy.

   (b) They're is playing in the snow.

In (4a), both the contracted copula 'm and the full form is are used, and in (4b) the contracted auxiliary 're and the full form is are used.

While Craig and Washington do not discuss the specific grades of speakers who use the constructions in (4b), considering their conclusion, we could take the view that these double copula/auxiliary sequences decline as a result of exposure to MAE contexts. However, I have not seen evidence that double copula/auxiliary persists in the language of adult AAE in speakers who do not have regular contact with MAE, so it is not clear to me how the decline of double auxiliaries says anything about loss of AAE, although it says something about development. Another view, which is from a developmental perspective, is that the use of the feature declines as the child's AAE grammar continues to develop. One way to check the developmental view is to look at the progression from double auxiliaries to a single form in the language of AAE-speaking children in pre-kindergarten groups to determine the pattern of declination before the children's exposure to school.

Another question about the features and DDM approach is whether it is actually possible to get a clear picture of decrease in use of AAE by appealing only to morphosyntactic features, especially in development in which children may be expanding their repertoire of AAE and exhibiting more complex patterns that are not represented in the feature list or complex patterns associated with features on the list. To that end, to complement the density measure, which is based on sheer rate of morphosyntactic features, there needs to be a density measure that is also based on complex structures beyond morphemes that could give a fuller picture that is in line with language use and development.

2.2 DUAL COMPONENTS OF AAE

The dual components view, such as that presented in Labov (1998), is based on the notion that AAE consists of two components.

The model in Figure 2.1 is intended to be a pictorial representation of the view of AAE presented in Labov (1998) and other proponents of a two-part AAE system. The view is that AAE consists of two components, a general English (GE) component and an African

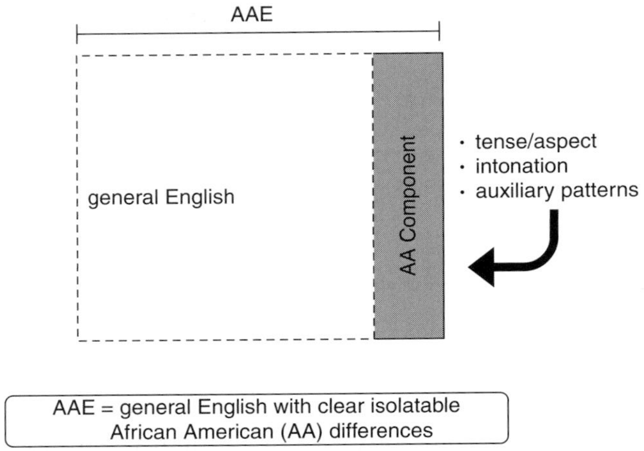

Figure 2.1 Dual components approach

American (AA) component, both of which contribute to the "flavor" of AAE, but they are not equal, as Labov explains. The GE component contributes the basic structure and grammar, which AAE shares with other varieties of English. It is the AA component that distinguishes AAE from other varieties and gives it the distinctively African American "flavor." For instance, the "unique" feature such as the Feature #10 invariant *be* on the list in (1), is part of the AA component, but not all of the features in the list are part of the AA component because some of the features may also be shared with other varieties of English. A crucial point to be made in a discussion of AAE as a two-part system is that although the features in the AA component are important in characterizing AAE, they cannot exist on their own; they do not comprise a language. To put it another way, according to this view, AAE speakers could not communicate by using elements from the AA component alone because the elements need to be buttressed by the GE component, or as Labov notes, the AA component coexists with the GE component.

In casting AAE in the dual components hypothesis, we can ask a number of questions about how the developmental properties fit into that model. In other words, do the children acquire the two components separately, or could they be said to acquire GE along with a set of the AA features that are integrated into the GE system? The dual components approach is certainly not intended to be a model of AAE acquisition, but it is natural to ask how development would proceed for children who are acquiring a system composed of two distinct components. It seems to be clear enough that the situation is not one of bidialectalism because only one of the two components is a complete dialect of English. The dual components view is quite intuitive in at least two ways at first glance. On the one hand, given the inclusion of the GE component, the characterization captures the fact that AAE shares similarities with other varieties of English. On the other hand, including a separate AA component allows for some differences that are found in AAE but not in other varieties. The feature list and the dual components model have in common the approach of highlighting features in AAE that are not shared by other varieties of English. In casting AAE in such terms, we get a clear sense of what stands apart in AAE from other varieties of English, but it is not so clear how the unique features (i.e., AA component) mesh with common American English to form a system that is acquired, developed, and used among speakers in a speech community. I want to move away from the feature list and dual components approaches with the understanding that they are models for characterizing AAE and highlighting points of divergence from other varieties of English. Also, they both indicate that AAE shares patterns with other English dialects; the dual components model expresses the link explicitly. There is no explicit statement about shared patterns between AAE and other American English dialects within the feature list model, but given the list of ways that AAE differs from other English varieties, such as MAE, it is implied that in all other ways (that are not enumerated in the lists) AAE is like general American English.

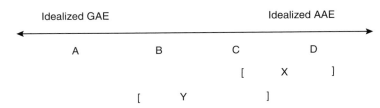

Figure 2.2 Speakers and the AAE continuum

2.3 PATTERNS AND SYSTEMS OF DEVELOPMENT

A third way of characterizing AAE is in terms of broader systems encompassing features that are part of the variety. The picture of AAE that I have in mind and that I would like to convey is one of a multidimensional, multifarious communicative system that is also developed by young children growing up in AAE-speaking communities. The terms multidimensional and multifarious in reference to AAE are intended to capture the fact that AAE, as a system of communication, has a range of uses and can be used by some, not all, speakers in varying degrees. While I am trying to focus on a broader characterization of AAE and am selecting terminology that refers to that approach, I am not the only or first person to take such an approach. For instance, I take Smitherman's (1977) work *Talkin and Testifyin: The Language of Black America* to be a characterization of AAE as a system of language use.

As noted in Baugh (1983) and Green (2002), AAE can be conceived of on a continuum, and speakers can have different relationships with respect to their places on it. Two relationships are indicated in Figure 2.2.

In the representation Figure 2.2, idealized general American English is on one end of the continuum, and idealized AAE is on the other. "X" and "Y" represent AAE speakers who have access to different ranges on the continuum. Speaker X has a more limited range, which is closer to the idealized AAE end of the spectrum, but has fluent skills in AAE and can use the variety with ease in different settings. On the other hand, speaker Y's range is more extended, and the point is that she has access to many more points on the

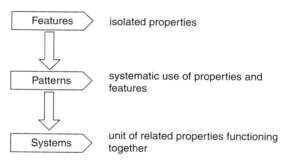

Figure 2.3 Three-level nested hierarchy in the patterns and systems approach

continuum, including those that approach the idealized general American English end of the spectrum. Speaker Y could be said to have access to the type of information it takes to function in a variety that is accepted or that passes in mainstream English environments. However, as the model shows, speaker Y also has access to AAE and can use the variety in some environments; perhaps the skills may or may not be as native-like as those of speaker X. By "use" AAE, I mean communicate with the sentence patterns, meanings, and phonology, not just insert common phrases and lexical items that are associated with AAE in conversation from time to time. Perhaps both speakers X and Y are native AAE speakers, but their experiences and perhaps personal decisions have led them to (gain access to) different places on the continuum. The notion of what it means to use AAE could be the topic of many discussions; here I am taking a very limited view to make the point about the continuum. Some of what is implicit in this continuum and speakers' relationships to it is code-shifting (and variable-shifting), which will be discussed in Chapter 7.

In conveying a multidimensional picture of AAE, I am going to take what I refer to as a patterns- and systems-based approach. Features, patterns, and systems are prominent in the description, and they are represented in a nested hierarchy (Figure 2.3).

Features, the type of isolated properties listed in (1), are used systematically and can then be identified with respect to patterns.

Consequently, patterns of related properties functioning together can be seen as units or systems. Although features do have a role in this patterns- and systems-based approach, they alone cannot characterize the system of AAE that is at the core of this book. Throughout the book, I want to shine the light on patterns of use of features and the systems that make up AAE. This approach builds on the definition of AAE in Green (2002):

5.   Definition of AAE: Patterns- and systems-based approach
     AAE is a system of syntactic, semantic (and pragmatic), phonological, morphological, and lexical patterns that are intertwined with patterns of general English.

As noted in Chapter 1, a number of patterns in phonological development have emerged in the data sets considered in this study, but they will not be discussed here. The major focus here will be on the syntactic, semantic, and morphological patterns, but pragmatic and rhetorical use will also be mentioned in relation to syntactic and semantic patterns. Certainly the pragmatic development of child AAE deserves attention in its own right, but the observations will be limited to language use and interpretation of particular constructions.

The involvement that I see of features, patterns, and systems and try to represent in the nested hierarchy in Figure 2.3 can be exemplified by the example in (2). That is, once a set of features relating to time and properties of events, such as whether they occur occasionally or whether the entire event ended in the far past, is isolated, then the specific patterns of these features can be studied to tell us something about the general tense and aspect system of child AAE. We can certainly get important information by studying the past tense –ed in developing AAE, but once we put those findings together with other ways that child AAE speakers talk about the past, the overall picture of the tense system begins to take shape.

There may be featural and systematic overlaps, so different options of subcategorization are available. For instance, Feature

#1 *ain't* could be classified along with features indicating tense and aspect marking as well as with features for negation. The subcategorization or arrangement of features should provide some insight into patterns in language. For instance, on the list in (1), *fitna/bouta/sposeta* are grouped together as Feature #7. *Fitna* (also *finna*, which occurs in the example at the beginning of the chapter) ('fixing to') and *bouta* ('about to') have a similar meaning: getting ready to, immediate future, or imminent. On the other hand, *sposeta* ('supposed to') does not share that meaning. They all share the common property of preceding an unmarked verb or verb in its bare form, as in *run, eat*: *fitna eat, bouta eat, sposeta eat*. In a patterns- and systems-based approach, it should be clear why the elements are grouped together.

The patterns- and systems-based approach assumes connections between and among features, which lead to patterns of language use of AAE and provide conditions for presenting AAE as a linguistic system. Secondly, the approach facilitates exploration into developmental patterns and stages in child AAE beyond the presence or absence of a particular feature. It does not yield a handy reference list of features, which would be redundant, given that there already exist numerous lists in the literature; however, the patterns- and systems-based approach can lead to descriptions that supplement feature lists in several ways.

Chapter 3 begins the exploration of child AAE by looking at the tense–aspect properties from the perspective of the patterns- and systems-based approach.

3 System of tense–aspect marking 1: non-past and habitual

Akila: 'Cause when I watch Blues Clues, my eyes be like this. <makes blinking motion with eyes>

INTRODUCTION

This chapter addresses some of the features and properties in the system of tense–aspect marking in child AAE. Tense refers to the time of an event, whether it takes place before, after, or during the speech time. For instance, we refer to past time or time prior to the moment the sentence *He left* is uttered, such that the leaving event took place before now or before the speech time. Aspect refers to other properties of events, such as whether the event occurs occasionally, whether it is represented as being in progress, or whether it is represented as being a complete event. An example of an aspect in general English is the progressive, as in *running*, which represents the running event as in progress or ongoing. The sequence *is running* indicates that the running event is in progress at speech time, present progressive, and the sequence *was running* indicates that the running event was in progress before speech time, past progressive. Specific tense–aspect marking has also been observed in child AAE. One of the issues in this chapter concerns the relationship between overt markers in the form of verbal elements (words), suffixes, or contracted forms and the tense–aspect meaning of sentences. To what extent do children use separate markers to indicate that an event is in the present or non-past, or that the event occurs on occasions?

An identifying characteristic of AAE is its tense–aspect properties. In fact, it has been claimed by researchers such as DeBose and Faraclas (1993) that AAE is aspect prominent; that is, in AAE aspectual properties are highlighted in sentences more so than tense properties. It is accurate to say that adult AAE expresses both tense and aspect and puts emphasis on certain aspectual properties.

3.1 PATTERN OF NON-PAST EVENT AND STATE MARKING: COPULA AND AUXILIARY *BE*

Arguably, the most studied patterns of adult AAE are those associated with the occurrence and absence of the copula and auxiliary *BE*. I use *BE* (written in capital letters) as an abstract form representing the different inflections of the copula and auxiliary forms. The reason that I am also considering these patterns in light of developing AAE is not so much due to their popularity in adult AAE as it is due to the type of information that we can learn about how developing AAE-speaking children talk about events and states when we study these forms in their speech. As noted in Chapters 1 and 2, copula use by child AAE speakers has been studied, especially from the perspective of whether the form is actually pronounced in certain situations or not. In addition to making observations about situations and contexts in which developing AAE speakers use the copula and auxiliary *BE*, I also want to draw attention to the way the verb forms are used in relation to the type and time of eventuality, where "eventuality" is a cover term that refers to states and events. The copula precedes nouns, adjectives, prepositions, or adverbs, as in the examples in (1), respectively.

1.   (a) He is a student.
      (b) They are tall.
      (c) The ball is in the yard.
      (d) The ball is right there.

The symbol "$\emptyset_{COP}$" is used to indicate that the copula is not pronounced, and is placed in the position in the sentence where the copula (*is, am, are*, etc.) would occur were it present:

2.   (a) He $\emptyset_{COP}$ a student.
        'He's a student'

(b) They $\emptyset_{COP}$ tall.
       'They're tall'
(c) The ball $\emptyset_{COP}$ in the yard.
       'The ball's in the yard'
(d) The ball $\emptyset_{COP}$ right there.
       'The ball's right there'

In its use as an auxiliary, the *BE* form precedes a V-*ing*, *gon/gonna* ('going to'), and *fitna/sposeta/bouta* ('fixing to,' 'supposed to,' 'about to,' respectively), as in the examples in (3).

3.   (a) Dee is talking.
        (b) Dee is gon leave.
               'Dee is going to leave'
        (c) She is finna read.
               'She is getting ready to read'

The symbol "$\emptyset_{AUX}$" is used to represent situations in which the auxiliary *BE* does not occur on the surface or is not pronounced, as in (4):

4.   (a) Dee $\emptyset_{AUX}$ talking.
               'Dee is talking'
        (b) Dee $\emptyset_{AUX}$ gon leave.
               'Dee is going to leave'
        (c) She $\emptyset_{AUX}$ finna read.
               'She is fixing (i.e., getting ready) to read'

In what follows, children's copula and auxiliary *BE* constructions that refer to present (or non-past) states or events are presented. These utterances were produced by children in the study as part of naturalistic speech or conversations with their peers and/or me and production or comprehension tasks. I will continue to use the symbol "$\emptyset$" to draw attention to the position where the *BE* form would occur were it present. Overwhelmingly, the $\emptyset_{COP}$ and $\emptyset_{AUX}$ are used with events or states that are in non-past (or present), as will be illustrated in children's language samples.

The data set in (5) consists of utterances from a description of pictures in *Good Dog, Carl*. Sometimes the participant commented on the characters and objects portrayed on the pages, and at other times, she asked questions about the pictures.[1]

5. Data Set 1: Excerpt, description of *Good Dog, Carl*
   (Alya, 3;4, F, AAE)
   1. (a) LJG: Hm hmm? What's what's happening?
      (b) Alya: What's happening?
   2. (a) LJG: Hm hmm? What are they doing?
      (b) Alya: They $\emptyset_{\text{AUX}}$ looking at you.
   3. Alya: And he $\emptyset_{\text{AUX}}$ trying get on the dog.
   4. (a) LJG: Hm hmm. What's Baby doing?
      (b) Alya: Baby $\emptyset_{\text{AUX}}$ looking at the dog.
   5. Alya: He $\emptyset_{\text{AUX}}$ gon bite.
   6. (a) Alya: He $\emptyset_{\text{COP}}$ a boy?[2]
      (b) LJG: Yeah, yeah. He's a boy. Um, hmm.
      (c) Alya: And he's a boy?
      (d) Alya: And they $\emptyset_{\text{COP}}$ brothers.
   7. (a) LJG: I-Is it a good dance?
      (b) Alya: No.
      (c) LJG: Why?
      (d) Alya: It's not a good dance.
   8. Alya: And that's bleet. ['bleet' for blood or bleeding.]

Alya's description is in the present context, but there are very few overt markers, such as inflected copula and auxiliary *BE*, to indicate tense. All of the overt *BE* forms are 's (contracted –s, forms of *is*), as in (1b), (6c), (7d), and (8). In (1b) she uses *what's*, which may be construed as *what* + contracted third singular auxiliary *BE* form (*what* + *is* →*what's*), or it may simply be an unanalyzed form that is a repetition of *what's* in LJG's preceding line. In (6c) Alya uses *he's*, which may have been prompted by *he's* in the preceding line and thus is an unanalyzed form. Overt contracted copulas are in *it's* and *that's* in (7d) and (8), respectively. These overt copula *BE* forms are quite

similar to the overt auxiliary *BE*, in that they could also be unanalyzed forms that occur on words ending in *t* (e.g., *that, it, what*). The
overwhelming majority of Alya's *be* forms are Ø. In addition, Ø$_{COP}$
occurs in her question in (6a) *He a boy?*, so instead of producing 'Is
he a boy?', with the copula at the beginning or 'He's a boy?', with the
contracted copula, she does not include the copula in the sentence.
The structure and intonation of yes–no questions will be addressed
in Chapter 6.

A similar pattern of copula and auxiliary *BE* is evident in
excerpts from Rayna's description of cartoon frames from a *SpongeBob
SquarePants* scenario developed as part of the materials for a comprehension task. Throughout the task, Rayna made observations about
the pictures.[3] Rayna uses overt auxiliary *BE* and copula *BE* (*was*) in
past tense environments, which will be addressed in Chapter 4; however, there is no overt *BE* in present tense environments.

6.   Data Set 2: Excerpt from description of *SpongeBob SquarePants*
      scenarios
      (Rayna, 4;8, F, AAE)
      1. Rayna: But they <u>was</u> screaming at him.
      2. (a) LJG: Right. Yeah, 'cause he's round and SpongeBob is
             square.
          (b) Rayna: And he Ø$_{COP}$ red.
      3. (a) Rayna: Sponge Bob Ø$_{COP}$ right there.
          (b) LJG: Right. Okay.
      4. Rayna: Look he Ø$_{AUX}$ dancing where he they cook the
             patties.
      5. (a) LJG: Yeah. You know that a lot, don't you.
          (b) Rayna: 'Cause I be watching it.
      6. Rayna: She Ø$_{AUX}$ cooking patties.
      7. Rayna: Guess what? Guess what? She she was sick. She had
             to go to the doctor, 'cause Sponge Sandy and-and
             Patrick was fighting over him.
      8. Rayna: Now he Ø$_{COP}$ in the tub.

9. Rayna: SpongeBob and him $\emptyset_{COP}$ in the tub.
10. Rayna: And nobody $\emptyset_{COP}$ in the tub.
11. Rayna: Now he $\emptyset_{COP}$ one.
12. Rayna: And Sandy $\emptyset_{COP}$ on her hands.
13. Rayna: He $\emptyset_{AUX}$ driving.
14. Rayna: And they pi – and guess what? They blow bubbles on-on-on Squidward when Squidward $\emptyset_{AUX}$ sleeping. And when Squidward $\emptyset_{AUX}$ blowing, they they pick the house up with a blowing with a blowing thing.

The only overt *BE* in a non-past environment is the uninflected form in example (5b), which precedes *watching*. There is some evidence that that *be* is invariant *be* (or habitual *be* or aspectual *be*), which will be discussed later in this chapter.

The final excerpt from Rayna includes her descriptions of and observations about picture frames in scenarios portraying created, not familiar cartoon characters.[4]

7. Data Set 3: Rayna's excerpt from descriptions of pictures in scenarios
(Rayna, 5;3, AAE)

1. Rayna: I know what color this is.
2. Rayna: They're going to this.
3. Rayna: And look his mama $\emptyset_{COP}$ in the car.
4. Rayna: Look he $\emptyset_{AUX}$ playing baseball with his daddy.
5. Rayna: 'Cause they $\emptyset_{AUX}$ bout to go into another they $\emptyset_{AUX}$ bout to go the store.
6. (a) Rayna: Look, that's John.
   (b) Rayna: That's the police.
       LJG: Ooo, let's see what he did.
   (c) Rayna: They $\emptyset_{AUX}$ gon put these two in jail.
       LJG: I hope not. Let's see.
   (d) Rayna: They $\emptyset_{AUX}$ gon go to jail.
7. Rayna: It's her big brother?
8. Rayna: That's Jesus doing that.

9. Rayna: Where $\emptyset_{\text{COP}}$ her sister?

10. Rayna: That's the walkie talkies.

11. Rayna: It's after the bike. After the bike one.

12. Rayna: It was under the pa – under the papers.

13. Rayna: We got to paint it first and then we $\emptyset_{\text{AUX}}$ gon do a lesson. Come on, we gotta paint.

Note that in all of the possible *it/that* + *BE* environments, Rayna uses the contracted forms (*it's/that's*) (Data Set 3 (6a), (6b), (7), (8), (10), (11)). The *'s* forms are uniformly produced, and again it is natural to raise the question about whether *it's*, *that's*, and *what's* are unanalyzed and learned as wholes and not as two parts, the words *it, that* and *what* + *'s*. Also, an obvious question is whether something about the meaning or function of *it* and *that* in examples such as (6a) and (8) requires *'s*. The other non-past overt *BE* form is in Data Set 3 (1) (copula) and (2) (auxiliary). The *BE* form in (2) differs from the ones that have been mentioned in that it is a contracted plural form (*'re*). Compare the sentences in Data Set 3 (2) and (6d), in which Rayna uses variable forms *'re going to* and $\emptyset_{\text{AUX}}$ *gon*. As it turns out, *'re* in (2) is the only (optional) *be* form that Rayna produces. The *BE* form in Data Set 3 (1) is obligatory, as it is required when it is the final word in a sentence. I have found no evidence in the data to suggest that the copula *BE* is optional when it is the final word in the sentence in child AAE.

The final copula and auxiliary *BE* data sets are three representative excerpts taken from responses from one child.

8. Data Set 4: Excerpt 1 from created characters scenarios (Zyrion, 5;2, M, AAE)

1. Zyrion: The other one is the white one.

2. Zyrion: And then I was the winner.

3. Zyrion: That's why I'm the winner.

4. Zyrion: Why they $\emptyset_{\text{AUX}}$ driving?[5]

5. Zyrion: Where I'm at?

6. Zyrion: And where's the other one that she broke her ankle?

7. Zyrion: This <u>is</u> a train.

8. Zyrion: Because she <u>was</u> riding her bike by herself.

Data Set 5: Excerpt 2 from created characters scenarios (Zyrion, 5;2, M, AAE)

9. Zyrion: This bear <u>is</u> not singing.

10. (a) LJG: These are the new bears.

    (b) Zyrion: These <u>are</u> not.

    (c) LJG: No.

11. Zyrion: They $\emptyset_{AUX}$ gon go in the trash, hunh?

12. (a) LJG: They're in the trash.

    (b) Zyrion: They $\emptyset_{COP}$ in the trash, hunh?

13. Zyrion: They $\emptyset_{COP}$ not.

14. (a) Zyrion: What color they <u>are</u>?

    (b) LJG: Brown.

    (c) Zyrion: Why they ($\emptyset_{COP}$) brown?

15. Zyrion: They don't have no ribbon because they, they $\emptyset_{COP}$ old.

Data Set 6: Excerpt 3 from *Good Dog, Carl* picture description (Zyrion, 5;2, M, AAE)

16. Zyrion: His name <u>is</u> just like Clifford.

17. Zyrion: He $\emptyset_{AUX}$ gon get on his back.

18. Zyrion: He <u>was</u> trying to put that thing on his back.

19. Zyrion: What's that?

20. Zyrion: Why he ($\emptyset_{AUX}$) doing that?

21. Zyrion: He $\emptyset_{AUX}$ trying to dance.

22. (a) Zyrion: They $\emptyset_{AUX}$ gon get in trouble, hunh?

    (b) LJG: I think they might be.

    (c) Zyrion: Yeah, they are.

23. Zyrion: And then Mama say, "Y'all $\emptyset_{AUX}$ gon catch a spanking!"

Zyrion consistently uses overt forms of the copula and auxiliary *BE* in the following contexts: past (e.g., *was* in (2), (8), (18)), first person singular (e.g., *I'm* in (3), (5)), sentence finally (e.g., *are* in (14a), (22c)), and *that's/what's* (e.g., (3), (19)). Variable forms of the non-past copula/ auxiliary *BE* occur in different contexts, including one instance of overt auxiliary preceding V-*ing* (e.g., (9)). However, note that Zyrion consistently uses $\emptyset_{\text{AUX}}$ preceding *gon* (e.g., (11), (17), (23)) and in all but one environment preceding V-*ing*. Also, there is variation in number marking, as Zyrion uses both singular (e.g., (1)) and plural (e.g., (10b)) *BE* forms. In the data sets Zyrion uses copula *BE* in three questions. In the question in (6), the *BE* form is contracted immediately follow- ing the *wh-* word *where* (*where's*). In (5) the *BE* form is also contracted but on *I* and not on the *wh-* word. That is, Zyrion produces *Where I'm?*, not *Where am I?* Finally in (14), the full form of the copula is at the end of the question. The latter two questions share the property of having the copula form after, not before, the subject. In (5) it is after the subject *I*, and in (14) it is after *they*. However, in (6) the *BE* form (*'s*) is contracted onto *where*, and it precedes the long subject *the other one that she broke her ankle* ('the other one who broke her ankle'). The auxiliary patterns in questions will be discussed in Chapter 6.

A number of general patterns are evident from the data sets in (1)–(6). The first is that while copula/auxiliary *BE* occurrence is variable (i.e. overt forms may or may not occur), the forms have a high (possibly obligatory) occurrence in past contexts; that is, the *BE* forms are necessary to express past tense, but no overt mark- ing is needed for non-past tense. Also, according to the data, there is (near) obligatory occurrence with *what*, *it*, and *that*, in that the copula occurs in its contracted form. These results are in line with the findings for adults. In fact, copula and auxiliary *BE* forms such as *I'm*, *what's*, *it's*, and *that's* are often omitted from quantitative analysis because the copula/auxiliary *BE* is almost always present in those contexts. These cases have been referred to in the literature as "don't count cases" (Wolfram 1969; Rickford 1999, for example). (See Blake (1997) for a discussion of the "don't count" cases.)

What can we say about optional contexts? There are instances of overt *BE* forms preceding V-*ing* in the non-past contexts (e.g., Data

Set 3: *They're going to this*. Data Set 5: *This bear is not singing*); however, in most cases, the children here use $\emptyset_{AUX}$ in that context. The high occurrence of $\emptyset_{AUX}$ preceding V-*ing* might be an indication of the relation between auxiliary *BE* and –*ing*. Labov (1972) made the following observation, which could explain why $\emptyset_{AUX}$, as opposed to an overt *BE* form, often precedes V-*ing*: "it seems likely that the deletion of that *BE* (in its finite forms) is connected with its redundant relation to the following –*ing* form" (p. 113). Another way to state the connection between $\emptyset_{AUX}$ and the following V –*ing* that Labov was making is to say that given that –*ing* already marks an event or indicates that some kind of verbal activity is occurring, the auxiliary *BE* is not required to give that information (Green, Wyatt, and Lopez 2007). That is, it is possible not to include the auxiliary preceding the V-*ing* simply because the purpose of the auxiliary (e.g., *is, are*) is to show that a verb follows; however, the –*ing* on the verb already does that. In that case, it might be preferable to leave out auxiliary *BE* to avoid it being redundant. Labov refers specifically to a deletion process, but I do not. I have no evidence that the *BE* form was ever present, so I prefer to describe the statements as instances in which *BE* does not occur or in which it is left out of the sentence – actually never made it into the sentences. For consideration, we can extend the observation about $\emptyset_{AUX}$ preceding V-*ing* to $\emptyset_{AUX}$ in other similar environments, such as those in which it precedes *gon* (e.g., Data Set 6 (17)), *fitna, sposeta*, and *bouta* (Data Set 3 (5)). In those constructions, *gon* and the other markers would be argued to indicate an event, so the overt verbal form (e.g., auxiliary *is*) is not required to occur on the surface.

Considering the copula and auxiliary *BE* in different environments in the speech of developing AAE-speaking children provides an opportunity to analyze properties and developmental patterns associated with these forms, which include their optional occurrence in certain linguistic environments. One of the overarching questions about the copula and auxiliary *BE* sentences is whether the variable occurrence of *BE* is developmental and subject to change as children advance through the AAE developmental stages, or whether the children's uses of $\emptyset_{COP}$ and $\emptyset_{AUX}$ are already representative of what is found in later stages of AAE. There are a number of directions to pursue in addressing this question. It might very well be that, in its earliest uses, auxiliary *BE* in child AAE is obligatory in past tense contexts (i.e. it must occur if it is used to indicate past tense, e.g., *was*). On the other hand, auxiliary *BE* is not required in non-past (or present) environments because the *–ing* on the following verb conveys the information that the event indicated by the verb is in progress. Therefore, one developmental trend that we may see in child AAE is that children start off early on with overt auxiliary *BE* in past contexts (e.g., *was*) and $\emptyset_{AUX}$ in non-past (or present) contexts. As children get older, they get evidence from the use of AAE in their speech communities that auxiliary *BE* is optional in non-past contexts. As a result, they use auxiliary *BE* optionally. The prediction here is that children go from $\emptyset_{COP}/\emptyset_{AUX}$ to a stage in which the forms are used optionally.

The copula also occurs in past tense contexts, as we see in Data Sets 2, 3, and 4 (e.g., *She she was sick*), but past contexts will be taken up in Chapter 4. As we look through the data, we also see that $\emptyset_{COP}$ occurs quite frequently. The most overt forms occur in Zyrion's Data Set 4; however, there are still $\emptyset_{COP}$ forms. In this way, $\emptyset_{COP}$ and $\emptyset_{AUX}$ do not seem to differ much. However, we might expect a difference because the auxiliary forms occur with V-*ing*, but the copula forms do not. If *–ing* makes it unnecessary for overt auxiliary *BE* to occur and creates an environment for $\emptyset_{AUX}$, then we might expect more occurrences of overt copula (or fewer occurrences of $\emptyset_{COP}$) simply because there is no element such as *–ing* redundantly contributing information added by the copula. Although overall there is evidence of more occurrences of overt copula *BE* forms, there are still significant incidences of non-past $\emptyset_{COP}$ among children at this stage of AAE development.

Child AAE speakers may start off treating the copula much like they treat the auxiliary *BE*. That is, they might assume that it only occurs in obligatory environments, in past tense contexts and at the end of the sentence. However, as the developmental process continues, the copula may be produced more and more as a variable form in certain environments. For instance, it might be that the overt copula will be produced in the environment preceding nouns, as in *The other one is the white one* (Zyrion, Data Set 4, – here it occurs in its full forms, but it is not stressed). Whether or not the copula (or auxiliary *BE*) is stressed will also affect its appearance, such that the stressed copula (or auxiliary *BE*) will be pronounced. Other issues to consider in the production of full forms (i.e. *is* v. *'s*) are related to prosodic properties of the phrases or sentences in which the forms occur, along the lines of Walker's (2000) claims that the prosodic complexity of the copular construction affects its overt occurrence. On the other hand, it might be that as the developmental process continues, children produce the copula as a variable form in other contexts, such as preceding prepositional phrases and adjectives. If this is part of the acquisition process, then it would be interesting to determine whether there is something about prepositional phrases, adjectives, and nouns that triggers variable copula use. Also, is this variable copula use the same preceding all categories, or do we expect to see more overt copula use in one of these environments? From the data considered here, it is clear that children of this AAE-speaking community acquire a grammar that can produce sentences without the copula/auxiliary *BE* and that can produce sentences with copula/ auxiliary *BE*. Henry (2002) addresses a similar situation of variable use of subject–verb agreement in Belfast English and notes the following: "A child is generally acquiring a grammar from the output of a number of different speakers, whose grammars are probably not identical; in order to do this, the child's acquisition device must be able to incorporate variation" (p. 281).

An obvious question that arises in relation to child copula and auxiliary *BE* data is whether the overwhelming use of Ø forms and the selected use of contracted *'s* as an unanalyzed form in some environments reflect AAE developmental patterns or whether the use is solely a reflection of general adult AAE. The data presented here are for children from ages 3, 4, and 5, so we do not have the range of developmental data beyond 5 years needed to check the predictions; however, results from adult AAE strongly suggest that a view along the lines of the one presented here is on the right track. That is, in adult AAE there is high incidence of $\emptyset_{\text{AUX}}$ forms preceding *gon* and V-*ing*. In addition, as presented in Green, Wyatt, and Lopez (2007), Becker's (2000) analysis of the acquisition of the copula in mainstream English is relevant to the development of the copula and auxiliary *BE* in AAE. In that work, Becker notes that children acquiring mainstream English produce variable copula according to the type of predicate that follows it. For instance, they are more likely to produce an overt copula form in instances in which it is followed by a predicate that indicates a more permanent property, such as a noun (e.g., *is a girl*), and $\emptyset_{\text{COP}}$ is more likely to occur in the environment in which a predicate that indicates a more transitory state, such as one marked by a prepositional phrase (e.g., $\emptyset_{COP}$ *in the kitchen*), follows. Becker does not directly address auxiliary *BE*; however, the connection between her observations for the acquisition of MAE copula and the AAE auxiliary *BE* observations is that both $\emptyset_{\text{COP}}$ in developmental MAE and $\emptyset_{\text{AUX}}$ in developmental AAE may be linked to the type of predicate that occurs with them.

The fact that the past form of the copula and auxiliary *BE* (*was*) is seemingly obligatory even in early AAE data presented here falls squarely within the explanation about why the *BE* forms are required to occur in some environments in children's sentences.[6] From the data sets above, the contracted forms *'m* and *'s* in *I'm, it's, that's,* and *what's* also seem to be overwhelmingly present. One view, put forth by DeBose and Faraclas (1993), is that the pronouns *I'm, it's,* and *that's* are actually variants of the pronouns *I, it,* and *that,* respectively, so the contracted forms (*'m* and *'s*) are not separate *BE* forms. Instead they are inherent parts of the pronoun. If this is the case, then these contracted forms do not count as separate *BE* forms; the developing AAE-speaking children, in learning *I'm, that's, it's,* and *what's* do not learn *I + am, that + is, it + is,* and *what + is;* they simply learn *I'm, it's, that's,* and *what's* as full, unanalyzed forms just as they learn *I, it, that,* and *what.* In this way these forms do not have the function of carrying tense. There is some support for this view in Data Set 4 example 5 (*Where I'm at?*). Note that in this question *I'm* is treated as a whole form that is not separated as *am* and *I,* as in *Where am I?.* However, even this form is subject to some variation in developing child AAE. Although not many speakers produced *I* with Ø *BE* forms as a variant of *I'm,* as in Data Set 7 below (and also in the example at the beginning of Chapter 2), a few did:

9.   Data Set 7: Excerpts from picture descriptions
      (Ray, 5;0, M, AAE)
      (a) I know what I gon be.
           'I know what I'm going to be'
      (b) I a smart boy.
           'I'm a smart boy'
One possible picture of the copula and auxiliary *BE* in child AAE is the following:

10.   Copula and Auxiliary *BE* in Child AAE
      Overt copula/auxiliary *BE* in past, prosodic contexts of stress, and word final contexts, and Ø elsewhere, with $\emptyset_{COP/AUX}$ subject to increasing variation.

Developing AAE-speaking children also use the verb form *go,* generally referred to as *go* copula in the communication disorders literature on AAE (Wyatt (1995) and Horton-Ikard and Weismar (2005)). This copular form occurs in presentational contexts, such as the following:

11.   (a) Here go your phone. (Bethany, 3, F, AAE)
           'Here is your phone'
      (b) Oh, here go the beeper right here. (Lenny, 5, M, AAE)
           'Oh the beeper is right here'

One important characteristic of *go* is that it occurs strictly in presentational contexts. As such, it differs from the regular copula (overt and $\emptyset_{COP}$), which can also occur in predicational contexts. In predicational contexts a property is associated with a subject, as the property of being a teacher is associated with Pat in *Pat is a teacher*, but an entity, such as *your phone* or *the beeper*, or an individual, is introduced in presentational contexts. Benedicto, Abdulkarim, Garrett, Johnson, and Seymour (1998) argue that the copula *BE* is more likely to occur in its overt form in presentational contexts. Considering that claim, it may be that the presence of some semantic information or requirement in presentational contexts also induces the presence of *go*.

In the next section I discuss an aspectual use of *be*, which requires that the marker be present. This aspectual *be* (also known as invariant *be* and habitual *be*) does not have a zero (Ø) counterpart in adult AAE, which is one way it differs from the copula/auxiliary *BE*.

3.2 MARKING RECURRING EVENTUALITIES

One of the characteristics of the copula and auxiliary *BE* in child AAE is that they can occur in their zero forms, $\emptyset_{COP}$ and $\emptyset_{AUX}$; however, aspectual *be* does not have a zero form. I will write *be* (in lower case) to indicate that I am referring to the actual word *be* in aspectual *be* sequences. Here I am making the strong claim that in Rayna's sentences in the previous section in (6) Data Set 2, example 14, while the $\emptyset_{AUX}$ form could also be realized as *is*, it could not be a variant of aspectual *be* and be realized as uninflected *be*. That is, the sentence could be ✓ *They blow bubbles on Squidward when Squidward $\emptyset_{AUX}$/is sleeping*. However, the following option is not available because $\emptyset_{AUX}$ and aspectual *be* are not variants, although the sentence is perfectly grammatical and has a felicitous reading: ✗ *They blow bubbles on Squidward when Squidward $\emptyset_{AUX}$/be sleeping.*

Aspectual *be* must always occur overtly in contexts in which it is used, and it does not occur in any other (inflected) form (such as *is*, *am*, *are*, etc.); it is always *be*. Thus the marker is referred to as invariant. It has one form, and that form always occurs overtly; it does not vary in forms or shapes. Aspectual *be* indicates that eventualities recur, happen from time to time or habitually (Green 2000, 2002). As I did in the previous chapter, here I am using "eventualities" as a cover term to include all of the different types of predicates indicating activities, events, and even states, that occur with aspectual *be*. It is referred to as an aspectual marker because it indicates that an eventuality recurs or occurs from time to time. It does not indicate that an eventuality occurred in the past, is occurring now, or will occur in the future, so it is not a tense marker. In the following example, the reading books eventuality recurs:

12.   Bruce be reading books.
         'Bruce is usually reading books'

The sentence contexts in which aspectual *be* occurs are preceding verb-*ing* (13a), adjective (13b), noun (13c), preposition (13d), adverb (13e), and sentence finally (13f). That is, it occurs in the same contexts in which the copula and auxiliary *BE* occur:

13.   (a) The students be singing.
            'The students are usually singing'
     (b) The eggs be soft.
            'The eggs are usually soft'
     (c) Dee be the leader.
            'Dee is usually the leader'
     (d) The marbles be in the jar.
            'The marbles are usually in the jar'
     (e) Bruce be there.
            'Bruce is usually there'
     (f) That's how much gas be.
            'That's how much gas usually is'

In all of the sentences in (13), the states or events indicated by the predicates recur. In other words, the singing (13a) occurs from time to time just as Dee's being the leader (13c) occurs from time to time. Also, as communicated by the sentence in (13f), gas is/costs a certain amount from time to time or generally.

Aspectual *be* is often taken to be unique to AAE. The marker, which is clearly identifiable as a point of difference between AAE and other varieties of English, has been the topic of a number of studies, although still it may not be well understood by people who are not members of the AAE-speaking community.[7] One difficulty that aspectual *be* presents for those for whom the marker is not part of their grammar is that it seems to be very close in meaning and use to the copula or auxiliary *BE*, so for many non-AAE speakers, people who use it appear to be misusing either the copula or auxiliary *BE* instead of using a *be* form that is actually grammatical in AAE. That is, AAE speakers are thought to be making a mistake in MAE or simply using "bad English."

In the southwest Louisiana data that are being considered here, some children produced the marker in spontaneous speech without hearing it in LJG's speech in a question directed to them, but others never produced the marker in spontaneous speech. 4- to 5-year-old developing AAE speakers comprehended the marker with varying degrees of success in comprehension tasks. Because aspectual *be* is such a robust marker in AAE, we might expect it to emerge very early in children's speech, and, at least, it is claimed to be part of the pre-kindergarten age group's grammar given that it occurs on feature lists (Feature #10 on the feature list in (1) in Chapter 2). As reported in (14) Data Set 8, a child produced what appeared to be aspectual *be* given the context; however, it may have been prompted by aspectual *be* in LJG's question in (14d):

14. Data Set 8: Excerpt from a conversation about a make-believe phone call
(Jamilla, 3;6, F, AAE)
(a) Jamilla: <*pretending to talk to her cousin on a toy cell phone*> What you want?

(b) LJG: What does J__Jr. want?

(c) Jamilla: That boy is crazy like a fool.

(d) LJG: What does he be doing?

(e) Jamilla: He be bad and fooling with me.

(f) LJG: What else?

(g) Jamilla: I don't know what he be doing, but he $\emptyset_{COP}$ bad though. (Green 2004, p. 64)

This excerpt is from Jamilla's comment about her recent (make-believe) phone call on a toy cell phone to her cousin, J__Jr. An uninflected *be* occurs in Jamilla's response to the question in (14d) "What does he doing?," which is intended to ask about J__Jr.'s usual "crazy like a fool" behavior. The extent to which uninflected *be* is part of Jamilla's grammar as an aspectual marker or the extent to which she uses it productively is not clear from her spontaneous speech, but the *be* in her response in (14e) could be habitual, a reading in which she intends to communicate that J__Jr. exhibits bad behavior on occasions and is "fooling" with her from time to time. Given that Jamilla uses the uninflected *be* construction in response to an aspectual *be* construction in LJG's line, her comprehension of aspectual *be* as a habitual marker is not clear, although she uses it in an appropriate sentence context, preceding an adjective *bad* and V-*ing fooling*. Note also the overt copula (14c) and $\emptyset_{COP}$ (14g) in the data set. Such data raise the question about whether Jamilla actually distinguishes uninflected *be* and forms of the copula, that is, whether the overt copula in (14c) and the $\emptyset_{COP}$ in (14g) are variants and the uninflected *be* in (14e) is aspectual *be*, such that Jamilla is using two BE forms, copula and aspectual *be*, with different meanings or whether she is using all three forms (*is*, *be*, and $\emptyset$) as variants of the copula. In the study there is no conclusive data to show that children comprehend and use aspectual *be* productively before they are 4 years old, and even at the older age children still seem to be in the process of acquiring it. Some children in the 4- to 5-year-old age group used invariant *be* in natural speech, without any prompting from a previous occurrence of the marker, as illustrated below:

15. Data Set 9: Commentary during comprehension task
   (Zeke, 4;8, M, AAE)
   (a) Zeke: <*pointing to the bike in the picture*> And I have – and I have a bike. Black right here, red right here, and green on my tire. And green right – and blue right there. I – It's different colors.
   (b) LJG: So you can race with those kids. You can race in the bicycle race. Wow!
   (c) Zeke: Sometimes I be going fast and falling off.
   (d) LJG: Oh, really?
   (e) Zeke: 'Cause I be having my knee pads – knee pads and my helmet.

The focus of the session with Zeke was on the comprehension of negative concord; none of the prompts or stories describing the pictures included aspectual *be*. (The picture that Zeke is commenting on is in Figure 5.1 in Chapter 5.) Nor was aspectual *be* used in LJG's lines, so Zeke was not prompted to use the marker by its previous occurrences in other parts of the exchange or in the story descriptions. It is clear that Zeke is not using the uninflected *be* (in (15c)) to refer to the present moment to indicate that he is going fast and falling off at the speech time because at that time, he was not engaged in bike riding. This is a clue that he is not using the uninflected *be* as a tense marker that indicates that the eventuality of bike riding is occurring at the present time. Secondly, he uses the adverbial *sometimes* with uninflected *be*, which could mean that he is linking *sometimes* to the 'from time to time' reading of aspectual *be* or specifying the time period – sometimes – when he is going fast and falling off his bike. Zeke seems to be talking about his instances of going fast and falling off during his bike-riding events, which would call for aspectual *be*. Again in his final line it is clear that he is not using the *be* to mean that he has his knee pads and a helmet with him at the moment during which he is talking, so the uninflected *be* is not used as auxiliary *BE* that refers to a present tense context. This *be* could indicate that the times that he goes fast and falls off of his bike are instances during which he has on his knee pads and helmet – an aspectual *be* reading. Taking Zeke's last example (be_{ASP} *having*) into consideration, I want to note that there appears to be a strong link between be_{ASP} and *–ing* on the following verb. *Have*, which is generally characterized as referring to a state, takes *–ing* as part of the sequence. At least from adult AAE perspective, BE_{AUX} cannot occur in this environment. The sentences ✗ *I'm having knee pads and my helmet/He having his knee pads and helmet* sound strange in adult AAE with a present progressive reading as well as with a habitual reading.

A similar example occurs in the following excerpt from Donovan's natural speech before the picture task began:

16.   Data Set 10: Spontaneous speech
       (Donovan, 5;0, M, AAE)
       Donovan: I can't um ride my bike without no training wheels.
       LJG: Well that's ok. That's fine. You can ride with the training
            wheels. That's good. That's a fun ride, isn't it?
       Donovan: I be going fast.
       LJG: Do you?

It is clear from the context that Donovan's *be going fast* does not refer to his activity at the speech time because, at that moment, he is not riding his bike. It may be possible to construe *be* in Donovan's response as a type of intensifier to mean that he can go really fast, but there are no obvious clues that point to this reading. It is clear that Donovan is not using uninflected *be* as a present tense marker, although some children may do so in earlier stages of AAE or at younger ages.

Information about the context in which child speakers use uninflected *be* is useful in making proposals about the type of meaning they associate with the marker. While it is true that children's use of uninflected *be* in natural conversation gives us information about production and about whether it is part of their grammar, we need more than production data to find out more about children's comprehension of the marker and the way *be* fits into their overall tense–aspect system.

To determine how children interpret and comprehend uninflected *be*, they were first tested on *SpongeBob SquarePants* scenarios, in which cartoon characters were portrayed as engaging in some activity or being in some state. They were asked questions pertaining to the characters to determine whether they associated uninflected *be* with activities that occur from time to time or states that hold from time to time. The scenarios were written in MAE, but the prompt or target question included aspectual *be*. The goal was to present the stories in a way that was natural for me and that was appropriate language for the setting. It was also my goal to present the stories in as interesting a manner as possible to engage participants and hold their attention. There were no attempts to write the scenarios in AAE or produce them in an affected AAE style. As is evident from the rich data collected from the child AAE speakers, the language used to deliver the stories did not present any problems for the participants.

Following work by Jackson (1998), in which *Sesame Street* characters were used to develop scenarios designed to elicit responses from children, a graduate student and I developed a line of scenarios based on the *SpongeBob SquarePants* cartoons. While the children showed great interest in the scenarios, and they often asked to read and reread the stories, it is not clear how much the children's pre-existing vast knowledge about the *SpongeBob* cartoon characters affected their responses. One of the concerns was that the participants might have relied more on the knowledge they gained about the cartoon and characters from having watched episodes of them so often than they would have used the information presented in the scenarios. While children's spontaneous speech and descriptions triggered by the *SpongeBob* scenarios serve as valuable data, the *SpongeBob* results on aspectual *be* comprehension tasks were not used simply because there were too many variables that were not sufficiently controlled. The following examples should convey the type of issues that came up with the scenarios and responses.

A sample scenario is given in which the participant was read the short story and asked the aspectual *be* target question at the end. Many of the participants told their own stories about the *Sponge Bob* cartoon, along the lines of Donovan's comments on a scenario about *Sponge Bob* characters Mr. Krabs and Pearl.

17. Data Set 11: Commentary on a *SpongeBob* scenario
     (Donovan, 5;0, M, AAE)
     LJG: Oh, okay. Why is Pearl crying?
     Donovan: Because she getting the krabby patties wet and wetter and wetter and wetter and then they going down then the (???). Mr. Krabs saying, "Why you did that? Stop crying, Pearl. Don't don't cry."[8]
     LJG: Who tells Pearl not to cry?
     Donovan: Mr. Krabs. That's that's Mr. Krabs daughter.
     LJG: Pearl is Mr. Krabs daughter? I didn't know that. But she's not a crab.
     Donovan: She STILL Mr. Krabs daughter.
     LJG: You sure about that?
     Donovan: Yeah, I'm sure. If you watch tonight, you'll know.
     LJG: Well, I need to watch it tonight, 'cause I don't know.
     Donovan: It's on um Nickelodeon.

This is just one example among many that reflects children's extensive background knowledge about the cartoon. My concern was that the children were very familiar with the *SpongeBob SquarePants* characters and their established behaviors, and such familiarity might give rise to responses that were not limited to the background information given in the scenarios. The target questions were based on the information in the scenarios, so they would provide insight into how the children interpreted the uninflected *be* in reference to the story they were provided.

Another example of children's interest in and knowledge about the *SpongeBob* cartoons is given below:

18.   Data Set 12: Commentary on *SpongeBob* scenario
       (Joya, 4;11, F, AAE)
       Joya: <*points to* SpongeBob *characters*> I watch this and that.
       LJG: You wat – Who are the people?
       Joya: Mr. Krab.
       LJG: Mr. Krab. Now, J__ I didn't know you knew Mr. Krab,
              too …
       Joya: And SpongeBob he he be silly.
       LJG: Do you like SpongeBob?
       Joya: Yeah.
       LJG: He's silly how? What does he do?
       Joya: He be, he be wearing a boot and, uh, and Mr. Krab give
              him the boot and he act silly with it.
       LJG: Wow.
       Joya: And the whole crabs burn up.

Just the sight of the *SpongeBob* pictures triggered a response from Joya. She identifies the character in the picture (Mr. Krab), and she adds information about a boot that is not included in any part of the scenario, so she must be reporting scenes from the actual cartoon. She uses invariant *be* (e.g., *be wearing*) as well as simple tense verbs that are not marked with third person singular –s morphology (e.g., *he act silly*). Without getting too far into a description of the excerpt, we can make the observation that it is possible that Joya uses invariant *be* constructions as well as the "unmarked" verbs or simple tense verbs to talk about events that generally happen. That is, it may be that *he be wearing a boot* (as in 'he generally wears a boot') is intended to indicate activity that occurs from time to time on the cartoon episodes. By the same token, it may be that in the case of *he act silly* ('he acts silly') and *the whole crabs burn up*, the reference is to eventualities that occur from time to time or have recurred on the episodes. While we have to speculate here because we are dealing with children's natural utterances and trying to link them to meanings, it is possible to explore questions about whether developing AAE-speaking children are acquiring two ways of marking habitual notions: with invariant *be* and with simple tense verbs. In other words, both invariant *be* and simple tense verbal constructions appear to be part of the AAE grammar for talking about recurring events. Perhaps there are other alternatives to consider, such as the following: Could it be that only invariant *be* verbal constructions (*be* V-*ing*) are part of the AAE grammar for talking about recurring events, but not simple tense verbal constructions? Another question to ask focuses mainly on morphology. That is, are both constructions part of the AAE grammar, but what is not part of the AAE grammar is third singular –*s* that would occur with simple tense verbs in singular subject contexts (e.g., *he acts* vs. *he act*). These questions are related to the issues about AAE, general English (or MAE), and code-shifting that are raised at the beginning of the book and then again in Chapter 7. I do not want to get too far off course here, but it is important to ask questions – with specific data in mind – about what researchers label as "true" AAE on the one hand and general American English on the other. Take, for instance, two sample sentences from the excerpt in (18), repeated as (19):

19. (a) Joya: He be, he be wearing a boot and, uh, and Mr. Krab give
         him the boot and he act silly with it.
     (b) Joya: And the whole crabs burn up.

In those analyses that rely on counting features to get at the depth or density of dialect, the AAE "features" in (19a, b) would have to be identified or tallied up. I assume that (19a) would include three features: 1-invariant *be*, 2-*give* (Ø third singular –*s*) vs. *gives*, 3-*act*

(Ø third singular –s) vs. *acts*. In such an analysis, the simple tense verbs would be included as "features" simply because they lack third singular –s marking. Following this line of analysis, are we to understand (19b) as not including any AAE "features" because there are no morphological indicators of AAE? In such an approach I do not see how the question about the type of forms that are used to indicate eventualities that recur come into the discussion. It is true that there is no third singular –s, but what more can be said about the verbs that are used in singular contexts, as well as the one in (19b) (*burn up*) that is used with a plural subject? As concrete as the counting method appears to be, it is no doubt quite simplistic in that it does not go beyond morphology; it does not provide a way to talk about whether or not these verbs are also used to mark habitual meaning. I note that in AAE simple tense verbs also indicate habituality, although they may not be morphologically marked with –s.

There is significant confirmation that 4- and 5-year-old developing AAE-speaking children produce invariant *be* in spontaneous speech, and often context strongly suggested that the marker was used to make a statement about eventualities that recurred. The *SpongeBob* scenarios proved quite useful in eliciting a significant amount of speech that provided more insight and raises interesting questions about the way children talk about events. However, to get consistent results that would help to determine whether children did indeed associate invariant *be* with a habitual reading ('is usually'), present ('is right now'), or past ('was before now') reading, they were tested on six scenarios based on new or created characters that were not featured in any cartoons to avoid the familiarity effect that was encountered with the *SpongeBob* scenarios. The scenarios consisted of a description of the pictures and a target question about the characters/objects in the scenarios. The children who were included in this study ranged in ages from 4;3 to 5;7. Initially, 3-year-olds were included in the study, but they were not able to handle the task, perhaps due to the length of the scenarios, the nature of the task itself, or cognitive development. Data from some children clearly show that developing AAE-speaking children in the 4- to-5-year-old age group have invariant *be* as an aspectual marker that refers to habits or recurrence of events as part of their developing grammar.

Two sample scenarios, including text and descriptive pictures, are given below. In the scenario in Figure 3.1, the character Bruce is portrayed in several frames as eating turkey sandwiches for lunch day after day; however, he is not eating turkey sandwiches at the speech time or present. The target question includes an aspectual *be* construction in which *be*$_{ASP}$ precedes V-*ing* (*having*). One instance of *be having* occurred in child spontaneous speech; although the spontaneous *having* had a different meaning than *having* (e.g, *eating*) in the scenario, it also occurred in a child's spontaneous speech. The prediction was that children who understood invariant *be* as a habitual marker would choose Bruce as the answer for the target question. Although Bruce decided to have soup and is not eating turkey now for a change, he is the one who *be eating/having turkey sandwiches for lunch*, that is, 'usually has (eats) / is usually having (eating) turkey sandwiches for lunch.' On the other hand, children who did not interpret the invariant *be* as a habitual marker were hypothesized to choose the person who is eating a turkey sandwich at the moment but who does not do so regularly, or perhaps they would choose all of the kids who have eaten turkey sandwiches before. Choosing the character who is eating the turkey sandwich at the moment could mean that the child understands *Who be eating turkey sandwiches?* to mean 'Who is eating turkey sandwiches now?,' which would count as a present progressive reading. A choice of all characters who have eaten turkey before, including those who are eating it now, could suggest that for the child, *Who be eating turkey sandwiches?* refers to any turkey-eating event, whether it is now or in the past. That interpretation also differs from the habitual reading.

In Figure 3.2, the focus of the scenario is on boxes and not on human characters. In this case it is not an activity that occurs from time to time; it is a box that is in some location from time to time

Figure 3.1 *Who be having turkey sandwiches for lunch?*

At lunchtime, all the kids eat together. Bruce always has turkey sandwiches because he loves turkey. He had turkey sandwiches last week
and this week. Jenny likes peanut butter and jelly or ham and cheese.
She doesn't eat turkey for lunch. Faye likes everything. She sometimes
has a cheese sandwich. Today, Faye has a turkey sandwich but Bruce
doesn't. He has soup.

Who be having turkey sandwiches for lunch?

Figure 3.2 *Which box be in the garage?*

Bruce has a box of toys he keeps in the garage. If there is no car in the garage, he plays with the box of toys there. Sometimes, John comes over and he and Bruce play with the toys in the box from the box in the garage. But, today, Bruce has to move his box of toys to the porch because he is keeping a box of John's baseball stuff in the garage.

Which box be in the garage?

or is generally in the garage. The target question includes an aspectual *be* construction in which be_{ASP} precedes a prepositional phrase. Bruce's toy box is generally in the garage because that is where he stores it; however, his friend John's box of baseball paraphernalia is being stored in the garage at the moment, so Bruce's toy box, which is usually in the garage, is now on the porch. If the child answered "the toy box" to the target question, "Which box be in the garage?," then the assumption was that he or she associated invariant *be* with habituality or with states that held from time to time. The children who gave the answer "the baseball box" to the question were assumed to take *be* as a tense marker associated with now, to mean 'Which box is in the garage?' Finally, children who chose both the toy box and the baseball box may have associated "be in the garage" with any event of ever having been in the garage, which is not compatible with the habitual reading.

The results for the invariant *be* comprehension tasks are reported in Green and Roeper (2007). Overall the children were tested on six scenarios. The be_{ASP} constructions in the target questions were: *be hiding, be getting to school, be having turkey sandwiches for lunch, be in the garage, train set be* (as in *Where does the train set be?* 'Where is the train set generally located?'). Although there were categories other than verbs, there were no instances of be_{ASP} + noun or be_{ASP} + adjective, constructions that should also be considered. In summary, "the developing AAE-speaking children have knowledge of aspectual *be*, so overall they associate it with eventualities that recur and with general states of affairs" (p. 305). As a group, the children scored at least .48 on each aspectual *be* scenario, and they scored as high as .72 on one scenario. When children answered the aspectual *be* target questions in the scenarios with a character who was habitually engaged in some activity or with an object that was generally in some state or place, that response was taken to indicate that they associated invariant *be* with habitual meaning. When children did not give such a response, they either chose the character who was currently engaged in the activity or they chose all characters described in the scenario. In the case of the former, in which they chose the character who was currently engaged in the activity, or an object that was currently in a particular place, children seemed to associate invariant *be* with a present ongoing activity, and such a response suggests that children are not making a distinction between invariant *be*, which indicates habitual occurrences, and auxiliary *be*, which can mark present tense and signal an event that is in progress or a state that is currently holding. When children chose all characters or objects, it seemed that they associated the marker with any representation of the event, regardless of whether it is currently in progress, in the past, or occurs from time to time. In such cases it was assumed that children did not associate invariant *be* with habitual occurrences of an eventuality.

This research on aspectual *be* provides an opportunity to compare developing AAE speakers' language and language of their non-AAE-speaking peers in the same geographical area (in the same child development center), especially given claims about the similarities between AAE and varieties of southern English. Although it has often been claimed that there is considerable overlap between AAE and English varieties spoken by whites in the southern United States, habitual *be*, as it is characterized in AAE, has not been linked to these southern varieties of American English. The overall results for the developing AAE-speaking children and their developing SwLVE-speaking peers are in Figure 3.3.

The SwLVE-speaking children's scores were not significantly different from chance (.33), so they do not appear to have developing knowledge of the marker. While AAE and varieties of English in the South share some similarities, the overlap does not seem to extend to habitual *be*, at least at this stage of development. The evidence that habitual *be* use is not a shared pattern between the two varieties comes from the significant difference in the results from the two populations of child speakers. The marker is part of the developing AAE-speaking children's grammar, but it does not seem to be part of the SwLVE-speaking children's grammar regardless of the contact

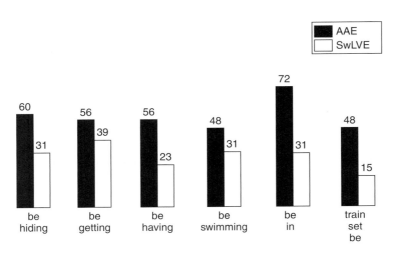

Figure 3.3 Results for AAE- and SwLVE-speaking children on aspectual *be* scenarios

between the two groups in the southern United States. The results of the aspectual *be* scenarios and the invariant *be* constructions produced by the children in spontaneous speech shed light on the treatment of aspectual *be* in the literature on child AAE. As has been shown in Chapter 2, the marker is included on feature lists for child AAE, but it is not generally discussed in the studies that reference the lists. Given the data that I have collected, the children are clearly developing the marker, along with its properties, but they have not mastered comprehension of the marker. Some children produce it in spontaneous speech, and some do not – at least not during the time allowed for the sessions with the children. It may be that at this stage (4 to 5 years old), the marker does not occur often enough in the course of speech samples to conclude very much about its nature in child AAE, so it is not widely discussed in work on child AAE. It is useful to supplement spontaneous speech data with elicitation tasks.

Developing AAE-speaking children are developing use and habitual meaning of be_{ASP}, and this marker increases their *BE* and *be* inventory. They also have copula and auxiliary *BE* in their grammars. An important point to note is that they make the distinction between the *BE* elements that are used in these contexts. For instance, they inflect the overt copula and auxiliary *BE* forms that are used in past tense constructions as well as in the limited non-past constructions, but they do not inflect the invariant *be* form that occurs in habitual constructions. At the developmental stage being considered, the meanings of the copula and auxiliary *BE* forms, on the one hand, and the invariant *be*, on the other, are clearly different for some children, although others are still developing comprehension of the marker. Rashandra's response to the invariant *be* scenario in Figure 3.4 is strong indication that she has a handle on the marker.

20.   Data Set 13 "Where does the train set be?"
       (Rashandra, 5;0, F, AAE)
       LJG: <*reads scenario and asks target question*> Where does the
          train set be?
       Rashandra: In his room.
       LJG: Where is the train set? Where is the train set, R__?
       Rashandra: ON the back porch.

In response to the question "Where does the train set be?" that is, 'where is the train set generally located,' Rashandra says "in his room." According to the scenario, this is precisely what is expected given an aspectual *be* interpretation because that is where Bruce keeps the train set, where it usually is. However, when asked where the train set is (meaning at the moment), Rashandra opts for "on the back porch," which is where the train set is now due to its having been moved temporarily because of the cleaning taking place in Bruce's room. These two responses provide evidence to support the claim that part of a child AAE speaker's developing knowledge is the difference between the tense–aspect properties of copula/auxiliary *BE* and aspectual *be*.

   Children use zero forms of the copula and auxiliary *BE* elements to talk about current states and events that are in progress, respectively. In developing aspectual *be*, children may very well go through a period in which they associate the invariant *be* with

Figure 3.4 *Where does the train set be?*

Bruce keeps a train set next to his bed so he can play with it when-
ever he wants. It's the only place in his bedroom that the train set fits.
Sometimes, Faye plays with him. Sometimes all the kids play with him
and the train set next to the bed. But, today, Bruce had to clean his room,
so the train set is on the back porch. Where does the train set be?

the same type of interpretation they give to auxiliary *BE* and even copula *BE* constructions. That is, they may take the invariant *be* to refer to events that are ongoing at present or during the time of speech, which may explain, in part, children's present ongoing interpretation of invariant *be* in combination with a following predicate. One of the claims made earlier in the chapter is that *–ing* in auxiliary *BE* constructions (e.g., *is running*, Ø *running*) gives the information about the verb being an event and makes it unnecessary for the auxiliary *BE* to occur in its overt form. There is no obvious evidence from the spontaneous speech samples to show that be_{ASP} occurs in a Ø form preceding verbs, although more data are in order before conclusions can be drawn. It would be useful to ask more questions about children's use of *–ing* in relation to auxiliary *BE* and aspectual *be*. First *–ing* must also indicate something about the event status of verbs in be_{ASP} constructions, but be_{ASP} always seems to be overt, unlike auxiliary *BE*. It may be that in developing be_{ASP}, children also must make the connection between be_{ASP} and *–ing*, such that the suffix occurs on verbs in aspectual sequences. They also have to learn that while *–ing* indicates that an activity is in progress in the case of auxiliary *BE* + V-*ing* (*is*/Ø *running*), it does not necessarily express that meaning of aspectual *be* + V-*ing* sequences. Compare the two sentence types (reported on in Green (2000)):

(a)　Bruce (is) crying when the teacher call his mother.
　　　Reading: Bruce's crying has already begun when the call is made.

(b)　Bruce be crying when the teacher call his mother.
　　　Reading 1: Bruce's crying has already begun when the call is made.
　　　Reading 2: Bruce's crying begins as a result of/after the call.

In the sentence in (a), which includes an auxiliary *BE* + V-*ing* sequence, Bruce's crying is in progress when the call is made. In the second sentence (b), Bruce's crying can be in progress when the call is made, or it can start when or after the call is made. It would be useful to follow the development of aspectual *be* to determine when children begin to make such subtle distinctions and determine whether the -*ing* in present progressive contexts differs from that in *be*$_{ASP}$ contexts.

The aspectual *be* experiment was not set up to test the extent to which children associate aspectual *be* constructions (e.g., *be running*) and simple tense verbs (e.g., *runs*) with the same situations, but some data from spontaneous speech suggest that children understand that aspectual *be* and verbs in non-past simple tense are used to talk about events that generally happen. Dawn (5;9, F, AAE) responds to a "what happens" question with an aspectual *be* construction:

21. LJG: What happens at the peanuts?
    Dawn: My teacher be telling us to pick them up, and I be in home living.

These lines are taken from an exchange between LJG and Dawn, in which Dawn talks about the different play centers (e.g., home living center) or areas in her classroom. My interpretation of her use of *be* is that it is in reference to what to her has become general practice in the classroom. Her teacher consistently reminds them to pick up the peanuts, and she generally plays in the home living center, a point that she had mentioned earlier in the conversation.

22. LJG: Do you like school?
    Dawn: Yes mam.
    LJG: What do you like about it?
    DAWN: Playing in home living.

Also, the children follow set daily routines that are intended to help them become familiar with classroom and community practices, and they have the opportunity to work and play in the various learning and activity centers set up in the classroom. Given the routines, it is highly probable that Dawn used "be telling us" and "be in home living" in reference to general classroom practices, an environment in which a simple tense verb (e.g., *my teacher tell(s) us*) could have also been used.

I raised the question about the extent to which both simple tense constructions and habitual *be* constructions are part of the AAE grammar. It would be useful to conduct a careful analysis of child AAE to get a sense of the way children use simple tense and habitual *be* to talk about general states of affairs and recurring events in addition to their comprehension of the structures. As the following excerpt shows, in some cases, at least, some children may be beginning to use the constructions interchangeably:

23. Akila (5;0, F, AAE)
    Akila: I never could watch *Blues Clues*.
    LJG: You never could watch *Blues Clues*?
    Akila: 'Cause when I when I watch *Blues Clues*, my eyes be like this.
    <makes blinking motion with eyes>
    LJG: Wait. Say that again.
    Akila: WHEN I GOT to watch *SpongeBob*, my eyes be like this.
    <makes blinking motion with eyes>
    LJG: Oh my goodness!
    Akila: 'Cause I be sleeping when *SpongeBob* come on.

At the outset, Akila establishes that she is talking about different opportunities to watch the television show *Blues Clues*. The *when* clauses (e.g., *when I watch* Blues Clues, *when* SpongeBob *come on*) can be analyzed as types of restrictors that specify the time period during which some particular event occurs, such as be sleeping or eyes be blinking. Data such as (23) show that children are developing a number of strategies for talking about recurring events. Aspectual *be* is generally barred from occurring in past contexts, but Akila seems to set the aspectual *be* reference in the past when she says: "When I got to watch *SpongeBob*, my eyes be like this." Just from that line it appears that Akila is referring to a one-time watching event; however, the last line clearly seems to refer to different occasions. Although it is not quite clear from the context what "my eyes be like this" means in the past context, there are a number of ways in which the statement could be taken to refer to recurring events. For instance, it could simply mean that her eyes blink over and over, a recurring event. The points here are that invariant *be* refers to recurring events and that the children also use simple tense verbs to mark recurrence. Aspectual *be* clearly does not occur in past contexts in adult AAE, but children may use it in such a context along the developmental path.

In this study no experiments were designed specifically to test children's knowledge and use of third singular –*s*. The data are clear in showing that developing AAE-speaking children at least associate simple tense verbs with habitual/generic contexts, but it is often the case that the verbs are not morphologically marked with verbal –*s* when the subjects are singular. In Chapter 7 I will return to the question of whether third singular –*s* is in the grammar of developing AAE and note work by de Villiers and Johnson (2007) and Terry, Evangelou, Smith, Roberts, and Zeisel (in press) that strongly suggests that it might not be. One informal conclusion that can be stated here is that developing AAE speakers seem to be more oriented toward grammaticalized markers, such as the preverbal marker invariant *be*, rather than to bound morphemes (e.g., third singular verbal –*s*) to indicate tense–aspect-related information in non-past contexts. In Chapter 4 it will be possible to make a similar observation about preverbal grammaticalized markers and bound morphemes that make reference to events in the past. By grammaticalized markers, I mean lexical items or words, such as markers that precede verbs (e.g., aspectual *be*), that have come to take on a specific meaning and distribution in sentences.

4 System of tense–aspect marking 2: past time

*Nia: I BIN learning that. I been reading books at home before I come
to school.*
LJG: Oh!
Nia: At nighttime.

INTRODUCTION

On any given AAE feature list such as the one in Chapter 2, designed
to capture prominent characteristics of child and adult AAE, there
will be entries relating to ways of marking events in the past. The
features on that list that refer to eventualities in the past are the
following: Feature #3 completive *done*, Feature #8 preterite *had*,
Feature #13 remote past *been*, and Feature #20 zero past tense. The
focus of this chapter is on patterns and strategies that child AAE
speakers use to talk about events in the past. The features pulled
from the Craig and Washington list will be represented in the discussion about children's interpretation and linguistic environments
in which certain past markers are used.

The marker completive *done*, which I define as indicating that
an eventuality is in its resultant state, that is, the state of having
ended, is included in the feature list in Chapter 2, but it will only be
briefly mentioned in this chapter because there is only one spontaneous resultant state *done* utterance in my corpus. In referring to the
marker, I generally represent it as being unstressed by spelling it with
a schwa (ə). That is my attempt to show that AAE speakers distinguish
the pronunciation of the marker *done* from the past participle verb
done. When speakers say *I done* (dən) *done my homework* to mean
'I finished my homework,' the first *done* is unstressed relative to the
past participle *done* that follows it. Although *dən* was not used exten-
sively by the developing AAE speakers in this study, comprehension

tasks could help to determine whether they understand the marker as referring to events that have ended or are over. It is not clear whether the marker is acquired at an older age or whether the children did not have occasion to produce it in spontaneous speech. Terry (2005) explains that completive *done* is a perfect marker in AAE, so *done left* 'already left' has a perfect reading in AAE just as *has left* marks the present perfect in general English. It would be especially important to determine when children acquire the *done* construction because that information could provide insight into AAE-speaking children's acquisition of the perfect. According to Craig and Washington (2006), completive *done*, "which indicates a recently completed action" (p. 120), is a feature of child AAE, but they do not give information about whether the marker is used by children in all age groups that the features in their list represent and whether its use also decreases as children go through school. However, the implication is that the marker occurs in the speech of even the youngest speakers (pre-kindergarten) represented in their data. They give a "recent past" definition for *done*, just one of its functions in adult AAE. It is not clear whether the description they give of *done* pertains specifically to the developing AAE speakers' use of the marker.

4.1 SIMPLEX AND COMPLEX FORMS FOR EVENTS IN THE PAST: SIMPLE PAST AND PREVERBAL *HAD*

Children use simplex and complex forms to talk about the past. I am using simplex here as a term for single verb forms, that is, one main verb without any preceding auxiliaries or other markers that refer to the past. These verbs may or may not bear overt past morphology, such as *–ed*. Overt past marking can occur with regular verbs (e.g., *looked*) and with irregular verbs (e.g., *came*). Verbs that are not morphologically marked for past may get past interpretation from the speech context or from adverbs. *Say* in the following sentence is not marked for past, but it receives past interpretation: *Yesterday she say she would leave early*. On the other hand, complex forms are those sequences of a verbal marker followed by a verb that is either overtly

Table 4.1 *Simplex and complex verb forms in contexts in child AAE*

	Verb Form	Example
1.	VERB (unmarked)	
	a. regular	a. *drop*
	b. irregular	b. *bite*
2.	VERB-*ed* (morphological past)	
SIMPLEX	a. regular	a. *looked*
	b. irregular	b. *ran*
3.	*had* + VERB (unmarked)	
	a. regular	a. *had start*
	b. irregular	b. *had hide*
COMPLEX		
4.	*had*+VERB-*ed* (morphological past)	
	a. regular	a. *had unlocked*
	b. irregular	b. *had did*
5.	BIN +VERB (-*ing*)	*BIN learning*

marked for past or not. Two verbal markers that occur with verbs in past contexts are *had* and *BIN*. A summary of these forms is given in Table 4.1, and data sets in which these forms occur will be discussed throughout this chapter.

The data sets (1) and (2) include representative examples of simplex and complex past marking in child AAE.

1.   Data Set 1: Commentary on scenarios
      (Zeke, 4;5, M, AAE)
      1.   Zeke: I <u>rode</u> it – But I <u>didn't rode</u> it right now, the bus <u>drop</u>
           me.
           Zeke: My bike <u>was broke</u> and I –
           LJG: Yours broke too?
           Zeke: And I <u>had to walk</u> too.
           LJG: Um hmm. <*continues to read scenario*> She walked
           but then today –

Zeke: And my, but my mama <u>walk</u> me to school.

2. Zeke: He live – He didn't – He <u>didn't did</u> that.

LJG: He didn't?

Zeke: No. He <u>didn't did</u> it.

LJG: He didn't do that? What did he do?

Zeke: He <u>didn't did</u> nothing.

3. Zeke: When we <u>played</u> hide-n-go-seek, I <u>had hide</u> behind the couch too.

LJG: <*continues to read scenario*> But – so now most of the time ...

Zeke: And I don't – they don't find me and I get base.

2. Data Set 2: Commentary and spontaneous speech

(Zeke, 4;8, M, AAE)

(Miss Dee, the duck puppet)

1. Zeke: I <u>dressed up</u> like this.

2. Zeke: I <u>ate</u> – I <u>ate</u> a ice cream from the Rocket with that plain ice cream with a – with a snow on it.

3. Zeke: Aw, he <u>bite</u> my hand.

LJG: Oh, Miss Dee don't bite his finger!

4. LJG: So you can race with those kids? You can race in the bicycle race. Wow.

Zeke: Sometimes I be going fast and falling off.

LJG: Oh, really?

Zeke: 'Cause I be having my knee pads – knee pads and my helmet.

LJG: That's what I like. Good. That's what I like, Z_.

Zeke: One-one-one day – one day uh I had – I <u>had got stuck</u> on top of the house.

LJG: Wow.

Zeke: And I <u>had</u> to jump off – off of there with my bike.

LJG: What?

Zeke: I had – I <u>had uh did</u> a trick off – off of the house.

LJG: Tell me that one more time. Say that loud. Listen Miss Dee.

Zeke: I <u>did</u> a trick off my house.

LJG: Whoa. And what else?

Zeke: And then when I <u>was coming</u> down and I <u>had twist</u>.

LJG: Wow. And now tell me about this twist.

Zeke: When I <u>was twisting</u>, um, um, I <u>had did</u> a flip up on my skateboard.

LJG: Wait. Say that again.

Zeke: I <u>was twisting</u> and then I <u>did</u> a back flip and then a front flip on my skateboard.

LJG: Wow. And what else?

Zeke: Umm, and I <u>jumped</u> off top of the house. I <u>went</u> on top – on top of the – the lil back house and <u>did</u> a – and <u>did</u> a trick. I <u>was</u> just <u>twisting</u>. I didn't never – I <u>didn't</u> never – I <u>kept twisting</u> that e – e – everyday.

LJG: Hmm. And then what – well what did your mom say?

Zeke: I <u>was rolling</u> on the ground. And then I <u>jumped</u> the fen – I <u>jumped</u> the fence with my skateboard.

5. Zeke: And one day, and one day when I, when I <u>had came</u> to roll on a tree. Um, I <u>had</u>, I <u>had landed</u> on the fence and – and my, I <u>kept going</u> on the fence.

LJG: Wow. I – I want to take a picture of you on this skateboard, uh, Z_ ... But you always wear your helmet, don't you?

Zeke: Sometimes I do, sometimes I do.

LJG: Sometimes you do? ...

Zeke: Sometimes I don't. But I don't be landing on my head. I be landing on my skateboard.

As the two different ages for Zeke indicate, he was recorded at different periods. He was always very engaged in the scenarios, which was evident from the questions he asked and the way he enthusiastically linked his own experiences and stories to the scenarios or created stories with similar themes. In the first line in Data Set 1, the simplex form *rode* is marked for past, but *drop* is not. Also, in that line Zeke marks past on both elements in the complex sequence *didn't rode*. In the group of examples in Data Set 1 (in (3)), a complex sequence of auxiliary followed by a main verb is used. I will refer to the *had* + v(ERB) sequence (e.g., *had ride*) as used in developing AAE as the preverbal *had* sequence. The *had* + VERB sequence is identical in "shape" to the pluperfect (or past perfect) in general English and in AAE, in that it is formed with *had* + VERB; however, it does not have the same interpretation as the pluperfect. Whereas the pluperfect indicates that an event happened farther in the past than some other event to which it is related, the *had* in AAE-speaking children's complex forms is used in contexts in which reference is to the simple past. The sentence *Bruce had left by the time the other students arrived*, in which the general English pluperfect *had left* is used, refers to a situation in which Bruce's leaving happened before the other students' arrival. On the other hand, AAE speakers use the verbal marker *had* followed by a verb in sentences such as *Bruce had left when the game started*. In that sentence, *had* does not necessarily mean that Bruce's leaving event is farther in the past relative to *when the game started*; in adolescent/adult AAE *had left* can simply indicate that the leaving event is past relative to the speech time. This means that the sentence can convey the message that Bruce left, and the leaving could have occurred right at the moment the game started.

Zeke uses the perfective and imperfective in talking about events in the past. The perfective refers to an action that is seen as a whole without focus on any single part or snapshot of part of the event at a certain time. On the other hand, the imperfective refers to parts of an event, such as a snapshot of an event that is in progress. Both perfective and imperfective examples are illustrated in (2) Data Set 2 example 4, in which Zeke talks about the having *jumped* (perfective) *off top of the house* event and the *was just twisting* and *kept twisting* (imperfective) events. In (1) Data Set 1 and (2) Data Set 2, some of Zeke's verbs that refer to perfective events are marked with past morphology; others are not: *drop* (Data set 1, example 1), *hide*

(Data set 1, example 3), *bite* (Data set 2, example 3), and *twist* (Data set 2, example 4). In a few cases, past is marked simultaneously on both the auxiliary and main verb (*didn't rode, didn't did*). Such double marking can be construed as a type of agreement that is common in general language development, not just in AAE. Neither *hide* nor *twist* has morphological past marking, but both verbs occur with the preverbal marker *had*. Both the past –*ed* morphology that does occur on some verbs and contexts of events Zeke recounts unquestionably confirm that he is talking about the past. Zeke also seems to be highlighting his achievement or accomplishment of the events. A stronger connection will be made between perfective/imperfective and different types of events, such as achievements and accomplishments.

In some examples, Zeke uses *had* + V (–*ed*) and V (–*ed*) interchangeably to talk about events that he has accomplished. For instance, in (2) Data Set 2, both *had did* and *did* are used to talk about the events of having performed a trick and having completed a flip. In both cases he marks the completed event with *had* on the first mention of it (*had did a trick, had did a flip*), but when asked to repeat the information, he refers to the actions with the simplex forms *did a trick* and *did a flip*, omitting *had*. It is tempting to pursue the hypothesis that *had* is somehow linked to the narrative mode, so Zeke does not use it when he is out of narrative mode and just clarifying a point in the event sequence. I will return to the question about the use of *had* in narrative mode in reference to work by Rickford and Théberge-Rafal (1999) and Ross, Oetting, and Stapleton (2004).

In the cases of preverbal *had* constructions, Zeke is focusing on the achievement of the event in the past. On the other hand, note that when he uses the past progressive (e.g., *was rolling*), the focus is not on an event he has completed or accomplished; instead the emphasis is on having been participating in an ongoing event. For instance in (2) Data Set 2, example 4, *was rolling* refers to an ongoing action in the past. Zeke also makes a morphological distinction between *twist* with a perfective reading (*had twist*), and an imperfective reading (*twisting*), in which the progressive *–ing* is used. In focusing on the ongoing event in the past – not the endpoint of the event – he uses *was twisting* or *kept twisting*.

While we have seen that overt past *was* occurs with the past progressive forms (e.g., *was twisting*), there might be some cases in which *was* is non-overt, as in the following excerpts from a story retell by Dawn (5;9, F, AAE):

3.   (a) Then the baby trying to get out of the umm bed.
      (b) And then the dog was eating some food.
      (c) The dog was seeing if the mama was coming.
      (d) Then his mama coming. He looking out the window.

In lines (3b) and (3d) Dawn uses what would appear to be the past progressive given the context, but there is no *was*, as in *was trying*, *was coming*, and *was looking* in (3a, d), although there are other cases in which the past progressive is overtly marked. Given the claim that the past *BE* form (i.e. *was*) is generally overtly expressed, one question that is raised here is whether it is possible to omit *was* if the past meaning can be constructed from the past context. There are few such examples in the database, so it is not clear how much can be drawn from the tokens. However, it might be the case that, at least in narratives, *was* can be omitted given the past context. More data should be analyzed in past contexts to determine the extent to which *was* can actually be omitted in narrative contexts.

In (4) Data Set 3 the only overt past marking is on *was* and *had*; however, Joya uses adverbials such as *just* (1) and *before* (4) for past reference.

4.   Data Set 3: Conversation and spontaneous speech
      (Joya, 5;7, F, AAE)
      1. Joya: My sister uh first name is um you just <u>say</u> that.
      2. LJG: Did you have that thing on your head?
         Joya: I <u>wear</u> em two times.
         Joya: I <u>wear</u> em at church and at and um at the store.

3. Joya: It <u>was</u> in the sink bowl.

   LJG: ... Umhmmm.

   Joya: And then the um the dressers <u>keep</u> coming open.

   LJG: Yeah ...

   Joya: And then he <u>close</u> it, the jar back up and it <u>keep</u> coming uh ...

4. Joya: I know how to play pinball.

   LJG: ... Wow!

   Joya: I <u>had start</u> the pinball before.

If the examples in (4) Data Set 3, example 2 are taken out of context, it might appear that the verb *wear* is intended to indicate that Joya generally wears them (i.e. pre-school graduation cap and gown) two times, to church and to the store, but given the context, it is clear that she is referring to having worn them two times in the past, once to church and once to the store. The simplex "unmarked" verbs (*keep* and *close*) (3) in Joya's retelling of part of a movie also refer to events that have happened. Finally, in (4) Joya also uses the marker *had* with a verb that is unmarked for past, complex form *had start*. Here, too, it would make sense to say that *had* marks a completed event or an event that Joya has accomplished, not simply past time. That is, while *start* is not tagged with –*ed*, there is still an overt past marker that associates it with past time. The adverb *before* serves the function of situating the having started the pinball event time in the past.

The following preverbal *had* constructions refer to the past, but the verbs themselves are not overtly marked for past:

5.   Data Set 4: Chuck E.

     (Nia, 5;9, F, AAE)

     LJG: What else did you do at Chuck E. Cheese? What else did you do?

     Nia: Chuck E. <u>had bring</u> me on the stage.

     LJG: And then what else?

     Nia: He he <u>had pick</u> me <u>up</u>.

LJG: No, girl, did he? And then what?

Nia: He <u>had uh uh went</u> up the slide with me.

LJG: Did he? That was so much fun. And then what else did you do?

Nia: <u>Slide</u> with him.

By virtue of talking about an event that has already taken place, Nia is recalling events in the context of the past, although the only overt past marking on verbs is on the irregular verb *went*. An analysis in which *had* is taken to serve as a general simple past is in line with Nia's recounting of the sequence of events. One piece of evidence against the view that *had* itself serves as a simple past marker comes in the last line of the exchange: *slide with him*. Presumably, *slide* is referring to the past context, but it is not marked with *had*, nor is the verb marked for past with *–ed* or in the past form *slid*. The variants for past marking are *–ed* and Ø, and *slide* just happens to take the latter form of past marking (Ø), in which the form used in the past is identical to that in the present. It is clear that *had* is compatible with past time marking, but it does not have the simple function of situating the event in the past or just marking it as past. The function of *had* is to indicate that an event has been achieved or accomplished. First it is clear that *slide* is in the past context, although it is not overtly marked for past. While the other verbs, *bring, pick up*, and *went* are in a *had* + VERB sequence, *slide* is not and it still manages to refer to the past. There are two reasons, among others, that *slide* might not occur with preverbal *had*. One explanation that I will not pursue is that *had* and Ø$_{had}$ are variants, and Ø$_{had}$ is used with *slide* in Nia's last line, not overt *had*. On an abstract level, Ø$_{had}$ is quite similar to Ø copula and Ø auxiliary *BE*, cases in which BE elements are left out of sentences. A different explanation is that the verb *slide* is used in the passage to refer to the continuous activity of back and forth sliding, not to refer to the activity of taking one or two slides and then completing or accomplishing the event. If *slide*, then, does not refer to the end part of the event, then there is another plausible explanation for the absence of *had* preceding *slide*, namely *had* is used only in contexts in reference to the accomplishment/achieve-ment of an event. As such, it does not occur with *slide* in this case because the sliding event is not an achievement; it is ongoing.

While parts of Zeke's and Nia's reports on events that they have performed (Data Sets 1 and 2) can be considered to be short narratives, Jasmine's "Dog Dream" story ((6) Data Set 5) is clearly a narrative with easily identifiable parts. For instance, according to Labov and Waletzky (1967), two components of narratives are com-plicating action, which gives specific events and actions, and a reso-lution or final outcome. Jasmine refers to a number of events and complicating action in the narrative, such as *had tried, had take, locked him up, unlocked, saved*, and she gives the outcome *came out the cage*. It is not the goal here to complete a narrative analysis, but it is possible to show that (6) is a narrative by pointing out its narrative properties.

6. Data Set 5: "Dog Dream"

   (Jasmine, 4;4, F, AAE)

   Then, then he <u>didn't</u> never reach me when my papa <u>hold</u> me.
   I <u>had</u> a bad dream. They <u>was trying</u> to get in my mama
   house. Then, they <u>had tried</u> to pull my leg. Then they
   <u>was trying</u> to bite my, my bones. And they <u>had</u> to and
   they <u>was</u>, <u>bite</u> my brother, too. Then I <u>pull</u> my brother.
   He take … The dog <u>had take, pull</u> my brother. He <u>take</u>
   him. He <u>put</u> him in a doggie cage. He <u>locked</u> him up.
   And I <u>had</u> the key in my hand. Then, then um I <u>unlocked</u>
   the door. Then I <u>had saved</u> my brother. I <u>had unlocked</u> it.
   Then I <u>had save</u> him. He <u>came</u> out the cage.

By virtue of the discourse being a narrative, it consists of a sequence of events. In some cases, the verbs indicating the sequence of events either are morphologically marked (e.g., *locked*), are not morphologic-ally marked (e.g., *pull, hold*), or either are or are not morphologically marked for past but are in a preverbal *had* construction (e.g., *had tried, had save*). These three situations are all different; nevertheless, they all, including the preverbal *had* construction, have in common the property that they refer to past events.

Preverbal *had* constructions also share another common property with simple past events. They move narratives along. In her discussion of discourse modes, Smith (2005) explains that a narrative includes sequencing of events that advance or move it along. This point can be illustrated with Jasmine's narrative, starting from where she says, "He take him." Note the sequencing of the events: "he take him," "he put him in a doggie cage," "he locked him up" ... "I had unlocked it," "I had save/saved him," "he came out." The story moves from one event to the next, and the verbs expressing the sequence of events refer to the simple past. Preverbal *had* constructions and other simple past verb forms move the narrative forward. We can pause here for a moment to compare the preverbal *had* construction to the pluperfect in the narrative mode. While the preverbal *had* construction moves the narrative along to the next event, pluperfect *had* constructions do not, as exemplified in the following short narrative. *I arrived home at 10 o'clock. I looked in the refrigerator. Bruce had eaten all of my cheese, so I went upstairs and did my homework.* The narrative moves along from one event to the next until the point of the past perfect construction. It stops at *Bruce had eaten all of my cheese*; an out-of-sequence event that had taken place at some point prior to the arrival home and looking in the refrigerator events. The narrative proceeds again with the sequence of events, *went upstairs and did my homework.*

Rickford and Théberge-Rafal (1999) have produced the most extensive study of preverbal *had*, although it is not the first study of the marker.[1] Earlier studies are in Labov, Cohen, Robbins, and Lewis (1968) and Cukor-Avila and Bailey (1995). In their discussion, Rickford and Théberge-Rafal consider the use and function of the marker in the speech of AAE-speaking adolescents and refer to it as preterite *had*. They observe that it is used mostly with verbs that are overtly marked for past tense, so it is not a substitute for overt past marking, because past is already being marked by *–ed* on verbs in the preverbal *had* construction. Rickford and Théberge-Rafal (1999) conclude that preterite *had* is used in the context of narratives to mark complicating action as well as to signal dramatic developments or descriptive peaks.

The *had* + VERB constructions presented in this chapter so far illustrate that developing AAE-speaking children do not always use preverbal *had* with verbs that are overtly marked for past. Rickford and Théberge-Rafal's conclusion that *had* is used predominantly with verbs marked with morphological past is based on data from adolescent AAE, and the preverbal *had* data in this chapter are from developing AAE speakers. There may be differences in the extent to which adolescents and developing AAE speakers mark past. This issue should be explored. There may be a correlation between language development and overt past tense marking on verbs in preverbal *had* constructions, and longitudinal studies can help reveal any changes in morphological marking that may occur in developmental stages.

While Rickford and Théberge-Rafal's observations may accurately account for the function of preterite *had* in narratives in adolescent AAE, something different may be going on with preverbal *had* in developing child AAE. Preverbal *had* in the child data is not limited to "complicating" actions or narratives, for that matter. It might be that in the beginning stages of the use of preverbal *had*, children do not discriminate on the basis of types of events or actions with respect to the parts of a narrative in which they occur or with respect to whether the event refers to complicating action. According to Ross, Oetting, and Stapleton (2004), preverbal *had* production increases as narrative skill develops. If the child AAE speakers represented here are still developing narrative skills, then they may not be expected to use preverbal *had* as a narrative discourse marker in the same way as it appears in adolescent AAE. What could be of consequence to the 4- to 5-year-old children is not whether there is a way for verbs to signal dramatic developments in narratives but whether there is a way to mark achievements and accomplishments. Several questions arise as we consider the preverbal *had* data. One question pertains to whether preverbal *had* constructions (e.g., *had saved*) and simplex past (*saved*) verbs are actually variants and can be used in the same contexts. By now it is obvious that both forms occur in simple past contexts, but preverbal *had* marks an achievement or accomplishment in discourse. It may be that as time progresses and language development continues, children begin to use preverbal *had* mostly in narratives in the way it is described by Rickford and Théberge-Rafal (1999). That is, what I am referring to here as preverbal *had* may develop into preterite *had* or develop the properties of preterite *had* over time. While I find enough evidence in the child data that cautions against equating the use of preverbal *had* with the description of preterite *had* reported for adolescents, Ross *et al.* (2004) report that the *had* used by the 4- and 6-year-old southeastern Louisiana AAE speakers in their study has the same function and properties of preterite *had* in the Rickford and Théberge-Rafal study. As it turns out, however, Ross *et al.* (2004) report the following finding – although they do not pursue it – that suggests that their participants also used *had* to mark the accomplishment of an event: "Notable, each of the 82 [had + V–ed tokens] referred to a completed event but included no relative temporal anchor as the standard pluperfect does" (p. 170). I take this statement to be clear evidence of preverbal *had* as an accomplishment marker in the Ross *et al.* developmental data.

The view that preverbal *had* may be used to talk about events that have been accomplished can account for the *had start* sequence in Joya's line in Data Set 3: *I had start the pinball before.* Also, given that Joya is not engaged in a narrative, her statement does not easily fall into the category of complicating actions. It is important to note that although preverbal *had* is not used in exactly the same way that preterite *had* is argued to be used, there is a major similarity. It seems to be clear that neither preverbal *had* nor preterite *had* is used simply as a past tense marker, but they are limited to past tense contexts, which is clearly why they are compatible with narratives.

The conversational data and spontaneous speech are excellent sources of preverbal *had* sequences; however, it is also necessary to design experiments or elicitation and comprehension tasks that will provide further insight into choices children make about using *had* sequences – perhaps in competition with simplex verb forms – and the interpretation they associate with them.

4.2 PREVERBAL *HAD* AND STORY RETELL

In the previous section the properties reported for preverbal *had* and past marking in developing AAE were based on constructions in spontaneous speech. Here I would like to review elicited data that will provide further insight into properties of preverbal *had*. One of the questions that are raised here relates to the nature of the verbs that developing AAE speakers use in preverbal *had* constructions and the context in which the verbs occur. In the preceding section the terms "achievement" and "accomplishment" were used as descriptors for the types of events developing AAE-speaking children associate with preverbal *had*. Here I want to focus more on these descriptors for preverbal *had* events from the perspective of elicited story retells.

The children's story retells are based on pictures in the picture book *Good Dog, Carl* and a corresponding story that was written to accompany the pictures. The story description read to each child is given in Appendix B. The story was told/read to the child in the simple past tense, and then the child was asked to retell the story to me while he/she was looking at the story book pictures. Two samples of pictures from the book are given in Figures 4.1 and 4.2, with descriptions from two children.

Segments of Angelle's (5;9, F, AAE) story description are below.

7.   Segments from Angelle's *Good Dog, Carl* story retell
       The baby <u>had went</u> to sleep.
       And the and the dog had <u>had</u> and uh <u>look</u> out the window if the
           mom <u>was coming</u>.

Figure 4.1 Illustration from *Good Dog, Carl*

And and the baby <u>was crawling</u> on the dog.
The puppy had had <u>had put</u> the baby uh <u>crawled</u> the baby in
     the room.
And and the baby <u>was jumping</u> on the on the bed with him.
The the baby <u>had put</u> some some powder on the on the dog.
And and they <u>looked</u> in the mirror.
The baby <u>had slide</u> down the slide.
And the dog <u>had went</u> down the stairs.
...
Put put some music on.
And they was dancing.
...

Figure 4.2 Illustration from *Good Dog, Carl*

The dog <u>had poured</u> some some uh milk in there.
And the dog <u>help</u> the baby get some cookies.
...
He <u>had get</u> back in.

Angelle uses three different forms to reference the past: *had* + VERB, simple past, and past progressive. The same range of variation that has been observed in previous speech samples is also evident here. The verb may or may not be marked for past, and, as in the case of *look*, the verb may be variably marked for past (e.g., *look*, *looked*). In comparing Nia's spontaneous speech in (5) to the retell in (7), we find that while *slide* did not occur with *had* in (5), it does occur with *had* in (7). It is clear that *slide down* in (7) refers to an event that has been completed – another example in which *had* could be taken as underscoring an event that has been accomplished. On the other hand, the use of the progressive (*was coming, was crawling, was jumping*) signals that the coming, crawling, and jumping events were ongoing as opposed to completed or accomplished.

Segments from another story retell are given below (Kerry, 5;11, M, AAE):

8.   Segments from Kerry's *Good Dog, Carl* story retell
This is the mama; this is the baby; and this is the dog.
The dog was looking out the window then the baby had woke up.
And then the baby had got on the bed and climb on the dog.
The baby went in the bed a bedroom.
And then it bounce, bounce, bounce.
And then the baby had put some makeup on the dog.
And they look at the mirror.
And then, he was right there saying, "Help."
And then the dog had took him.
And then they had um slide on the rug.
And then they was looking at the fish tank.
And then they was swimming in the fish tank.
And then they had turn on the music radio and was dancing.

Kerry expresses the looking, swimming, and dancing events as past progressive, and the other events are expressed in the simple past, either with or without *had*. In comparing (7) and (8), note that Angelle expresses Carl and the baby as "was jumping," and Kerry expresses the event in simple past as "bounce, bounce, bounce." While it is conceivable that Kerry uses multiple bounces to indicate the ongoing activity of jumping or bouncing on the bed, it is quite likely that he chooses to express the activity with a repetition of the word *bounce* because that is similar to the way it was presented

in the story description read to him: "They bounced and bounced."
(See Appendix B.) Kerry expresses events in the progressive that are
clearly ongoing in the story: *looking at, swimming,* and *dancing.*
However, the first instance of *look at* (i.e. *look at the mirror*) is in the
past not the progressive, at least given the context not with respect to
morphological marking because the verb *look* does not end in *–ed.*

   Some children leaned more toward the past progressive, but
even those children expressed some events in the simple past, with
or without overt past morphology. Dawn (5;9, F, AAE) moves back
and forth between past progressive and simple past, although she
does not use preverbal *had* in the description.

9.   Segments from Dawn's *Good Dog, Carl* story retell
     They, the dog <u>was showing</u> the baby how to swim.
     Now he <u>turned up</u> some music.
     He was dancing.
     And the baby was just <u>a-watching</u> him.
     The he <u>open up</u> the icebox and then Carl <u>got</u> the bread, <u>open</u> it
          up, and then the baby <u>got</u> a bread. Then he <u>ate</u> it.
     And then um the baby the dog was um got <u>got</u> the grapes and
          the baby <u>pull</u> some off.
     And the and the dog <u>was pouring</u> chocolate milk in his cup.

Dawn expresses *showing, dancing,* and *watching* (which includes
the *a*-prefix, a marker associated with southern US varieties and
used in ongoing contexts) in the past progressive, as other children
do, but she also expresses activities indicated by verbs such as <u>get</u>,
<u>open</u>, and <u>turn up</u> in the simple past.[2] There is no across-the-board
consistency such that children express particular verbs in the simple past or past progressive; however, there is overlap in some cases
such that different children consistently mark certain verbs as progressive. I do not take the overlap to mean that children only express
certain verbs in the simple past and others in the past progressive.
However, I do think that the overlap and consistency in treatment
of some verbs by the children say something about the way children

perceive the events expressed by the verbs. Specifically, events that are expressed in *had* + VERB constructions are seen by the children as being completed or accomplished, and those in progressive contexts are seen as ongoing.

Table 4.2 summarizes all of the verbs used by children in past contexts in fifteen narrative descriptions. As shown in Table 4.2, some verbs are either expressed in the *had* + V(ERB)–*ed* sequence, in the V (–*ed*) form (without *had*), in the past progressive *was* V-*ing*, or in any combination of the three. The type of past the child used is due, in part, to the nature of the verb type and the event it indicates, but it is also due to the perspective from which the children viewed the events. Some saw them as having been completed, and others saw them as being in progress. For some verbs, all that can be said of them is that they occur in a certain form because the child used that form, past or past progressive, to tell the story, but for other verbs children seemed to have made choices about the viewpoint of the event. For instance, even those children who described the majority of the events in the past perfective still chose to talk about some events in the progressive. One example is the verb *dance*, which all children expressed as *dancing* in the present or past progressive, including those children who used preverbal *had* throughout the narrative. Carl's dancing is clearly depicted in the picture as being in progress. (See Figure 4.2.) What is important here is not just where the children use the *had* sequence or regular past marking V(–*ed*) but where they do not use it or an alternative simple past form, as in *dancing*.

The evidence is strong that the children are indeed paying attention to the viewpoint of the event, as in Smith (1997), in which the event is seen in its entirety or in part. According to Smith, situation types such as activity, accomplishment, and achievement are presented from perfective and imperfective viewpoint aspect. When an event is seen from the perfective viewpoint, the event is seen in its entirety; its endpoint is included. On the other hand, when an event is seen from the imperfective viewpoint, only part of it is focused; its endpoint is not

Table 4.2 *Summary of verbs in* Good Dog, Carl *story retells*

had + V–*ed*	Simple Past (V–*ed*/Ø)	Past Progressive
had went	went	was going
had got	got	
had poed [poured]	poured	was pouring
	pour	
had dried	dried	
had said	said	
	say	
had woke up		
had took	took	
had sprayed		
had + V–Ø		
had look out	looked	was looking
	look	
had rub	rubbed	was rubbing
had git [get]	get	was getting
had slide	slide	was sliding
had put	put	was putting
had turn	turned	
	turn, turn on	
had open	opened	
	open	
had pick up	pick	
had wipe		was wiping
	bounced	
	bounce	
	climbed	
	climb	
	blowed	
	fixed	

Table 4.2 (*cont.*)

had + V–*ed*	Simple Past (V–*ed*/Ø)	Past Progressive
	digged	
	walked	
	sucked up	
	straightened	
	stepped	
	hopped	
	falled	
	helped	
	help	
	tore	
	told	
	drunk	
	cut	
	lick	
	pull	
	throw	
	flip	
	dump	
	mess	
	pet	
	listen	
	grab	
	fix	
	had	
	was	
	jumped	was jumping
	jump off	
	cleaned	was cleaning
	clean	
	crawled	was crawling

Table 4.2 (*cont.*)

had + V–*ed*	Simple Past (V–*ed*/Ø)	Past Progressive
	ran, runned	was running
	made, maked	was making
	used	was using
	came	was coming
	laid, lay	was laying
	saw, seen	was seeing
	did	was doing
	swim	was swimming
	pat	was patting
		was holding
		was showing
		was watching
		was trying
		was eating
		was leaning
		was washing
		was sitting
		was giving
		was playing
		was waiting
		was being
		was dancing
		was sleeping

included. The events expressed by verbs can be categorized in terms of semantic characterization or situation types. Examples of the situation type activity are "stroll in the park," "laugh," "think about," and "eat cherries" (p. 23). Unlike activities, the accomplishment situation type has a final endpoint. Examples of accomplishments are "build

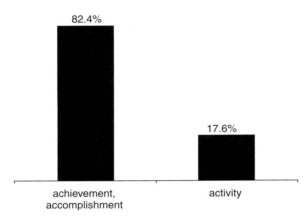

82.4%

17.6%

achievement,
accomplishment

activity

Figure 4.3 Percentage preverbal *had* by situation type

a bridge," "walk to school," and "drink a glass of wine" (p. 26). The achievement situation type is similar to accomplishments; however, the change in states or results of events in the situation type accomplishment category occur very quickly. Examples are "find," "recognize," "break a glass," and "reach the top" (p. 30).

I have already implicated "accomplishment" and "achievement" in the description of events used in preverbal *had* constructions, and it is useful to try to make a stronger connection by taking a closer look at the situation types of verbs used with preverbal *had*. In comparison to the activity situation type on the one hand, verbs of achievement and accomplishment situation types, on the other hand, occur more frequently with preverbal *had*. The results, based on verbs in the *Good Dog, Carl* story retells, are given in Figure 4.3.

The picture that emerges here is one in which preverbal *had* occurs in simple past contexts mostly with accomplishment and achievement situation types, but not exclusively. As is evident from the list of verbs in Table 4.2, it is not that the children do not use activity verbs; it is that they use them more often in the (past) progressive. What can be seen by peering into the situation types is that events with a final endpoint are more likely to occur with preverbal *had*, while those without an endpoint are more compatible with the past progressive or imperfective viewpoint; they can be easily construed as ongoing. In this case the line is drawn between situation types that prefer preverbal *had* as well as viewpoints. That is to say that in situations in which preverbal *had* is used, the event is seen from the perfective viewpoint, such that the endpoints are included. If it is the case that preverbal *had* focuses on endpoints, then it is clear why achievement and accomplishment situation types occur with the marker more so than verbs of the activity situation type. Achievement and accomplishment situation types seem to stand out in preverbal *had* constructions, and this observation is reminiscent of hypotheses about lexical aspect and tense–aspect in developmental patterns in general English and other languages (e.g., Bronckart and Sinclair 1973; Antinucci and Miller 1976; Olsen and Weinberg 1999; Behrens 2001; Wagner 2001). For instance, in Shirai and Andersen (1995) it is noted that children use past marking mainly with achievement and accomplishment verbs first and then extend the past marking to other verb types. Ogiela, Casby, and Schmitt (2005) cast these observations in terms of event realization, as presented in Bohnemeyer and Swift (2004), noting that the type of predicates that are initially marked for past are those that express that an event has been realized. The difference, though, is that although the 4- to 5-year-old AAE-speaking children's use of *had* may be developmental, their use of general past marking is not in the sense that they seem to be beyond the stage at which past is only used with predicates that mark completed events.

So far, nothing has suggested that preverbal *had* is obligatory even for some speakers. For instance, Dina (4;11, F, AAE) uses a couple of very salient properties (i.e. *say* to mark direct speech, zero copula *he not here*) of AAE, yet she does not use preverbal *had* in her narrative, in which she clearly uses morphological past marking:

10.   Data Set 6: "The Bulldog and the Tree"
       Dina: He just *climbed* up.
       LJG: Uhmm. Hmm.

> Dina: A_, my cousin, A_, she uh, they <u>had</u> a lady and she <u>had</u>,
> they <u>had</u> a lady and the lady <u>had</u> a bulldog and it <u>was uh</u>
> <u>trying</u> to chase her and she <u>jumped</u> on the tree, <u>climbed</u>
> the tree and the bulldog <u>bit</u> the tree and she <u>fell</u> … the
> bulldog, the bulldog …
>
> …
>
> She uh <u>ran</u> home. The lady <u>say</u>, "What <u>happened</u>?" "Your
> bulldog <u>bit</u> me." The lady <u>say</u>, "Come here, Bulldog! I'm
> bout to put you back on your chain." And she <u>did</u>. A_ <u>came</u>
> back and <u>looked</u>. A_ <u>say</u>, "Oh, I'm glad he not here …"

Most of the events are indicated by verbs that are morphologically marked for past. All of the verbs, which present a sequence of events, reflect the perfective point of view except *was uh trying*, which is imperfective. The verb *say* is consistently morphologically unmarked for past, but from the context the interpretation of *say* is perfective ('said') and it, too, introduces an event in the sequence. Dina talks about the actions of three characters: her cousin, the lady, and the bulldog; and she keeps all of them straight. The sequence of events is important: as a result of the chase, the girl jumped on the tree, climbed it, the dog bit the tree, and the girl fell. In addition, Dina switches to talk about events from the cousin's and lady's perspectives. Here past time, not just event completion, is important, and this is evident given the way Dina establishes a point in the past and then refers to future and present events within that time period. At the end of the story she establishes a point in the past with "the lady say," and then goes on to code the lady's reference to the future, *I'm bout to* ('I'm about to'). Finally, she establishes that A_'s comment was in the past ("A_ say"), but in reporting A_'s speech, she seems to quote her, including using A_'s reference to the present, "I'm glad …". The most obvious and logical response to any questions about why child AAE speakers do not use preverbal *had* in contexts that are well suited to it is that the marker is optional. Secondly, variation may also play a role such that speakers vary, even those in

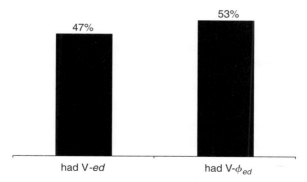

Figure 4.4 Percentage *–ed* in preverbal *had* constructions

developmental stages, in their use of the marker. Ross *et al.* (2004) linked the productivity of the marker to narrative skill, a correlation that is likely to be real and valid. However, clear variation, and perhaps other factors that may be non- or extra-linguistic, are related to the use of the marker. Although I have only presented a snippet of Dina's spontaneous language, it should be clear that her narrative skill is well on its developmental path, and her lack of use of *had* does not seem to be linked to her storytelling ability.

The data presented in the first part of this chapter are useful in addressing the question about whether developing AAE-speaking children use preverbal *had* to mark endpoints as in the accomplishment and achievement of an event. Questions along these lines have been raised for children developing past tense in MAE, especially given the claim that children first use the past tense with verbs that intrinsically encode a complete event or the accomplishment/ achievement of an event. Also, AAE-speaking children are developing a variety that has a number of options for marking events in the past, simple past with variable *–ed* marking and preverbal *had*. The variable *–ed* marking is also evident in preverbal *had* constructions. Figure 4.4 shows the percentage of *–ed* morphological marking on verbs in preverbal *had* constructions (from *Good Dog, Carl* story retells).

There may be parallels between overt past marking in developing MAE and preverbal *had* in child AAE with respect to the situation types of verbs with which these markers occur. Many more questions should be addressed in exploring this issue, and many more insightful questions may be raised in relation to variable *–ed* marking. The variable input that AAE-speaking children get from their speech communities must account, in part, for some of their developmental patterns. Finally, it is clear that the past perfect is also part of AAE and is acquired after the preverbal *had* construction has been acquired. Developmentally speaking, there are a number of questions that should be asked in reference to when children begin to use *had* + VERB in past perfect contexts and the extent to which they make changes in the way they use preverbal *had* constructions once they acquire past perfect.

4.3   REMOTE PAST

Child AAE speakers produce simplex [VERB (*–ed*)] and complex [*had* + VERB (*–ed*)] constructions that refer to events that have already been completed or performed, that is, achieved or accomplished. Another marker that occurs in the spontaneous speech samples produced by developing AAE speakers is stressed *been*. Here I will follow the convention of writing the marker stressed *been* in capital letters (*BIN*) to indicate that it is pronounced with stress relative to other words in the sentence with it and to distinguish it from *been* that occurs in perfect contexts (e.g., *She has been running* or *She been running* in AAE[3]) and from the unstressed *been* that occurs in AAE (*He been had that car for seven or eight years.* 'He has had that car for seven or eight years'). In adolescent and adult AAE, *BIN* indicates that some event started or occurred a long time ago, or some state has held for a long time. For instance, *Bruce BIN running* means that 'Bruce started running a long time ago and he is still running,' and *That mouse BIN dead* means 'That mouse has been dead for a long time.'

Given the data from adult AAE, *BIN* can occur with all predicate types:

11.   *BIN* and following predicate
  (a)   BIN + VERB -*ing*
          Bruce BIN reading mystery novels.
          'Bruce has been reading mystery novels for a long time'
  (b)   BIN + VERB –*ed*, where –*ed* is optional in some contexts
          Bruce BIN parked his car in the garage.
          'Bruce parked his car in the garage a long time ago'
  (c)   BIN + Adjective
          Her hair BIN black.
          'Her hair has been black for a long time'
  (d)   BIN + Preposition/Adverb
          That folder BIN on the table.
          'That folder has been on the table for a long time'
          That car BIN there.
          'That car has been there for a long time'
  (e)   BIN + Noun
          Dee BIN the leader.
          'Dee has been the leader for a long time'

BIN constructions are glossed either as 'for a long time,' for eventualities that started a long time ago and are still in progress or are holding at the present time (e.g., (11a, c, d, e)) or 'a long time ago' for eventualities that started and ended in the distant past (e.g., (11b)). The long period signaled by *BIN* is relative, as explained in Green (2002, p. 55): "The remote past is relative, so it can refer to a time period of fifteen minutes ago or fifteen years ago. One way to put it is that *BIN* is used to indicate that the time period referred to is longer than normal for an activity, or it can be used to affirm that a state has indeed held for a long time."

One observation that can be made about child AAE speakers' use of the complex form *BIN* + VERB is that they produce the marker with stress and link it to some notion of distant past. The following is an example of *BIN* in the spontaneous speech of a developing AAE speaker (Jamal, 4;8, M, AAE):

12.   LJG: Ooh, I like that jogging suit. Is that a new jogging suit?
         Hmm, or an old one?
      Jamal: A new jacket.
      LJG: A new jacket? You just got it? You just got it? Hmm?
      Jamal: I BIN havin it. (Green 2004, p. 65)

If Jamal's understanding of *BIN* is that it situates an eventuality in the distant past or that it is associated with a long period, then what he intends to communicate is that he has had the jacket for a long time, although it is not clear what type of long period a 4-year-old is referring to when he uses *BIN*, especially in reference to his/her ownership of a piece of clothing that he/she still wears.

A similar example occurs in the speech of Jasmine (4;4, F, AAE). In the following example from Jasmine, she gives a paraphrase of *BIN*, which could serve as direct evidence that she associates the marker with the distant past.

13.   LJG: Ooh, J__, I love those pants. Ooh they're so nice. Did ya
         just get em or you BIN having em?
      Jasmine: I BIN having em.
      LJG: Ooh, well when did you get em?
      Jasmine: My mama bought em.
      LJG: When?
      Jasmine: Umm.
      LJG: A long time ago or yesterday?
      Jasmine: A long time, a long time ago.
      LJG: Alright. (Green 2004, pp. 65–66)

From the two options given to her as a possible length of time she has had the pants (i.e. *just get em* or *BIN having em*), Jasmine chooses to answer with *BIN*. In choosing a response to clarify what she means by "I BIN having em," she opts for "a long time ago" as opposed to "yesterday," a response that could suggest that yesterday is not far enough in the past. From an adult perspective, it is the case that yesterday can certainly refer to the far past for some events, but it does not appear to be long enough ago to capture the time Jasmine has had those pants.

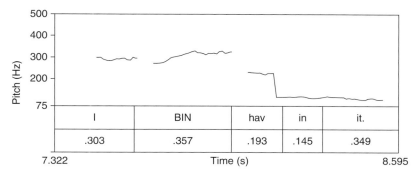

Figure 4.5 Pitch track of *I BIN havin it*. (Jamal)

Note also that Jamal and Jasmine use *having* instead of *had* following *BIN*. While AAE speakers from other areas of the United States may use *BIN had* to mean 'have had for a long time,' *BIN having* commonly occurs in areas in southwestern Louisiana and in neighboring areas in parts of Texas (Green 1998), although *BIN had* may be used, also, which will be shown in part of the data from comprehension tasks (Figure 4.7).[4] Developing AAE speakers in this area also use *BIN having* as expected because it is part of the input from their speech communities.

In both (12) and (13) the children stress *BIN* relative to other words in the sentences (or place stronger emphasis on it or mark it with a pitch accent), which suggests that they understand stress to be a crucial part of the meaning of the marker. Consider the pitch tracks of the *BIN* sentences in Figures 4.5 and 4.6 and note the duration of *BIN* as compared to duration of the first words in the sentence. In each case, the duration of *BIN* is longer.[5]

While at first glance, it seems that the two examples are simply instances in which *BIN* is used in the context of the distant past, they are certainly worthy of further discussion. Jamal (12) says that the jacket is new, yet he declares, "I BIN having it." Certainly more information would be needed to determine whether Jamal has had the jacket for a long time although he had not worn it before that day – to determine why the jacket is characterized as being new and has been in his possession for a long time.

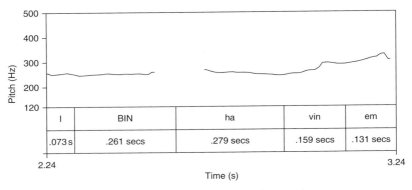

Figure 4.6 Pitch track of *I BIN havin em*. (Jasmine)

In (13) Jasmine does not immediately respond to the "when" question with information about the time she got the pants until she is prompted by LJG to choose an appropriate time from two answers. She chooses "a long time ago," which is in line with *BIN*. It is not clear how precise about time developing speakers can be in certain situations, nor is it clear what "a long time" means to them – 4- and 5-year-olds – but it is clear that the children are developing *BIN* as a marker that relates, at least in part, to some notion of length of time.

4.3.1 Remote past and elicitation tasks

Utterances from developing AAE speakers' spontaneous speech samples provide clear evidence that the children do indeed produce *BIN* in a way that indicates their sensitivity to the way stress influences meaning. In addition, contexts in which they use *BIN* can be interpreted as being compatible with distant past readings. However, in order to get more reliable information about the extent to which 3-, 4-, and 5-year-olds have *BIN* in their grammars and actually associate it with the distant past, they were tested on ten scenarios in the form of comprehension tasks. The advantage of the comprehension tasks is that they could be devised to test the children's interpretation of *BIN*, and they could potentially lead to considerably more results with fewer questions about children's intended meanings.

In short, data from them could supplement the spontaneous speech data. The ten scenarios used in the *BIN* comprehension study consisted of pictures accompanied by short descriptions and prompts or questions about the scenarios that included the marker *BIN*. Samples of these scenarios are included in Figures 4.7, 4.8, and 4.9.[6] The scenarios are written in MAE, and the target question or prompt includes *BIN*. In all of the cases, I (LJG) read the story description to the child while pointing to the corresponding pictures and then asked questions about the scenario. The goal was to present the scenarios in storytelling mode in a voice that would be "normal" for a member (perhaps a teacher) of the children's speech community and natural for me. For the record, there were no exaggerations in the direction of affected AAE or affected MAE. During the task the child was allowed to ask questions and comment on the story. The story or part of it was repeated if the child's focus moved away from listening to the *BIN* scenario to telling his/her own story. In some *BIN* scenarios characters/objects were portrayed as having been in a state for a longer time than other characters/objects, and in other scenarios some characters were portrayed as having been participating in an activity longer than other characters. The scenario in Figure 4.7 features two characters (an old man and John) who can fix bikes. The old man has been fixing bikes for a long time, but John just learned how to fix bikes at school. (See the short story that accompanies the pictures.)

The target response to the prompt "Who BIN fixing bikes?" is "the old man." Some participants' responses to follow-up questions provided further insight into their understanding of *BIN* as a distant past marker, and other participants asked questions and naturally elaborated on the stories, giving more information about their interpretations. For instance, Talia (4;2, F, AAE) answered "the old man" to the prompt after being read the story in the scenario in Figure 4.7, and she also answered a follow-up question as repeated below:

14. "Who BIN fixing bikes?"
     LJG: <after reading the story> Who BIN fixing bikes?

Figure 4.7 *Who BIN fixing bikes?*

There is an old man in town who fixes bikes. Many kids take their bikes to the old man to get them fixed. John broke his bike before and took it to the old man to fix. Then, John broke his bike again and told his older cousin Jeremy. His older cousin, Jeremy, learned how to fix bikes in school this week, so he said, "I can fix your bike for you, John." So John is letting Jeremy fix his bike this time?

Who BIN fixing bikes?

Talia: The old man.

LJG: Why you say the old man?

Talia: 'Cause he old.

Talia's response suggests that she links some notion of *BIN* with being old relative to schoolboy Jeremy's state. It is not clear whether Talia also used the background information in the scenario about Jeremy's just learning how to fix bikes at school, along with the man being old, to determine that the targeted response was the old man, or whether the property of being old was enough for her to link the old man to *BIN fixing bikes* ('fixing bikes for a long time'). Other children also gave "old" as the reason for choosing "the old man" as the target answer.

Along these same lines, before Jabari (4;9, M, AAE) answers the prompt in the scenario in Figure 4.8, he asks a series of questions for clarification about the distance in the past, so to speak.

15.   "Bruce BIN had which shoes?"

LJG: *<after reading the story>* Bruce BIN had which shoes?

Jabari: All day long?

LJG: All day long. Bruce BIN had which shoes?

Jabari: For a long time?

LJG: Yeah. For a long time.

Jabari: Since I got here?

LJG: Umhmmm! Which ones?

Jabari: Them, them.

LJG: Them?

Jabari: Them old ones. (Green and Roeper 2007, p. 295)

Given the adverbials Jabari uses to paraphrase the time period he thinks may be associated with *BIN had which shoes*, "all day long?," "for a long time?," and "since I got here?," it is clear that he links *BIN* to an extended or long period. After he is clear about what is intended, he settles on the target answer 'old shoes' ("them old ones").

The developing AAE-speaking children scored above chance on all *BIN* scenarios. Overall the AAE-speaking children's score

Figure 4.8 *Bruce BIN had which shoes?*[7]

Bruce has a pair of tennis shoes that he wears all the time. Even though they are raggedy, he still likes to wear them. Finally, his dad noticed Bruce's shoes were falling apart and bought him a new pair. Bruce wears the new pair sometimes but he still likes to wear the old ones.

Bruce BIN had which shoes?

was .73. While there was not a significant interaction of age with predicate type, age was significant overall, such that the older children scored higher than the younger children on all *BIN* scenarios. The conclusion here is that developing AAE-speaking children have knowledge of the function, meaning, and use of *BIN* as a remote past marker, which increases with age. In further research more scenarios with different types of predicates should be tested to determine the extent to which there are differences in the development of *BIN* with different types of verbs and other predicates. One case in point is the *BIN* V–*ed* construction or *BIN* followed by a verb that refers to an event in the past, such as the *BIN went* construction in Figure 4.9.

The children scored lowest on the *BIN went* scenario (.52). Children who did not choose the target answer "Bruce," chose either "Mom" or both "Mom and Bruce." The fact that mothers in the real world may be associated with going to the store may have influenced the children's responses. Also, they may have had a difficult time with the scenario given that the predicate is in the V–*ed* form. Also, it is not clear what the interaction is between *BIN* and –*ed*. It might be the case that for some children *BIN went to the store* does not refer to who has been away at the store the longest, but who is actually at the store or simply who has gone to the store. The picture shows that both Mom and Bruce are at the store at one point in time, so children may choose to respond with either or both characters. It would be useful to test additional *BIN* V–*ed* scenarios to determine whether children actually master these constructions later with respect to other *BIN* constructions, such as those in (11).

Research on *BIN* and following predicates provides insight into the development of tense–aspect properties in child AAE, and it also sheds some light on dialectal differences among different varieties of English. From the very early research on AAE, the claim has been made that AAE and varieties of English spoken in the southern United States share similar patterns and for some researchers there is a question about whether any properties actually distinguish the

Figure 4.9 *Who BIN went to the store?*

Bruce's mom asked him to go to the store because she needed some flour and chicken and vegetables to make a pie for dinner. So, Bruce left the house and went to the store for his mom. It was nice day so he walked slowly through the park on the way to the store. Then Jenny went over to the neighbor's house. After both kids left, Mom realized that she also needed eggs. So, she told Dad that she will quickly go to the store, get the eggs and bring Bruce home with her. She picked up her purse and went out the door to go to the store.

Who BIN went to the store?

two. (See the discussion of this and related issues in Wolfram and Schilling-Estes (1998).) In addition to *BIN* results for developing AAE speakers, we also have data on developing SwLVE speakers' knowledge of *BIN*. Overall the SwLVE-speaking children scored almost as well on the *BIN* scenarios as the developing AAE-speaking children, and these results confirm that they use the marker to refer to the distant past in certain contexts, also. However, there is a significant difference between the two groups in the *BIN went* scenario. Both the AAE-speaking and the SwLVE-speaking children scored lower on the *BIN went* scenario than they did on the other scenarios; however, the SwLVE-speaking children's score was .27, which was well below chance (.33). The AAE-speaking children's score was above chance (.52). The SwLVE-speaking children may do well on most *BIN* scenarios because they, like their AAE-speaking peers in their geographical region, are developing *BIN* as part of their grammar. On the other hand, it may be that the SwLVE-speaking children do well on the *BIN* constructions that are quite similar to *been* constructions in general English (and regional varieties of English). For instance, in general English it is possible to say, *That box has been under the bed (for a long time)*, a sentence with unstressed *been* that is quite similar to the stressed *BIN* construction *That box BIN under the bed*. On the other hand, in general English it is not possible to say, **That girl has been went to the store (a long time ago)*, although in AAE it is natural to say *That girl BIN went to the store* to mean 'That girl went to the store a long time ago.' That is to say that SwLVE-speaking children may be able to rely on their knowledge of *been* in most *BIN* scenarios, but it does not help much where *BIN* V–*ed* is concerned. The AAE-speaking children may have a better hold on *BIN went* because they are developing the marker in their grammars as a separate tense–aspect marker that is linked to the remote or distant past.

In addition to using simplex forms or, in other words, verbs that are overtly marked (–*ed*) or covertly marked ($\emptyset_{-ed}$) for past, child AAE speakers also use complex forms consisting of preverbal markers (*had*, *BIN*) followed by a verb bearing overt or covert morphology. The children produce and interpret these markers as referring to some eventuality in the past at least as early as 4 years old. Spontaneous speech data show that developing AAE-speaking children have a number of ways of talking about and referring to eventualities in the past or events that they have accomplished or achieved. The large corpus of spontaneous and directed speech that I have amassed does not reveal the same findings for the resultant state marker *done* (which I represent as *dən*). Of all of the child speakers represented, only one produced the marker *dən*, although the children do use the past participle *done* to indicate "finished" (e.g., *I'm done playing*) or a type of experiential perfect reading (e.g., *I already done all of that stuff*. Donovan, 5;0, M, AAE). The following resultant state *dən* token was produced by Lenny (5, M, AAE):

16.   LJG: Talk to your mama, L__.
      Lenny: She dən hanged up.

The exchange between LJG and Lenny took place when LJG tried to prompt Lenny to have a pretend conversation on a toy cell phone with his mother. Rather than have the make-believe conversation, Lenny reported that his mother was no longer on the telephone by using *dən* + *hanged up* ('has already hung up'). It would be useful to collect systematic data on the marker *dən*, along the lines of what has been collected for *BIN*, to determine the extent to which children actually produce and comprehend it. The virtual non-existence of *dən* constructions may be due to the lack of focus on the marker in the data collection or the limited contexts for its use as well as developmental and cognitive constraints. It was relatively easy to set up contexts for eliciting *BIN*; however, I did not take the opportunity to set up contexts for *dən*.

4.3.2 The past: pragmatics and rhetorical marking

Children acquiring systems in AAE tense–aspect marking must develop grammatical uses of markers such as *BIN* to use them in appropriate linguistic contexts in reference to properties of events in the past. In addition, they must also use them in appropriate pragmatic contexts. The data from elicitation tasks and spontaneous speech clearly point to children's association of *BIN* with some meaning that extends beyond reference to the past. In particular, there is a strong suggestion that some children use *BIN* in the type of aggrandizement context mentioned by Rickford (1975). He notes that *BIN* occurs in pragmatic contexts in which speakers use it for "dramatization and self-aggrandizement, or styling" (p. 117). Children can be heard using *BIN* in contexts that also highlight their expertise in a particular area or their familiarity with a topic or process. A case in point follows:

17.   LJG: You said that was the wrong way. How did you know that was the wrong way? *<in reference to Jabari's response to the incorrect way LJG was trying to put the cassette into the recorder>*
      Jabari: I BIN knowing.

First it should be noted that Jabari gave the response in (17) before the *BIN* elicitation tasks began (e.g., as in (15)), so it was not triggered by previous *BIN* constructions in connection with the scenarios. As the example illustrates, Jabari does not explicitly or directly answer the "How?" question that he was asked, but the answer he gives conveys his attitude and knowledge. By using *BIN*, he could be communicating that the knowledge is just second nature; it is as if he has always had it. Also, his intent could be to communicate that he is just smart at figuring things out, and he figured out how to determine the wrong way of things a long time ago.

Nia (5;4, F, AAE) also uses *BIN* in a similar context:

18.   LJG: Where you learn to tell stories like that? Where did you learn to tell stories like that? *<question in response to Nia's retelling of* Good Dog, Carl*>*
      Nia: I BIN learnin that. I been readin books at home before I come to school.
      LJG: Oh!

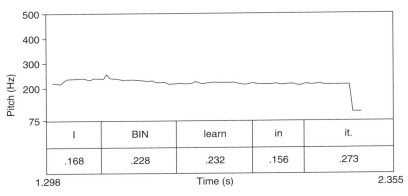

Figure 4.10 Pitch track for *I BIN learnin that*.

Nia: At nighttime.

She uses stressed *BIN* to communicate that her storytelling ability has been developing for a long time, but she uses unstressed *been* in the perfect context to explain that she has been participating (as in the habitual sense) in a reading activity at home. There is no explicit expression of distant past in the second sentence as there is in the first sentence. The first sentence, which includes stressed *BIN*, indicates that the learning has been in progress for quite some time, but the second sentence simply states the form of learning that has taken place. She highlights that she has been working on her storytelling for some time at home. The pitch tracks for Nia's *BIN* sentence and for her *been* sentence are different. See Figures 4.10 and 4.11.

The first point to note is that the contour associated with *BIN* and that associated with *been* are different. The *BIN* contour is relatively flat, but the one associated with *been* indicates some movement on the syllable. Here again the duration of *BIN* is longer than the duration of the subject *I*, which is what we would expect for a stressed *BIN*, although other prosodic properties may help to define the marker. Just comparing the duration of *been* and the subject *I* in Figure 4.11, we find that *been* is also longer; however, it is not

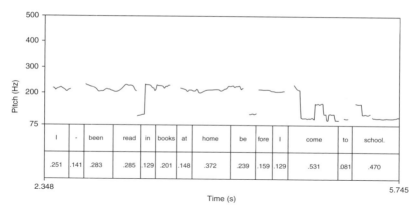

Figure 4.11 Pitch track for *I been reading books at home before I come to school.*

clear what to make of the syllable immediately preceding *been*, that is, whether it should be construed as part of *I* or not. In addition to duration, it would appear that other characteristics define a *been* as being stressed or unstressed. *Been* in Figure 4.11 is certainly heard as an unstressed *been;* perhaps the actual movement on that syllable contributes to the interpretation.

Nia uses *BIN* in another context, which may be understood as a type of aggrandizement, in which the marker is contrasted with "just started":

19.   LJG: I love those barrettes ...You just started wearing these barrettes?

Nia: I BIN wearing barrettes.

LJG: Oh, okay.

Nia: ... I like a lot of balls. *<in reference to hair adornment items>*

In this case Nia explicitly answers the question, and her response could certainly be taken to mean that she has worn barrettes for a long time – literally – especially given the fact that such adornment for little girls' hair in that community is quite common, and the girls can begin to wear barrettes very early, at one or two years old. Nia may not recollect her earliest memories of wearing barrettes, but she may not remember a day when she has not worn them either. Her response is almost certainly laced with a touch of pride; however, *BIN* likely refers to a literal long period.

It is possible to devise elicitation and other experimental tasks to determine the type of semantic meaning children associate with *BIN*, but the marker may also have pragmatic meaning and rhetorical uses that cannot be explained by semantics alone. The goal of the *BIN* study was not to collect the possible pragmatic and rhetorical uses of *BIN* simply because it was necessary to get an understanding of children's grammatical uses of the marker first. However, it is useful to think about and begin to investigate different uses of the marker by developing AAE-speaking children, especially with respect to the types of indirect and embedded messages the children may be able to convey with *BIN* as well as possible developing rhetorical strategies they may be acquiring.

In what follows, Dawn seems to be able to communicate an indirect message with the use of *BIN*:

20.   Dawn: L__ gon tell you about this one?
      LJG: Umhmm.
      Dawn: I wanna stay in here while L__ doing that. Alright?
      LJG: Why? Tell me why.
      Dawn: 'Cause. My teacher is nice.
      LJG: I know she is nice. I love her, too.
      Dawn: You BIN knowing her?
      LJG: Hmm?
      Dawn: You BIN knowing her?
      LJG: Umhmm.

In this excerpt Dawn informs me that she would like to stay in the room while her classmate (L_) participates in the elicitation tasks, and the conversation turns to her teacher, possibly because she thinks her teacher is nice enough to allow her to be out of the class for an extended period. To my response about her teacher being nice,

Dawn asks whether I have known her for a long time (i.e. "You BIN knowing her?"), as if to suggest that I must really be acquainted with the teacher to speak about her in such familiar terms. It could also be that Dawn is alluding to the way she has seen me interact with her teacher, whom I have known for many years. In any case, it is not a stretch to read implied messages into the *BIN* construction. These *BIN* examples are offered as observations about possible pragmatic meaning and rhetorical strategies associated with the marker. More data should be collected on pragmatics and developing AAE that might help to answer questions about additional meaning beyond the semantics that is associated with tense–aspect markers.

One major observation that can be made given the discussion in this chapter as well as in Chapter 3 is that grammaticalized markers are prominent in the tense–aspect system of developing AAE-speaking children. For instance, there is evidence that the children are beginning to use preverbal markers such as aspectual *be*, preverbal *had*, and remote past *BIN* in tense–aspect contexts. Preverbal *had* only refers to events indicated by verbs, but aspectual *be* and remote past *BIN* can apply to states and events in adult AAE, so they can precede just about any predicate type including nouns, adjectives, and prepositional phrases. There is evidence that children understand sequences of aspectual *be*/remote past *BIN* and following nonverbal predicates, although they seem to produce the markers with verbs more often in the beginning stages. The children in this study ranged in ages from 3;6 to 5;7. The 3-year-olds seemed to fare better on the *BIN* tasks than they did on the aspectual *be* tasks, which raises the question about whether *BIN* is acquired before aspectual *be*. It is the case that the children also use the bound morphemes (i.e. some form of *–ed*) to mark the past, although the occurrence is variable. In acquiring the AAE tense–aspect system, children have to pay attention to preverbal grammaticalized free morphemes (e.g., aspectual *be*, *BIN*, and *had*) as well as to bound morphemes such as *–ing* and forms of the past.

5 Negation: focus on negative concord

Dawn: I don't wanna be no doctor. I wanna be a mailman.

INTRODUCTION

This chapter considers negation marking in child AAE, with a focus on negative concord. One general pattern that AAE shares with some languages, such as Romance and Slavic languages, as well as other non-standard varieties of English, is the use of multiple negative elements within a clause to convey a single negative meaning. For instance, in the sentence *They didn't have no books*, negation is indicated on the auxiliary *didn't* as well as within the noun phrase *no books*; however, the meaning of the sentence is the same as that of the corresponding single negation sentence with the negated auxiliary and polarity item *any*: *They didn't have any books*. Thus the term for this type of multiple negation is generally known as negative concord given that the multiple negative elements are in agreement or concord with each other rather than each indicating separate negative meaning or each contributing further negative import to the sentence. Simply put, agreement or concord refers to the choice of a following negative element based on the preceding one. For instance, instead of *no* in *They didn't have no books* canceling out the negative *didn't*, resulting in the positive sentence *They did have books*, *no* occurs because there is a preceding negative (*didn't*), not to add any negative meaning but to agree with the negative that is already present. Because multiple negative elements are used without changing the negative meaning of the sentence, negative concord has often been associated with emphatic interpretation, which would mean that the sentence in (1) is more emphatic than the one in (2):

1. Bruce <u>didn't</u> have <u>no</u> book.
2. Bruce <u>didn't</u> have a book.

While the sentence in (1) can certainly be emphatic, it is not necessarily so, and (2) can be as emphatic as (1), especially with emphasis on *a book*. Although negative concord is a stigmatized pattern, it does not present the type of interpretation challenges for speakers who do not understand AAE patterns that constructions such as aspectual *be* sequences present. That is, American English speakers who do not speak varieties of English in which negative concord is acceptable generally do not have problems understanding it. Charles Yang (2006, p. 120) goes even farther and notes the following: "Third, it is possible that everyone in America spoke a fragment of African American English at one point. Many children learning English, regardless of demographics, make frequent use of double or multiple negatives:

> Daddy's not being nothing.
> I don't want no milk!
> He didn't do nothing.

As is the case in other varieties of English, negative concord in AAE is generally optional, so the frequency with which speakers choose either (1) or (2) above may depend on a number of factors. This type of variation within AAE speech communities is particularly interesting from the angle of the type of impact it has on the negative concord patterns developing child AAE speakers acquire in their speech communities. While negative concord patterns may be quite similar in varieties of English, certain developmental properties in the acquisition of negative concord may differ. Henry, Maclaren, Wilson, and Finlay (1997) make just this point in their discussion of negative concord in Belfast English and Bristol English. They note that children developing Bristol English master negative concord around the age of 3;3, but children who are developing Belfast English begin to use negative concord later, around 4;6. The researchers suggest that the difference in development of negative concord in the two varieties is due to subtle linguistic differences rather than to socio-linguistic factors.

5.1 NEGATIVE CONCORD PRODUCTION

Children in the study produced negative concord sentences with two negative elements, so only one of the elements had the force of negation.

3. Joya: Uhhuh. But my mama um at home.
    LJG: Mmhmmm ...
    Joya: But she don't got no work today.
        'But she doesn't have (any) work today'

The first negation (*don't*) marks the sentence negative, and the following negative element (*no*) simply agrees with the first or is licensed by the first. The combination of two negatives in the construction is quite common in the southwestern Louisiana data.

Some of the examples from the database, in which negation is represented on the auxiliary and the following noun phrase, are given below:

4. (a) I don't have no dog. (Tyra, 5;3, F, AAE)
    (b) I don't have no training wheels. (Tyra, 5; 3, F, AAE)
    (c) They don't have no ribbon because they, they old. (Zyrion, 5;2, M, AAE)
    (d) He don't have no eye, hunh? (Zyrion, 5; 2, M, AAE)
    (e) I don't wanna to be no doctor. (Dawn)
    (f) I didn't see no snakes. (Valencia, 5;6, F, AAE)
    (g) But they don't have no apples on that. (Valencia, 5; 6, F, AAE)
    (h) They don't have no reading on there. (Valencia, 5; 6, F, AAE)
    (i) LJG: Turn the page.
        Ray: Ain't got no more page. (5, M, AAE)
    (j) LJG: What happened when you were going fast?
        Darnell: I didn't wreck nobody. (5;3, M, AAE)
    (k) Darnell: And second it didn't have no gas.

LJG: Wait a minute!

Darnell: They didn't have no gas in my bike.

Similar constructions are also produced in which the first negative element is a negated auxiliary (e.g., *didn't*) and the following is an adverbial element (e.g., *nowhere*), as in (5):

5. (a) 'Cause I didn't go nowhere. (Rashandra, 5, F, AAE)
   (b) We not playing with blocks no more. (Nia, 5;9, F, AAE)
   (c) I didn't have nowhere to put them. (Mitchell, 5, M, AAE)

A third concord pattern is one in which the negated indefinite noun, which is the subject of the sentence (e.g., *nobody*), is followed by a negated auxiliary:

6. (a) Nobody can't get in this. (Zeke)
   (b) And nobody ain't gon get me 'cause I be riding my bike. (Zeke)
   (c) Nobody didn't steal it. (Deon, 3;10, M, AAE)

The use of multiple negative elements is quite productive in the developing AAE speakers' spontaneous speech, and given the context in which it is used, it is easy to interpret the multiple negation as in (3)–(6) as negative concord. To supplement the data from spontaneous speech, elicitation tasks were used to determine whether children really assign multiple negative elements a concord interpretation. The elicitation scenarios consisted of a short story and corresponding pictures. After hearing the stories while looking at the pictures, the children were asked to answer questions about the scenarios. Two of the four elicitation scenarios administered to the participants are given as examples in Figures 5.1 and 5.2:

In the scenario in Figure 5.1, a bike with training wheels is contrasted with a bike without training wheels, and the target question is worded in such a way in which it could elicit a negative response containing two negative elements. The children were expected to give a response that alluded to the fact that the chosen bike did not

Figure 5.1 *Negative concord elicitation: "Bikes and Training Wheels"*

One day, Bruce was riding his bike with training wheels. See, here? He was getting too big for his bike with training wheels, and he started thinking about getting a bike without training wheels. He really wanted a bike without training wheels. Bruce went to the bike store and looked at the different bikes they had. He saw a bike with training wheels. See, here? And he saw another bike without training wheels. He really wanted that bike without training wheels.

Why did he want this bike? [points to bike without training wheels]

Figure 5.2 *Negative concord elicitation: "Box of Books"*

Bruce won a big box of books. He is so happy because he wants a book about SpongeBob. Bruce loves SpongeBob. He really wants a book about SpongeBob, so he looks through the box of books. He finds a book about birds, a book about stars, and the last book in the box is about flowers. See all the books here? But he really wants a book about SpongeBob, so he gives the box of books to his friend John.

Why does Bruce give the box of books to his friend John?

have training wheels. Some of the children's responses to the scenario question are given in (7):

7. (a) Because they didn't have no training wheels. (Tiffini, 5;5, F, AAE)
   (b) They don't have no training wheels. (Thomas, 4;6, M, AAE)
   (c) Don't have no training wheels on there. (Raven, 5;1, F, AAE)
   (d) 'Cause he don't want no training wheels on his bike. (Marcus, 5;1, M, AAE)
   (e) Because he want to get a bike without no training wheels. (Valencia, 5;6, F, AAE)
   (f) Don't have training wheels on it. (Kara, 4;11, F, AAE)
   (g) This one don't have training wheels. (James, 5;2, M, AAE)

The responses in (7) are all negative, some with negative concord and the others with only one negative element. In the first four negative concord sentences (7a–d), the auxiliary is negated and followed by a noun phrase (*no training wheels*) negated by *no*. The sentence in (7e) includes the preposition *without* followed by *no training wheels*. I take that sentence to be an example of negative concord, also, in which *without no training wheels* has the reading "without training wheels." Children also produce similar sentences with a negative element within the prepositional phrase headed by *with*: *You don't have to defeat him with, with no machines and no* <unintelligible> *bombs* (Terry, 5;11, M, AAE). The remaining sentences (7f, g) are non-negative concord (i.e. single negation), which show that negative concord is also optional for speakers in the community.

In the scenario in Figure 5.2, the focus is on a box of books that does not contain the desired book about SpongeBob. The goal was also to elicit a negative response communicating that the box does not contain a book about SpongeBob. Some of children's responses to the scenario question in Figure 5.2 are given in (8):

8. (a) He didn't have no more in here. (Thomas, 4;6, M, AAE)
   (b) This box of books don't got no cars. (Joya, 5;1, F, AAE)

(c) Because they didn't even have SpongeBob. (Tiffini, 5;5, F, AAE)

(d) He don't have SpongeBob in it. (Kara, 4;11, F, AAE)

(e) He don't like em. (James, 5;2, M, AAE)

(f) He don't like em. (Marcus, 5;1, M, AAE)

(g) 'Cause he already have books and he want to give some to his friends. (Valencia, 5;6, F, AAE)

While negative concord is indeed very common, it is not obligatory, so children are not limited to negative concord in producing negative sentences, as the examples in (8) show. As in (7), they use both negative concord in (8a, b) and single negative elements in (8c–g). The same children who use negative concord also use single negation, and the occurrence of these dual strategies for marking negation in child speech indicates the variation in the grammar, in which one strategy is just as much part of the grammar as the other. That is, moving from negative concord to single negation does not necessarily mean that children are shifting to a "standard" variety or moving from single negation to negative concord does not mean that they are shifting from one dialect to another. While this is not a sociolinguistic study, it seems to be within the lines of the data to say that a number of factors may contribute to the choice of the answers to be expressed in single negation or in negative concord, and to the content of the answer. For instance, all of the children gave on-target responses that addressed the training wheels in the scenario about the bikes. On the other hand, there were different types of responses to the SpongeBob book scenario question, as exemplified in (8). While some children directly addressed the absence of a SpongeBob book in the box, others went in different directions to talk about cars not being in the box (8b), not liking the books (8e, f), and wanting to give some books away (8g). Without further analysis of the test scenarios, it is difficult to draw solid conclusions about all of the responses. I bring up the point about conditions that might affect a child's production of negative concord, including there being optionality in the grammar and the child's familiarity with the subject (e.g., training wheels), to underscore the fact that children who are developing AAE also develop what may appear to be mainstream English forms. Their use of just a single negative element vs. negative concord may not indicate a shift to MAE; the use could show optionality in AAE. It is important to consider optionality in discussions of child AAE, especially given the claims about code-shifting that are addressed in Chapter 7. Also, because AAE is often characterized strictly by patterns that are markedly different from MAE and are argued not to occur in the "standard," often overlap in constructions produced by AAE speakers and constructions that also occur in MAE is taken to be a switch into the "standard" variety. However, if AAE is a "complete" grammar, which is what I am presenting it as here, then it includes constructions that are found in other varieties of English as well as those that are not. The bottom line is that it is possible to produce single negation while speaking AAE.

The overall percentage of negative concord production in the four scenarios was 48 percent; however, it is not clear how much and exactly what to read into these results. This means that the children gave negative concord responses to the scenario questions 48 percent of the time. The other responses were either in single negation form or positive, as in (8g). It is clear that the results show that children do indeed produce negative concord spontaneously, but that it is not obligatory. They can also use single negation in the same context. What is clear is that the results of the elicitation tasks are in line with the children's spontaneous negation: They use negative concord variably in negative contexts.

One negative concord pattern that was not attested in the child data is the initial negated auxiliary (e.g., *can't*) followed by a negative indefinite noun (e.g., *nobody*), such as the following:

9.   <u>Can't nobody</u> get in this.

Going back to (6), we see that the children have the opposite concord pattern, a sentence with an initial negative indefinite noun followed by a negated auxiliary (e.g., *nobody can't*). As it turns out, there are some sentence initial negated auxiliary negative concord construction tions in the dataset, but they are not quite the same as the structure in (9). Look at the existential sentences in (4i), (*Ain't got no more page*) and (7c), (*Don't have no training wheels on there*), which refer to the (non)existence of entities, pages, and training wheels in these cases. These sentences come to have sentence initial negated auxiliaries due to the missing expletive subject. Given the expletive subjects (e.g., *it, they*) produced by the developing AAE speakers, possible renditions of the sentences are the following:

It/They ain't got no more page. (cf. (4i))
It/They don't have no training wheels on there. (cf. (7c))

Both *it* and *they* (*they* is often pronounced as *dey*, with an initial *d* vs. *th*) occur as expletive subjects in the data. As expletives, the pronouns are merely placeholders in subject position. Although they look like the referential pronouns that actually refer to objects or humans, as in *It* (i.e. the book) *is on the table*, and *They* (i.e. the students) *are in the gym*, they are simply placeholders and do not refer to actual entities in the world. The expletives that are purported to be dropped from the sentences in (4i) and (7c) are different in that they do not refer to an object or human or have any real meaning; they just stand in the place of subjects. Presumably, one reason they can be dropped from the sentences is that they do not refer to any object or human; they just serve as placeholders. Once they are dropped, the first element is a negated auxiliary that is in concord with a negated noun phrase that is separated from it by a special verb that occurs in expletive or existential constructions (e.g., *have*).

Expletive Drop: It/They don't have no training wheels on there.
(cf. (7c))

Ø = Don't have no training wheels on there.
'There aren't any training wheels on there'

By virtue of the expletive "drop" process, we end up with a negative concord sentence that superficially begins with a negated auxiliary. Empirical data from adults as well as child AAE strongly support the claim that something along the lines of expletive "drop" does apply. For instance, examples such as (4h) and (4d) show that children also produce the expletive initial constructions, in which case the expletive is not dropped (e.g., *It didn't have no gas.* 'There wasn't any gas'). In effect, sentences with the initial negated auxiliaries, as in (4i) and (7c), are only superficially similar to the type of negative concord structures in (9). The expletive/existential sentences in (4i) and (7c) only have an initial auxiliary due to expletive "drop." Secondly, the negative indefinite noun does not immediately follow the negated auxiliary, which is the case in the genuine negative initial sentence (9). I will return to a discussion of the sentence type in (9) in the next chapter and speculate about why the pattern may not appear until later in development.

5.2   NEGATIVE CONCORD COMPREHENSION

In the previous section the examples of children's multiple negative elements provide strong evidence to support the claim that developing AAE-speaking children produce negative concord. Scenarios, such as the ones in Figures 5.1 and 5.2, are quite useful in setting up contexts that elicit negative responses as further support of children's use of multiple negative elements to communicate a single negation meaning. However, tasks actually designed to get at children's interpretation and comprehension of multiple negative elements in sentences can provide even stronger evidence that developing AAE-speaking children not only produce negative concord structures, but they also interpret multiple negative elements as negative concord.

The scenarios for the negative concord comprehension task included a short story and illustrative pictures. After simultaneously hearing the stories and seeing the corresponding pictures, the children were prompted to select from possible choices, which would be in line either with a negative concord or non-negative concord interpretation. Two sample scenarios are given in Figures 5.3 and 5.4.

In order to be certain that the child was indeed paying attention and followed the story in the scenario, questions irrelevant to negation (i.e. distracter questions) were also asked. In addition to asking the questions to the child, a duck puppet (Miss Dee) was also questioned, and the child was asked whether the puppet's response was correct. Note that there are no morphologically marked negative elements in the stories themselves, such as *don't, didn't,* or *no,* but they are introduced in the scenario questions. For instance, *don't* and *no,* which are used to negate the verb and a noun, respectively, are included in the questions. The assumption was that children who had negative concord readings would answer in one way and those who assigned negative meaning to both *don't* and *no,* a true double negation reading, instead of treating *don't* as the true negation and *no* as a marker that agrees with it, would choose another response. For instance, for the scenario in Figure 5.3, children who had a negative concord reading for *Who don't have no red snow cone?* would choose "Bruce," and those who leaned toward a double negation reading would choose "Jenny." All participants (100 percent) chose "Bruce," a result that we interpret as being compatible with negative concord interpretation, and they consistently counted the duck puppet's negative concord response ("Bruce") as correct.

Let me pause here to say that in reading the scenarios, I did not use any special emphasis on the negative elements to try to force a double negation reading in which children would select "Jenny." Admittedly, some manipulation of prosodic cues may have had a positive effect in triggering double negation readings.[1] My delivery may have had a strong effect on the 100 percent negative concord readings for the scenario. However, considering the extensive negative concord production data, I do not find the results surprising. Given the "universality" of negative concord in developing language, these results do not seem to be extraordinary.

Figure 5.3 *Negative concord comprehension: "Red Snow Cones and Purple Snow Cones"*

After school, Bruce and Jenny's dad takes them to get snow cones. They have to walk a long way to the snow code stand and it's hot! There are lots of flavors at the snow cone stand, and Bruce and Jenny have to choose which flavors they want. Jenny gets a red snow cone, because she loves red. Bruce hates red flavor so he gets a purple snow cone.

Who didn't get no purple snow cone?

Figure 5.4 *Negative concord comprehension: "Cookies and Rainbow Sprinkles"*

Bruce and Jenny went to the store with their mom. They brought their friend John with them. They were all in the bakery section, and they saw a case full of cookies. John didn't want a cookie with rainbow sprinkles because he wasn't hungry, but Bruce and Jenny wanted a cookie. Jenny got a cookie with rainbow sprinkles because she loved rainbow sprinkles. Bruce didn't want a cookie with rainbow sprinkles on top, so he got a plain cookie.

Who didn't get no cookie with no rainbow sprinkles on top?

The question prompt in the scenario in Figure 5.4 is slightly different from the one in the scenario in Figure 5.3. The question *Who didn't get no cookie with no rainbow sprinkles on top?* includes multiple negative elements, in which the auxiliary verb (*didn't*) and the two noun phrases (*no cookie, no rainbow sprinkles*) are negated. In the scenario in Figure 5.3, we have already seen that children get a negative concord reading of two negative elements in the same sentence, but the scenario in Figure 5.4 presents three negative elements. The first negated noun phrase directly follows the verb, and the second negated noun phrase is the object of the preposition within the following prepositional phrase (*with no rainbow sprinkles*). What is noteworthy about the sentence in the question prompt is that the final negative element is within a prepositional phrase that separates it from the preceding negated verb (*didn't get*) and noun phrase (*no cookie ...*). A question that can be raised here, along with how many negatives children allow to agree in a concord reading in a sentence, is under what sentence conditions the negative elements are allowed to relate to each other. That is, we have already seen that negative elements can relate to each other when they are only separated by a verb, as in the question in the scenario in Figure 5.3, but what about the relation between two negative elements that are separated by a preposition? As it turns out, the result for the scenario in Figures 5.4 was 92 percent negative concord readings (e.g., "Bruce" (and/or "John")), which strongly suggests that children allow negative elements to agree with each other or enter into a concord relationship even when they are separated by a prepositional phrase.

These are not the results presented in previous work by Coles-White, de Villiers, and Roeper (2004), in which the same type of negative concord constructions were examined. Coles-White *et al.* suggest that it is difficult for negative elements to relate to or agree with each other when they are separated by a boundary such as a prepositional phrase. For our purposes, this would mean that while children would be expected to associate the negative elements in *didn't get no cookies* with each other to get a concord reading ('didn't get any cookies'), the concord reading of *didn't* and *no cookies* might not extend across the preposition *with* to form a concord relation with *no rainbow sprinkles*. This is a technical issue, so I will avoid the details and present a brief version of the point about how prepositions can be relevant for negative concord. The main idea is that, in some sentences, a preposition (within a prepositional phrase) can serve as a boundary between information preceding and following it. The boundary can prevent the information on either side of the preposition from being related. We can illustrate with the prompt in the scenario in Figure 5.4. Depending on how the negative elements are related, the sentence in (10) can have two readings. I will refer to one reading as the negative concord reading (Reading 1), which has been discussed, and to the other reading as the partial negative concord with double negation reading (Reading 2):

10. Who didn't get no cookie with no rainbow sprinkles on top?
     Reading 1 Negative Concord (paraphrase): 'Who didn't get a cookie with rainbow sprinkles on top?'
     Reading 2 Partial Negative Concord with Double Negation (paraphrase): 'Who didn't get a cookie that had NO rainbow sprinkles on top/without rainbow sprinkles on top?'

Note that in the paraphrase of the Negative Concord Reading (1), there is only one negative element (*didn't*), which is what we expect given that, in the concord cases, only one negative does the work, as illustrated below:

> Negative Concord illustration:
> Who didn't get no cookie with no rainbow sprinkles on top?
> True neg (*didn't*) – *no* Agrees with True neg (*didn't*) – *no* Agrees with True neg (*didn't*)

The illustration shows that in the interpretation of the sentence only one negative will be represented given that there is only one "true negation," and this is exactly what is shown in Reading 1 in (10); the only negative introduced in the paraphrase is also the "true negation," *didn't*. On the other hand, in the Partial Negative Concord with Double Negation Reading (2), we should see a case in which there is a "true negation" with which a negative element agrees, which results in negative concord. In this same sentence we should also see a case in which an additional element has independent negative meaning. There will be more than one negative element contributing true negation, so I will refer to this case as double negation.

> Partial Negative Concord with Double Negation Illustration:
> Who didn't get no cookie with no rainbow sprinkles on top?
> True neg 1 (*didn't*) – *no* Agrees with True neg 1 (*didn't*) – True neg 2 (*no*)

The illustration above represents a reading in which two of the three negative elements receive a true negation reading; one, not both of the following negatives, agrees with the first true negation. The final negative element in the sentence contributes its own negative meaning, resulting in Reading 2 in (10). While the sentence in (10) is ambiguous, context and intonation can generally determine whether the speaker intends Reading 1 or Reading 2. For instance, the double negation reading often occurs when the negative element is stressed. This means that it is quite possible that Reading 2 can be distinguished from Reading 1 when the *no* in *no rainbow sprinkles* is stressed. One explanation for why the final negative element can be on its own as a true negation for one reading, not agreeing with the previous negative elements outside of the prepositional phrase that includes the final negative, is that the imaginary boundary prevents such association. Obviously, however, the boundary is not impenetrable because there is a reading in which the negative element included in the prepositional phrase (*no rainbow sprinkles*) can actually be associated with the other negatives, yielding a negative concord reading.

In her study of negation in child AAE, Coles (1998) noted that thirty-nine out of sixty-one 5- to 7-year-old children obeyed the boundary by not allowing negative concord between the preceding negative and the negative element within the prepositional phrase that modified the NP (noun phrase) (e.g., *cookies with no rainbow sprinkles on top*), resulting in the double negation reading. The children did allow concord between the preceding negative and other prepositional structure, in which the prepositional phrase does not modify the NP. Coles's claim is that this result is consistent with the view that young children's grammars may also reflect a universal principle about the types of structure in which concord and other similar constructions are allowed. However, she also notes that many 4-year-olds allowed negative concord across the boundary, results that are in line with the results I have reported. Coles suggests that given the age difference, the younger children might allow concord across boundaries due to the nature of development. Of course, a number of questions have to be addressed in light of the possible explanations for the results with the 4-year-olds, on the one hand, as well as with the 5- to 7-year-olds on the other. For instance, if it is the case that developing AAE speakers generally allow concord across boundaries as a stage in the developmental process, then it is interesting to determine what the situation is with respect to negative concord in adult AAE. Do adult AAE speakers allow negative concord across boundaries? If so, then it is not clear that children who allow negative concord across boundaries do so due to being in a developmental phase, although development may be an important factor in the interpretation of negation. Another point that should be addressed is that about the interaction between intonational patterns and negation that could lead to a negative concord or double negation reading. That is, intonation and stress may play a role in the way negatives are interpreted. It is clear even with AAE adult speech that speakers may favor a type of reading – concord or non-concord – given the type of intonation that the speaker uses. By no means is the suggestion that child negation and adult AAE negation work the same way, but a number of issues should be addressed in claims about the acquisition path to negation in general and negative concord in particular.

One special property about the prepositional phrase (*with no rainbow sprinkles on top*) in (10) is that it modifies the preceding noun *no cookie*; it tells that the cookie did not have any rainbow sprinkles on top of it. The prepositional phrase in (11) below (*with no plastic gloves*) does not have the role of describing the cookie. It tells about what was used/not used to get or pick up the cookie. According to Coles (1998), the children in her study allowed negative concord to occur over the type of prepositional boundary in (11), but not in (10).

11.   He didn't get no cookie with no plastic gloves.

The sentence in (11) also has three readings: negative concord, partial negative concord with double negation, and full double negation, as listed below:

12.   He didn't get no cookie with no plastic gloves.
       Reading 1 Negative Concord: 'He did not get a cookie by using
           plastic gloves'
       Reading 2 Partial Negative Concord with Double Negation: 'He
           did not get a cookie without using any plastic gloves.'
       Reading 3 Full Double Negation: 'He got a cookie by using
           plastic gloves.'

The full double negation reading has not been addressed, and it should also be noted that such reading is available for the sentence in (10). One simple description of the full double negation reading is that together several negatives make a positive, so, as reflected in the way Reading 3 is written, the combination of the negative elements results in a canceling out of the negatives and gives way to a sentence with all "positives." This reading will not be discussed further; however, some work should be conducted on it in relation to the acquisition path AAE-speaking children take in developing their negation system.

    The final point that I would like to make regarding the sentence in (11) is that it is argued to differ from the sentence in (10) in that *with no plastic gloves* is not part of the preceding noun phrase (*no cookie*). The prepositional phrase does not describe the noun phrase, so the claim is that it should not introduce the type of boundary that would prevent negation in the preceding part of the sentence from relating to words within the prepositional phrase. For that reason, it should be possible to get a negative concord reading, in which all of the negative elements in the sentence enter into an agreement with each other. The prediction is definitely borne out given the negative concord reading shown in Reading 1 in (12). An interesting prediction, given the Coles (1998) and Coles-White, de Villiers, and Roeper (2004) story, is that there should be a difference in the negative interpretations for the sentences in (10) and (11). That is, given that the prepositional phrase in (10) is part of the preceding noun phrase, it is argued to be a type of boundary that prevents an element outside of it from relating to the negative element contained within the prepositional phrase. On the other hand, the prepositional phrase in (11) is different and does not block other negative elements from relating to the negative element inside the prepositional phrase. However, strong evidence suggesting that the purported boundary in (11) does not prevent the preceding negative element from entering into a negative concord relationship with the negative element in the prepositional phrase is that the children in the negation comprehension tasks in the southwest Louisiana data gave negative concord readings for the sentence, although the claim in the Coles-White *et al.* study is that the boundary prevents a negative concord reading. This type of result raises a number of questions. Two obvious questions are the following: (1) Do children simply ignore the boundary in early developmental stages as they did in the negative concord comprehension tasks? (2) Is there a difference in language varieties, as well as regional difference with AAE, in what are considered to be boundaries in negative concord contexts? These, among a number of additional factors, should be considered in discussions of negative concord; however, the developmental and dialect-specific questions about negation are especially relevant for our purposes here.

5.3   HOW DIALECT UNIVERSAL IS NEGATIVE CONCORD

In her work on negation, Bellugi (1967) explains that the data from Adam and Sarah, in their later periods of forming negation constructions, can be characterized as "a thick layer of negation spread over negative sentences" (p. 137).[2] She uses "thick layer" to refer to the negative elements (e.g., *nothing, nobody*) that occur in the sentences rather than indefinite polarity items such as *anything* and *anybody*. The negation process is so pervasive that Bellugi associates an across-the-board rule with the process: "Apply negatives wherever possible in single propositions" (p. 143). Her characterization has the flavor of Labov's (1972) observation of "proliferation of negation." She reports examples such as the following from Adam and Sarah and notes that at age 5, Adam continues to use a combination of multiple negatives:

13. (a) Sarah: Nothing can't reach it, see? (p. 147)
    (b) Sarah: I don't got no paper today. (p. 148)
    (c) Adam: No one's not going to do what I'm doing. (p. 147)
    (d) Adam: I wasn't no baby. (p. 147)

The examples in (13) are the type of sentences reported for child AAE, and, from the data given for child AAE, there do not seem to be differences between negative concord in child AAE and that used by Sarah and Adam. Bellugi only considered production data, so it is not clear whether Sarah and Adam also had the same type of readings of negative concord into certain prepositional phrases. One hint that we get from Bellugi is that the negative concord or "thick layer" of negation in child speech may stop at around age 5 for children developing MAE. Obviously, the use of negative concord continues to develop in child AAE, and is used in adult AAE.

Stokes (1976) makes this same point in her study of negation of 3-, 4-, and 5-year-old AAE-speaking children. In comparing the data in her study to the findings in Bellugi (1967), she notes, "We cannot say that the acquisition of negation by VBE [Vernacular Black English] speaking children totally mirrors that of SE [Standard

English] speaking children, but we can say that in acquiring some of the various structures within negation there are many points of overlap" (p. 171). Stokes takes negative concord to be a "regular or unmarked way of negativizing" (p. 24), which is attributed to its use by developing AAE-speaking and MAE-speaking children. One point of difference between developing AAE-speaking and SE-speaking children that Stokes identified was the higher percentage of use of negative concord by the AAE-speaking children at earlier as well as later stages.

As has been noted in this study of developmental speech in southwestern Louisiana, negative concord also occurs in the spontaneous speech of the SwLVE-speaking children, as in the following representative example:

14. LJG: What did she say?
    Ryan: She didn't say nothing. (4, M, SwLVE)

This exchange was in the context of a toy cell phone conversation, in which LJG asked Ryan what the party on the other end of his cell phone said. The difference that we found between the AAE-speaking and the SwLVE-speaking children was in the rate of production on the negation elicitation tasks. While the SwLVE-speaking children produced some negative concord in negative elicitation tasks, their incidence of production was not as high as that of the AAE-speaking children. It would also be useful to analyze the SwLVE-speaking children's negative concord in spontaneous speech. Data such as that presented in Bellugi, for instance, provide sound evidence that negative concord is not unique to AAE varieties in American English or to other non-standard English varieties, at least in child language; it also occurs among speakers who are developing mainstream American English varieties.

In evaluating the data for this chapter, I find that negation boundaries or possible barriers for negative concord should be further analyzed to provide more insight into variation in the use of negative concord. In relation to environments more conducive to or environments constraining negative concord, questions arise about the extent to which concord is allowed to "skip" possible negation sites. For instance, sentences such as the following (15d), in which negation is expressed in only one of two possible sites, are produced in spontaneous speech.

15.   (a) LJG: That's called a retainer, so my teeth won't move.
      (b) Dawn: My teeth moving?
      (c) LJG: Yeah. 'Cause you a big girl.
      (d) Dawn: You not a big girl?

In (15d) *not* is associated with a Ø auxiliary *BE* form, (cf. the overt *BE* form *is/are*, as in *You is/are not a big girl?*). The noun phrase *a big girl* is not negated, as in *no big girl*. A variation of Dawn's sentence (15d) is the negative concord version, *You not no big girl?*, in which negation is expressed on all possible sites, which she did not produce. The question is whether the variation in the single negation construction in (15d) and the concord structure is due to syntactic properties or extralinguistic and social factors that influence language use. In (15d) there are two "possible" negation sites, and one is negated. However, if there are at least three possible sites for negation marking, is it possible to negate the first and third positions and, at the same time, skip the second site, as in *a book* (16a), or is (16b), in which negation is produced in all three sites, including *no book*, more desirable?

16.   (a) They <u>don't</u> have **a book** on <u>no</u> table.
           'There isn't a book on the/any table'
      (b) They <u>don't</u> have <u>no book</u> on <u>no table</u>.
           'There isn't a book on the/any table'

The major focus in this section is on developmental patterns, but it is obvious that some of the questions about the acquisition path of negation could be answered by more spontaneous speech and experimental data from speakers beyond age 5.

6 Asking questions: seeking clarification and requesting elaboration

LJG: Now what movies does she have?
Julius: She say what movies do you have.

INTRODUCTION

In previous research on early question patterns in child English, issues concerning the development of inversion patterns, that is, the stages children go through in producing questions that have the structure initial auxiliary followed by the subject of the sentence are at the forefront. Consider the following examples, in which the sentences in (1) are declarative and those in (2) are yes–no questions, so named because they elicit yes–no responses:

1. Declarative:
    (a) That is a cake.
    (b) He can fly.
2. Question:
    (a) Is that a cake?
        That is a cake.
        Is_1 that $_{is_1}$ a cake
    (b) Can he fly?
        He can fly.
        Can_1 he $_{can_1}$ fly

In the declaratives (1a, b), the subject (i.e. *that, he*) is followed by the auxiliary (i.e., *is, can*), and in the questions (2a, b), the auxiliary precedes the subject. The inversion process is illustrated to show that the auxiliary inverts to the position preceding the subject. Here I am using the convention of the small print and subscripts to show that the auxiliary started off in the position following the subject and ends up in the position preceding the subject. Two elements with the same subscript are linked or represent a single element. The one in small print is just a copy of the element that once occupied the position. It is not pronounced. The element in regular print at the beginning of the sentence is pronounced. Inversion also occurs in *wh*-questions such as *Why did they leave?*, which begin with *wh*-words, such as *what, when, why, where,* and *how. How come* questions (e.g, *How come he left?*) are different in that they do not exhibit such inversion as they include a main verb (e.g., *left*) but not an auxiliary. The literature on questions in children developing MAE is extensive, and data have been used to address claims about a number of issues, including the use of auxiliaries in child language. Given some of the patterns that have already been described in developing AAE-speaking children's language, it would also be interesting to consider questions in this population. For instance, the data have shown that the auxiliary *BE* and the copula are clearly optional in some environments in child AAE. Following the description of these verb forms, it would be worthwhile to see data that reflect the status of auxiliaries in questions in child AAE as well as shed some light on the overall use of auxiliaries in questions. It is necessary to guard against focusing on a description of child AAE questions solely in reference to adult AAE, but it is useful to consider questions in the latter as it is the target language. Along such lines, a number of points about adult AAE questions should be considered because it will be useful to compare children's questions to the adult target, as they go through stages of question formation. At least four patterns in AAE adult questions can be brought to the forefront: Yes–no questions (1) are variably produced with inverted auxiliaries, (2) are variably produced with uninverted auxiliaries or auxiliaries that remain in place and do not precede the subject, (3) may be produced without auxiliaries, so tense will be marked on the main verb, and (4) can be produced with final level or falling intonation (Green 2002; Jun and Foreman 1996).

Reviewing adult AAE questions shines the light on the variable question input that children in AAE-speaking communities get. The child AAE questions also reflect the range of variation in the properties listed in (1–4), and they contribute to a data set that could provide insight into general patterns that children in the population display in developing variable questions strategies. Examples of sentences that illustrate the properties in (1–4) are given below:

3.   Did he buy the book?
4.   He was taking too long?
5.   He bought the book?
6.   You traded your other one in?

The sentence in (3) is generally assumed to be the prototypical yes–no question with respect to the inverted auxiliary (*did*) and the following subject (*he*). The question in (4) includes an auxiliary although it is not inverted to the position preceding the subject. The structure in (5) is another way of asking the question in (3); it does not have an auxiliary. In (3) the auxiliary *did* expresses past tense, but in (5) there is no auxiliary, so the main verb *bought* expresses past tense. As reported in Green (2002), the question in (6) is a true yes–no question, which the speaker uses to request information about whether the listener actually traded his other one [car] in or not. The intonational pattern associated with the question in (6) is pretty much level, without much of a final rise (at the end of the sentence), as shown in Figure 6.1.

A distinction has been made among different types of yes–no questions according to the contexts in which they are used or the meaning they are intended to convey and the type of intonational patterns or rhythmic contours associated with them. For instance, questions can be placed into three broad basic categories based on intonational contours that characterize the ends of questions: those that end in rising contours, those that end in falling contours, and those that end in level contours. In a study of questions in natural discourse, Hedberg and Sosa (2002) noted that contrary to what had been shown in previous research on American English questions, they found that an overwhelming majority of positive declarative

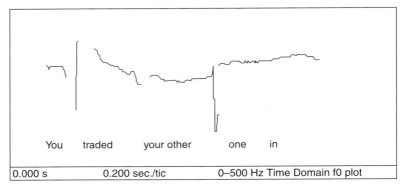

Figure 6.1 Pitch track for *You traded your other one in*? (Green 2002, p. 129)

questions were produced with falling or level tones as opposed to a final rise. However, Hedberg, Sosa, and Fadden (2006) reported that the most common type of terminal contour is the low rise. The different results in the two studies may be due to the fact that the 2002 study focused on questions in natural discourse produced during episodes of news shows in which journalists talked about political issues. Hedberg and Sosa suggest that due to the adversarial and less cooperative nature of the natural conversation in the 2002 study, more falling and level tones characterized the questions in that database.

In keeping in mind the general types of final contours that have been associated with questions, I would like to consider some yes–no questions produced by child AAE speakers. I am not assuming that the same types of contours that are found in adult questions also occur in children's questions, nor am I assuming that the contours reported for American English corpora are the standard against which questions produced by child AAE speakers should be measured. Instead the goal of the discussion is to present a description of yes–no questions in the child AAE database, and, where possible, to make some general observations about the intonational contours. Given the claims about question intonation and the variation in structure of yes–no questions in AAE, it is important to raise questions about intonational patterns in child AAE – again, not for the benefit of simply comparing adult AAE and child AAE, but to consider different properties of questions in developmental stages with an eye to the target structures.

6.1 CHILD AAE YES–NO QUESTIONS

The first questions to be considered in this section were produced by Alisa (5;3, F, AAE). The questions in (7) are part of spontaneous speech during an exchange between Alisa and LJG that focuses on Alisa's birthday party:

7.   LJG: Did you have cake at your party?
      Alisa: Umhum. And some pupcakes.
      LJG: What kind of cakes?
      Alisa: Pupcakes.
      LJG: Really? Where'd you get those?
      Alisa: At the ummm they was bake in the oven.
      LJG: Mmmmm. Cupcakes yummy. What color?
      Alisa: Blue.
      LJG: That was a good thing to make blue cupcakes.
   (a) Alisa: They good?
      LJG: They are delicious ... not just good. Delicious ... When something is delicious it tastes what?
      Alisa: Good!
      LJG: Umhmm. Like cupcakes, delicious.
      Alisa: And cake.
      LJG: Cake too. What about ice cream?
   (b) Alisa: They all good?
      LJG: They are all good, girl. Yes, indeed. Umhmm! <affirmative response>

The following excerpt is also from an exchange between Alisa and LJG:

8.   LJG: She just polished your fingernails?
      Alisa: Umhmm.

> LJG: Wow!
> Alisa: They pretty?
> LJG: Very pretty, girl! *<affirmative response>*

Alisa's spontaneous questions in (9) and (10) were produced in transition between elicitation tasks:

9. LJG: OK. Turn the page.
   Alisa: I can do this one? *<refers to scenario on new page>*
10. LJG: I like your shamrock.
    Alisa: We almost done?
    LJG: Umhmm.

The first point to note here is that Alisa's questions in (7–10) are all what might be referred to as non-prototypical yes–no questions. That is, the questions have a structure identical to that of declaratives, in which case there is no overt auxiliary *BE* in (7), (8), and (10). The overt auxiliary *can* in (9) follows the subject as it does in declaratives. As has already been established, the copula and auxiliary *BE* are often non-overt, so questions without the copula (7), (8), and (10) should be predicted. The structure and order of words in the sentences alone do not tell us that the string is a question, especially given that the questions are superficially similar to declaratives. However, context and intonation set these sentences apart as questions. I will return to a discussion of intonation after making some observations about the contexts in which Alisa produced the questions. In (7) Alisa's two questions are in reference to cupcakes, cake, and ice cream. She asks whether they are good, and, at first glance, the questions may seem to be rhetorical in nature because, in general, kids like sweets. In effect, the judgment might be that the utterances are not genuine questions because she already knows the answers to them, but I think they are true yes–no questions in that Alisa is seeking my view on the sweets, to see if they are in line with her own views. As the "teacher," I can be seen as having the "right" answer and to the extent that my view is in agreement with hers – perhaps that makes things all the better. Given the context, relation or hierarchy between the participant and me, it does not seem right to take (9a, b) to be anything other than true yes–no questions, in which Alisa is requesting an answer from me, or at the very least confirmation that she is indeed right. I take this to be the obvious assessment, in part, because of the context but more so because of the teacher (LJG)–student (Alisa) relationship, in which the teacher knows the answers and tries to get the correct response from the student. The segment including Alisa's question "They all good?" was an informal exchange in which LJG was checking to determine whether Alisa knew the meaning of "delicious" and could give examples of food items that were indeed delicious. In this context, Alisa was challenged to give the correct response, as indicated in the exchange. Alisa's question was in response to LJG's question, "What about ice cream?", as if to check to determine whether her view that they are all good is indeed correct or not. While these foods might be good in her view, she wants to check to determine whether her view is in line with LJG's view or whether she gave the response that LJG was seeking. For this reason, I take the question to be a true yes–no question, although it is not in the prototypical structure usually assumed to be associated with questions. It is not formed by inversion of the auxiliary to the position before the subject (as in "Are they all good?"); in fact, there is no overt auxiliary. Actually, children in the study consistently produced yes–no questions using the same type of non-prototypical structure we see in the exchange with Alisa.

The questions in (8) can be seen in a similar light. Alisa thinks her nails are pretty, and my "Wow!" response may also suggest that my view is the same. Nevertheless, her direct question requests confirmation that I think they are pretty, or it solicits my genuine view – whatever my view. The questions in (9) and (10) are not about personal preference; they are about the classroom activities, and only the person in charge can answer them. It may be that Alisa hopes that the answer to the questions will be "yes," but these questions certainly cannot be seen as rhetorical because she really has no way of knowing what the response will be. The utterances are genuine requests for permission – true yes–no questions – although they have a non-prototypical structure. In asking *I can do this one?* ('May I do this one?'), Alisa is requesting permission to work on a scenario and illustrations that look interesting to her, although I decided to skip it. Alisa's sentences look like declaratives, but they are very much interrogatives.

The remaining questions were produced by Alisa during structured elicitation tasks in order to get more information about events or situations in the scenarios that were being read to her. For the most part, in each data set only the line before Alisa's questions is given, not the entire preceding conversation.

11.   LJG: Who BIN went to the store? *<reads scenario prompt>*
      Alisa: That's the store? *<points to picture of character's house in background>*
      LJG: That's the house. *<notes that the building is the house not the store>*

12.   LJG: She has a favorite tree to climb at the park. *<reads scenario>*
      Alisa: She like climbing up trees?
      LJG: Umhmm. She loves it. *<affirmative response>*

13.   LJG: Now he and Jenny can climb trees together. *<reads scenario>*
      Alisa: She know how climb trees?[1] *<Before the necessary description is given for all characters, Alisa points to girl in the story who is characterized as not knowing how to climb trees.>*
      LJG: Un Un. Un Un. *<negative response>*

14.   LJG: He teaches these policemen what to do. See here's ... *<reads scenario >*
      Alisa: That's the dad? *<points to picture of the dad>*
      LJG: Umhmm. That's the dad. *<affirmative response>*

15.   LJG: See Faye and Jenny? *<points to characters in scenario>*

Alisa: She know how to climb up trees? *<points to girl in tree>*

LJG: Umhmm. Now she learned, finally. Thank goodness! *<affirmative response>*

16. LJG: They go there to talk about all their toys ...

Alisa: This the house? *<points to picture of house in background>*

LJG: Umhmm. *<affirmative response>*

17. LJG: Now they have two secret places, one in Faye's backyard and the one in the park with the droopy branches.

(a) Alisa: She Faye?

LJG: Umhmm. That's Faye. Umhmm. *<affirmative response>*

(b) Alisa: That's her house?

LJG: Umhmm. That's her house. *<affirmative response>*

18. LJG: See John?

Alisa: That's his bike?

LJG: Umhmm. *<affirmative response>*

19. LJG: *<reads part of scenario>* Mr. Henry was a little clumsy so sometimes he knocked things over and broke them. See? See this blue piggy bank on the shelf behind Mr. Henry?

(a) Alisa: He angry?

LJG: No. He's not angry. *<negative response>* *<continues to read scenario>* But you know what happened to this piggy bank, A__? He broke it a long time ago and he still hasn't fixed it. But look at this yellow piggy bank. See this yellow piggy bank in front of him on the counter? Mr. Henry broke this bank yesterday.

(b) Alisa: He didn't broke this one? *<points to a non-broken piggy bank>*

LJG: Un Un. *<negative response confirms negative question>*

The questions in (11–19) are identical in structure to the ones just discussed (7–10) in that they also either have the order of the subject as the first word in the sentence followed by the auxiliary, as in (11), (14), (17b), (18), and (19b), or there is no overt auxiliary at all, as in (12), (13), (15), (16), (17a), and (19a). The overt auxiliaries are contracted forms of *is* ('s), and in the case of (19b), it is *did* plus the contracted form of *not* (*n't*). While the production of auxiliaries is sparse here, I do not take the limited number in Alisa's questions to be representative of a situation in which she has not acquired auxiliaries. The auxiliaries and the environments in which they occur are of note. While contracted 's occurs with *that*, as in (14) and (18), no other copular forms surface, which is in line with the type of copula constructions that were discussed in Chapter 3. That is, out of the eleven possible copular environments, Alisa only produces 's in the environment of *that*. Neither the plural nor singular *BE* forms are produced in questions such as *They pretty?* and *She Faye?*, respectively. The bottom line is that the children's variable *BE* use is also reflected in questions. My hypothesis here is that these questions are not truncated or reduced in the sense that they are merely variations on prototypical questions. The alternative to the truncation story is that the questions follow a general pattern in AAE. For instance, from what has been shown in adult AAE and in child AAE, 's that occurs on *that's* is almost categorical (see Chapter 3), and that it occurs in questions here is no surprise.[2] *Did* is used to support negation (*n't*) in (19b), so it is required in the sentence. In short, we see that auxiliaries in questions are uninverted, but they do occur, especially if they are required for some meaning (e.g., past or permission or other modality) or function (e.g., to support negation). The auxiliary *can* (9) expresses permission, and without it the sentence would have a different meaning.

The questions in (7–10) were characterized as serving as requests for confirmation and as true interrogatives in the sense that Alisa had no idea about whether the answer would be "yes" or "no." The questions in (11–19) can be characterized as serving a clarification function and as facilitating elaboration. For instance, the question in (12) seems to request more information about the character and more information than the story gives. Alisa chooses to address Jenny's feelings about climbing trees. The scenario is more about Jenny's ability to climb trees than it is about her enjoyment of the activity, which is what Alisa wants to clarify. In the question in (15) Alisa asks about another character who is in the tree in the current scenario but who was portrayed as not being able to climb trees in a previous scenario. She wants to clarify that the character now knows how to climb trees, as she sees the character sitting in the tree.

The children constantly interpret the pictures and raise questions about the way situations and events are represented, and their questions may get negative responses from me if they have misconstrued the situation, as in (13) and (19a). In the case of the scenarios, children were permitted to use their imagination to go beyond the story if their additions would not interfere with the interpretation of the story in relation to the target questions. In some cases the interpretations and character traits were specific and had to be understood as presented for the elicitation tasks to be successful, so children's content was corrected in those contexts. It is quite useful to study questions in different contexts because the questions will have different functions, and we might gain more insight by considering the functions of questions in relation to their structure and intonation.

6.1.1 Declaratives, questions, and declarative questions

As has been noted in the previous section, one obvious issue that arises in the study of questions such as the ones produced by Alisa is related to the type of function they serve. That is, given that the questions are not in the prototypical yes–no question form, that is, they are not of the form in which the subject precedes the auxiliary, it might be that they are not perceived as "genuine" information-seeking questions. The non-prototypical questions might be construed as being biased toward a "yes" answer or just uttered for confirmation about a belief that the child already has. The pragmatic function of questions has not been specifically addressed in work on adult AAE, and it certainly has not been addressed in child AAE. However, there is some work on the function of MAE questions, in which the focus is on the relationship between the meaning and function of yes–no questions and the type of intonational patterns that characterize them. In particular, the discussion has focused largely on the different contexts in which prototypical questions and non-prototypical questions, which are more akin to declaratives at least in structure, are used. However, by providing child questions in different contexts, I showed that these subject-initial questions can have different functions, which is clearly in line with being a genuine question requesting an explicit yes or no answer.

Gunlogson (2008) discusses the restrictions on a type of general English subject-initial question, which she refers to as declarative questions: "Declarative questions pattern in some respects with other types of interrogatives widely recognized as "biased" or, using Bolinger's (1957) term, *conducive* to a particular answer" (p. 2). For instance, she considers the contexts in which three different types of sentences are felicitous: polar interrogative (20a), rising declarative (20b), and falling declarative (20c):[3]

20. (a) Is the weather supposed to be good this weekend?
        Polar interrogative
    (b) The weather's supposed to be good this weekend?
        Rising declarative
    (c) The weather's supposed to be good this weekend.
        Falling declarative

In accounting for the use of the sentences in (20), Gunlogson points to factors such as the difference in authority of the addressee and the speaker, commitment of the speaker, the context of the question, and role of the intonational rise. Her view is that the difference between the addressee and the questioner along the lines of the addressee's authority and the questioner's dependency is a direct effect of the prototypical question, as in (20a). On the other hand, she argues that such relationship does not hold between the addressee and questioner when a declarative question is used, so context as well as the rising intonation gives the interpretation as a question for sentences such as (20b). Specifically, the rise signals that the statement is an utterance that needs to be verified, which makes it more question-like. The falling declarative (20c), not having the properties of the prototypical question and rising declarative, must rely on context and other verbal markers to be felicitous in question environments.

One interesting question – among several others – is raised when we consider subject-initial questions in AAE from the perspective of Gunlogson's assessment of declarative questions. Does the intonation associated with the AAE subject-initial questions sufficiently mark them as questions, or do they rely strictly on context for question interpretation? In order to begin to answer this question, of course, it is necessary to know something about the type of intonation that is used with question in AAE. Just as it is possible to talk about prototypical question structure in reference to word order in which the auxiliary is followed by the subject, we find that the final rising intonational pattern is commonly associated with interrogatives in general English. Some reports have also been made about question intonation patterns in AAE.

Jun and Foreman (1996) noted that in asking yes–no questions, although AAE speakers used the prototypical final rise, they also used the final flat or level tone. In addition, they found that the speakers also used the falling tonal pattern in yes–no questions that is associated with declarative sentences in general English as well as in AAE. Similar observations about the intonational patterns of questions were reported in Tarone (1972) and Green (1990). When we consider the more standard claim that English questions are marked with a final rise, AAE question intonation seems to differ quite a bit from general English question intonation – given the summary of previous research just noted. However, when the Hedberg and Sosa (2002) finding that positive interrogatives were produced with level or falling tones is taken into consideration, at least at first glance,

AAE question intonation does not seem to be different from general English intonation at all. Hedberg and Sosa link the level and falling tones of yes–no questions in natural speech from videotaped television discussion programs to the context of the discussion groups during which they were produced.[4] In other words, they suggest that the large number of level and falling tones, which may be characteristic of questions used in heated discussions, may be a result of the contentious conditions under which the questions were produced. Nothing in the literature suggests that the level and falling tones reported for adult AAE questions are linked to adversarial discourse, although I must pause here to ask whether some questions may be perceived as adversarial by those who are not accustomed to hearing AAE. It is important to note that given the lag in research on AAE intonation, it is impossible to address all of the issues that arise about the pragmatic contexts in which different intonational patterns associated with questions are used. The studies that report the level and falling patterns in adult AAE do not focus specifically on functions of the questions and contexts in which they were used.

It is tempting to make general comparisons between the type of questions that are produced by the child AAE and adult AAE speakers, but only limited comparisons can be made with the limited details about questions for both groups of speakers. As noted in Thomas (2007), salient intonational features have been attributed to AAE. It would be useful to determine the extent to which developing AAE-speaking children exhibit (some of) these patterns. In particular more research is needed, especially in addressing the issue of the type of input child AAE speakers get with respect to the intonational patterns that are used with questions, but that is not to say that questions in developing AAE questions should only be studied in the context of adult AAE questions.

6.1.2 A word about questions and intonation

In the introduction to the child AAE questions produced by Alisa in Section 6.1, it was noted that her questions were uttered in different

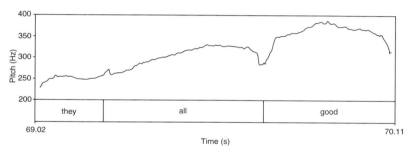

Figure 6.2 Pitch track for *They all good?*

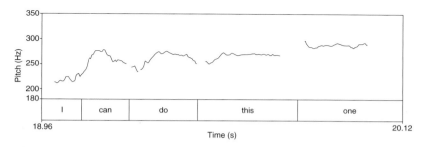

Figure 6.3 Pitch track for *I can do this one?*

contexts but they all had in common the property of being subject-initial. Consider once again the questions in (7b) and (9), repeated in (21a) and (21b), respectively, which I determined to be genuine requests for a yes or no response:

21.   (a) They all good?
       (b) I can do this one?

The intonational patterns for the questions in (21a, b) are given in Figure 6.2 and Figure 6.3, respectively.

The shape of the contours in the pitch tracks give us a general idea about how the questions were pronounced. That is, the contours give a pictorial representation of the stress or movement patterns associated with the words that account for the overall rhythm of sentences. From an impressionistic view of the pitch tracks as opposed to a theoretical analysis within a framework for analyzing intonational patterns, which would require some technicalities about the type of tones and combinations of tones that are used to describe the contours, we can make some very general observations about the structures.[5]

One similarity between the two intonational patterns in Figures 6.2 and 6.3 is that beginning with the utterance of the first word in each sentence, there is a rise or upward tendency as the sentences progress. The difference is in the endings. In the sentence in Figure 6.2 (21a), the shape at the end of the sentence on the last word *good* is rising then falling. On the other hand, in the sentence in Figure 6.3 (21b), the shape of the contour at the end of the sentence is level, neither rising nor falling. There is, however, a rise from *this* to *one*, but not just on the final word (*one*) itself. These patterns, at least at the ends of the sentences, seem to be a general trend in the questions in the child data, and some interesting issues arise based on observations about them. For instance, are the two (falling and level (or neither rising nor falling)) patterns both associated with genuine yes–no questions, or are these contours used mostly with any type of subject-initial question regardless of function? Do the two contours really have different meanings and are thus used in different pragmatic contexts? Is the different contour shape related to the presence or absence of auxiliaries? Note that the auxiliary *can* is in (21b), but there is no overt auxiliary in (21a). The type of data and analysis necessary to answer these questions are not available; however, it does seem to be that in the case of the children, both contours occur with genuine yes–no questions, although the contours may also occur with other questions with different functions. These contours might also be used with different sentence types in addition to questions. Finally, the question about whether these contours reflect general developmental patterns should also be raised.

Alisa's questions were overwhelmingly subject-initial; however, there are prototypical yes–no questions in the data set, in which the auxiliary is sentence-initial. Before considering this structure in the child data, I would like to make some introductory

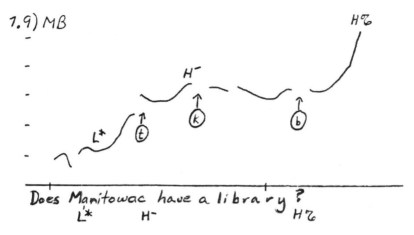

Figure 6.4 Pitch track for *Does Manitowac have a library?*

remarks about the auxiliary-initial yes–no questions, such as that in (22):

22.   Will Bruce read the story? (cf. declarative: *Bruce will read the story.*)

In MAE the intonational pattern often reported to accompany these inverted questions is the final rise. The example of the question intonation rising pattern in Figure 6.4 presented here is taken from Pierrehumbert (1980, p. 265).

   The final rise is represented in the diagram by the upward line associated with *library*. In comparison, the rises that have been observed in the child questions were preceding and leading up to, but not at, the end of the sentence. However, in the question in Figure 6.4 the rise continues to the end of the sentence, and it is this final rise that is often associated with yes–no questions in English, although it has been shown that they may have other final intonational contours, including level and falling tones. This rise is assumed to contribute to the interpretation of the sentence as a question.

   While some inverted structures, in which the auxiliary precedes the subject, do indeed occur in the child data, there are very few instances of them. What I want to put forth here is that it is not that children have not begun to use inversion, but it may be that a number of non-developmental factors contribute to the low production of such question structures. One factor may be the nature of the setting in which the data were being collected. That is, the context of the teacher–student relations and scenarios with elicitation tasks, during which participants may have been seeking clarification, may have been conducive to the production of the subject-initial questions. Another factor may be that in AAE there is a low rate of production of questions with inverted auxiliaries, and the children's results of the overwhelming number of subject-initial questions may be a direct result of the type of input-limited inversion they get from their surrounding community of AAE speakers. What remains to be figured out is whether children (and adults) associate a special intonation with these subject-initial questions that contributes to their interpretation as questions and/or whether the intonational patterns associated with them are indicative of certain pragmatic contexts. It is also useful to compare the subject-initial question intonation to the auxiliary-initial intonation to determine whether such a difference exists in these yes–no question types in child AAE.

Now look at the intonational pattern in Figure 6.5 for the question in (23):

23.   Can I use the duck talk to huh?[6] (*huh* 'her') (Valencia, 5;6, F, AAE)

This sentence was a request to use the duck puppet to ask the monkey puppet a question in a similar way that I had demonstrated with the puppets in an earlier elicitation task.

What is evident from the pitch track (Figure 6.5) for the auxiliary-initial question in (23) is that the kind of rise starting at the beginning of the sentence that has been associated with prototypical yes–no questions in general English (as in Figure 6.4) also occurs with the child AAE questions. The difference, however, is in the

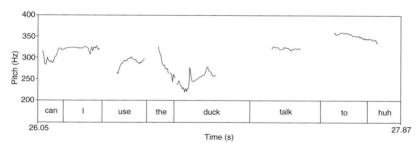

Figure 6.5 Pitch track for *Can I use the duck talk to huh?*

final tone of the sentence. Note that while the sentence begins and progresses with an upward trend, the sentence final tone is level; the rise does not continue to the end of the sentence. The difference between the intonational pattern for the general English question (Figure 6.4) and the pattern for the AAE child English question (Figure 6.5) is apparent, especially in taking the final tones into consideration. Simply put, the rise continues throughout the end of the sentence in the question in Figure 6.4, but it only continues up to and not through the final tone in the question in Figure 6.5. To what extent is the difference that is represented in the contour of the final tones perceived by listeners? As more research is conducted on intonation in child and adult AAE issues about the inventory of final tones in yes–no questions, the nature of the different tones that are associated with yes–no questions should be studied. Also, as more research is conducted on AAE intonation, we may be able to engage in more substantial discussions about the link between variation in question structure (as shown in (24), all from Dawn, 5;9, F, AAE) and type of question intonational pattern that may be associated with each question structure.

24. (a) Auxiliary-initial: Can I read one of them books?
        'May I read one of those books'
     (b) Subject-initial (and zero auxiliary): You want me to go answer the phone?
        'Do you want me to answer the phone?

(c) Non-inverted auxiliary (and zero auxiliary): You could stick your eye in there?
> 'Can you stick your eye in there?'

6.1.3 Eliciting questions

Auxiliary-initial yes–no questions are not as common in the data as other yes–no question structures; however, they are part of children's question grammar. Children produced some auxiliary-initial questions in spontaneous speech, but they seemed to have leaned toward subject-initial questions in elicitation exercises, in which they were instructed to request information. In one elicitation activity, a participant (4;4, M, AAE) was given a toy cell phone and instructed to call a popular store in the area to find out about particular products and items in the store. The following is an example of the participant's questions in the exercise in which he was instructed to call the local Wal-Mart:

25.　(a) LJG: I want to call back to Wal-Mart but this time I want J_ to ask her something. OK J_ ask em if they just got in, ask her if they just got their bikes in, if they just got them in or what.
　　(b) Julius: Y'all just got y'all bikes in?
　　(c) LJG: What she said? No or what?
　　(d) Julius: She said "yeah."
　　(e) LJG: Just got em in? Umhmm. What about basketballs? They got em in or they BIN having em in?
　　(f) Julius: They BIN having em in.
　　(g) LJG: OK. Ask em.
　　(h) Julius: Y'all BIN having them basketballs in? And they said, "Yeah."

Julius was given the instruction in an indirect question: "Ask her if ...". His question in (25b), which he asked in response to the instructions he was given, is a subject-initial zero auxiliary direct question, with past tense marked on the verb *got*. In the second set of instructions (25g), he was directed to ask about the length of the time period the store has had the basketballs. The remote past marker *BIN* is used in the question Julius was given in the instructions (25e). It is evident that Julius is reluctant to ask that question because, as someone who is familiar with some of the items in the store, he is certain about the answer. In (25f) he gives the answer without asking the question. Nevertheless, he can be persuaded to ask the question in (25h). The question may be assumed to have the subject-initial structure due to the nature of Julius's view about the information. That is, one assessment may be that because Julius already thinks that he knows the answer to the question, he uses a subject-initial direct question instead of an inverted auxiliary question. However, in this case the question context or the child's certainty about the answer may not be the only factor that determines the structure. In adult AAE remote past *BIN* does not generally occur with an auxiliary in non-negative contexts, so many adult speakers would produce the question as Julius produced it. However, some speakers may produce the following question, in which *have* is the supporting auxiliary, and the question is auxiliary-initial: *Have they BIN having those basketballs?* It is not clear how common such *have BIN* sequences are, or even how widely used the auxiliary *have* is in AAE, and this is important information, especially when considering what input children get. To what extent would children be predicted to produce *have BIN* questions in any pragmatic context? In this child data we have information on the production and comprehension of tense–aspect markers such as remote past *BIN*, but we also need to conduct longitudinal studies to chart the development of auxiliaries that occur with these markers in negation and question contexts, for example.

Myron (5;6, M, AAE) was given the same instructions in an indirect question to ask about Playstations (26a), and he also asked by using a subject-initial zero auxiliary direct question.

26. (a) LJG: I want you to ask Wal-Mart if they have any Playstations.

(b) Myron: They have some play – ? You have some Play-
     stations?

(c) LJG: Yeah ask. Wait. Ask em again. Say it loud.

(d) Myron: They have some Playstations?

(e) LJG: Umhmm. What she say?

(f) Myron: She say "yeah."

It is clear that Myron's questions were prompted by instructions from LJG; however, he did have some independence in choosing the form or structure of the question, and, of course, the question intonation, as he was not participating in a repetition task in which he was required to say just what I said the way I said it. While there may be a propensity toward zero auxiliary direct questions in the cell phone task, the children also produced some overt auxiliary questions.

In a similar exercise, instead of talking to a make-believe sales clerk, Lenny (5, M, AAE) spoke to one of his peers (Kendra, 4, F, AAE) who was also participating in the elicitation session and who also had a toy cell phone:

27. (a) LJG: L__ OK before we go, I want you to call Wal-Mart for
          me. Call Wal-Mart and ask if they have any ask em
          what they have in the store.

     (b) Lenny: Hello. What do you have?

     (c) Kendra: I have a sofa set.

     (d) Lenny: That's all you got?

In the exercise Lenny asks a contracted *BE* question (27d). We have already established that there are questions about whether 's on *that's* is a separate auxiliary form. I will return to *wh*-questions, such as (27b), in Section 6.2, but note that Lenny produces the "prototypical" structure following *what*, with the auxiliary *do* inverted and followed by the subject *you*.

A call for more research on the place of prototypical question structure in the inventory of AAE yes–no questions has already been made. There are certainly a number of ways of approaching this issue. One reading of the data is that the subject-initial (non-prototypical) questions represent a stage in development prior to the point at which children get question inversion (prototypical auxiliary-initial), and the non-prototypical questions facilitate the development of prototypical questions (Estigarribia 2007). Such analysis is certainly plausible, especially in earlier stages of AAE question development; however, I do not think that it applies to all of the subject-initial questions here. Estigarribia (2007) is particularly relevant for a discussion of AAE yes–no questions in that the work pays a good deal of attention to non-prototypical yes–no questions and does not dismiss them in favor of a discussion based only on prototypical questions. Also, it considers the effect that parental input and the type of questions children hear have on the type of questions they produce. It is clear that there is a good deal of variation in the structure of AAE questions, and it is important to consider the role of variation in input in children's production of questions.

Throughout this book I have noted that there was no systematic attempt to conduct a controlled comparative study of the range of structures used in developing AAE and SwLVE because the goal was to describe patterns in the speech of children growing up in the AAE-speaking community; however, in addition to analysis of some specific constructions, some comparative observations were made and data are also still being analyzed. Below Ryan (4, M, SwLVE) is given directions to make a phone call to Wal-Mart to inquire about fishing poles and Playstations:

28. (a) LJG: R_ I want you to ask the Wal-Mart lady if she has any fishing poles to sell.
     (b) Ryan: Do you have any fishing poles?
     (c) LJG: What did she say?
     (d) Ryan: She didn't say nothing.
     (e) LJG: She didn't say nothing?
     (f) Ryan: What? She hunged up.

(g) LJG: Well, we have to call her again because I have some more questions to ask. Good grief! *<speaks into toy cell phone>* Oh operator, could you connect me to the Wal-Mart in J_? OK. Oh Hello Miss Miss Hebert. I have somebody here. I'm gonna ask him to ask you some questions please. OK. Ask her where her uh ask her where the toys are in the store.

(h) Ryan: Where where are your toys at in the store?

(i) Ryan: Where're your toys at in the store? Talk to me. I know you're there.

(j) LJG: Ask her if they have any uh Playstations?

(k) Ryan: D'you have any Playstations?

Ryan asked direct questions in response to the instructions he was given, and he used inverted auxiliary questions (prototypical auxiliary-initial) (28b, k). Bobby (4;1, M, SwLVE), from the SwLVE-speaking community, also participated in the same task and asked a direct inverted auxiliary question (29b) in response to the instructions:

29. (a) LJG: Ask em if they have any pizza.

     (b) Bobby: Do y'all have any pizza? He didn't *<unintelligible>*

     (c) LJG: OK well ask her where their store, ask them where their store is. I wanna go.

     (d) Bobby: Where's the store at?

Although there is limited data from the children growing up in SwLVE-speaking communities, nothing in the data suggests that those children only produce inverted auxiliary or auxiliary-initial questions. The SwLVE-speaking children also produced some subject-initial questions. The difference in question structure and intonational patterns among children developing different varieties of English, AAE and SwLVE, may be apparent only in the rate of production. That is, it may be that AAE has a preference for certain question structures and particular intonational patterns, although the variety may not be limited to just those patterns. The data from child AAE strongly suggest that the children produce auxiliary-initial and subject-initial yes–no questions. The auxiliary in subject-initial questions may be overt or covert (zero auxiliary). Some properties of these questions may be due to development; however, given the input the children get from adult AAE, not all subject-initial, including zero auxiliary, yes–no questions should be taken as points in the developmental stages of questions. It should be clear that the reference to auxiliary-initial questions as prototypical does not mean that they are the type of questions that are most common in AAE, although they might be taken as the typical yes–no question type.

6.2 CHILD AAE *WH*–QUESTIONS

Some of the same properties of child AAE yes–no questions are also associated with child AAE *wh*-questions. In general English *wh*-questions, such as *What is he reading?* and *Why can she go outside?*, are characterized as questions that begin with *wh*-words *who, what, where, when, why,* and *how,* which are followed by an inverted auxiliary (e.g., *is, can*) and subject (e.g., *he, she*). That leads to a prototypical *wh*-question with the following structure: *wh*-word – auxiliary – subject. Focus in research on the development of *wh*-questions in general English has been placed on issues ranging from auxiliary inversion to the development of *wh*-questions with respect to the *wh*-words that introduce them. For instance, claims have been made about the link between auxiliary inversion and specific *wh*-words in *wh*-questions (e.g., Stromswold 1990, 1995; de Villiers 1991). Still other approaches link the auxiliary inversion errors in *wh*-questions to specific auxiliaries (e.g., Santelmann, Berk, Austin, Somashekar, and Lust 2002). Van Valin (2002) also considers differences in auxiliaries in *wh*-questions, with a focus on tense marking. For instance, the present/past tense opposition is reflected in *do/did* but not in *can/can*. On the other hand, in other analyses it has been claimed that children learn specific *wh*-word + lexical auxiliary sequences together such as *what + do* and *why + can* (e.g., Ambridge, Rowland,

Theakson, and Tomasello 2006). In addition, it is important to note that the interpretation of *wh*-words in different parts of the sentence (e.g., de Villiers, Roeper, and Vainikka 1990; de Villiers and Roeper 1996) has also received attention in child language acquisition studies, and more recently, de Villiers, de Villiers, and Roeper (in press) report on data from child AAE speakers in this area of study of *wh*-questions. In that research, which is based on a large data set as part of field testing of the Dialect Sensitive Language Test (DSLT) (Seymour, Roeper, and de Villiers 2000), they found that certain properties of embedded questions in AAE give AAE-speaking children an early edge in correctly interpreting sentences such as *How did John ask what he wanted* (p. 21) by answering the "how did John ask" part of the question rather than the "what he wanted" question.

6.2.1 Inventory of *wh*-questions in child AAE

As in the previous section on yes–no questions, I want to consider the structure of *wh*-questions in this section with respect to various components such as the *wh*-word, auxiliary, and subject. If we consider forms of the auxiliary/copula *BE* and *DO*, it might appear that the children produce *BE* forms more often as overt auxiliaries in *wh*-questions. *Can* has to be addressed separately because it carries semantic import which makes its occurrence obligatory in contexts in which *BE* and *DO* are optional. Realistically speaking, auxiliaries *BE* and *DO* are not on an equal footing either, although both seem to be optional in similar contexts. There are some differences in their overt distribution or optional contexts, and these factors must be taken into consideration in descriptions of the child AAE data. These general patterns of auxiliaries in *wh*-questions are reflected in the composite picture of *wh*-questions produced by the child AAE speakers and categorized according to *wh*-words.

If some of the *wh*-questions in Table 6.1 were presented as a general list of questions not specifically associated with child AAE, they might be taken to be representative of early stages of children acquiring general English auxiliaries and subject–auxiliary

Table 6.1 *Inventory of samples of* wh-*questions by* wh-*word*

Wh-question by word	Example sentences by presence of overt auxiliary	
Who	Overt auxiliary	
	(a) Who is this?	Tyra
	(b) Who this is?	
	(c) Who's Faye?	
	Ø auxiliary	
	(d) Who here?	Valencia
What	Overt auxiliary	
	(a) What's that right there?	Valencia
	(b) What's they number?	Akila
	(c) What's this?	Kendra
	(d) Hello, what are you doing?	Akila
	(e) What did you say?	
	(f) What is that room?	Lenny
	(g) What is that?	Kendra
	(h) Hello, what do you have?	
	(i) What color they are?	Zyrion
	(j) What this is?	Tyra, Dawn
	(k) What else I'ma do now?	Nia
	Ø auxiliary	
	(l) What you do with this?	Valencia
	(m) What they said on my phone?	Rashanna
	(n) What Miss D doing?	Terrell
	(o) What else we gon do?	Dina
	(p) What you do with this?	Kendra
	(q) What time you gon meet me, boy?	Jamal
	(r) What you want?	Jamilla
	(s) What they number?	Akila
	(t) What her name?	Zeke
	(u) What Big K__ just read?	Terry

Table 6.1 (*cont.*)

Wh-question by word	Example sentences by presence of overt auxiliary	
Where	Overt auxiliary	
	(a) Where was SpongeBob book at?	Zeke
	(b) Where I'm at?	Zyrion
	(c) And where's the other one that she broke her ankle?	
	(d) Where's my coffee?	Omar
	Ø auxiliary	
	(e) Where her brother?	Ray
	(f) Where another book I can read?	
	(g) B__, where you put that phone?	Rashanna
	(h) Where that man?	Jamilla
	(i) Where the dog head?	Dawn
	(j) Where you got that one from?	Akila
How	Ø auxiliary	
	(a) How they broke it?	Alisa
	(b) How she broke her leg?	Talia
	(c) How you knew how to spell?	Rashandra
	(d) How it do?	Jamal
	(e) How you open this?	Kendra
Why	Overt auxiliary	
	(a) Why you don't like it?	Valencia
	(b) Why she don't want to race with 'em?	Zeke
	(c) Why I can't stay?	
	(d) Why he can't look in there?	Ray
	(e) Why he was doing that?	Zyrion
	(f) Why you ain't gon give me a sticker?	Omar
	Ø auxiliary	
	(g) Why this not working?	Valencia
	(h) Why you got another Bruce one?	Ray
	(i) Why they scratch it out?	Zyrion
	(j) Why he doing that?	
	(k) Hey, why these cars roll?	Omar

inversion or, according to analyses such as that in Ambridge *et al.* (2006), children acquiring sequences of *wh*-words followed by auxiliaries. However, if by the age of 4 years AAE-speaking children are already beyond the stage of acquiring inversion, then there is little reason to think that all of the questions represented in Table 6.1 are due to developmental patterns with auxiliary inversion.

A major feature of the data is variability, within and across speakers as well as within the *wh*-word category and across *wh*-words. The variability occurs with auxiliaries in *wh*-questions. For instance, overt *wh*-words occur in *wh*-questions that begin with *what* (examples (a–k)), but as indicated in examples (l–u) under *what*, the auxiliaries are not obligatory. All of those *wh*-questions occur without auxiliaries. For example, compare (e), in which the auxiliary *did* occurs in the past tense, and (m), in which there is no overt auxiliary *did*. Past tense is indicated on the verb *said*. In (g) the auxiliary (*is*) immediately follows *what* or immediately precedes the subject *that*, but in (j) the auxiliary (*is*) immediately follows, does not precede, the subject *this*. Note the same type of variability with auxiliaries in *who* and *why* questions, for example. What is interesting about the *why* questions is that all of the overt auxiliaries follow the subject; they are not inverted to the position following *why* and preceding the subject. The *why* questions have the non-prototypical subject–auxiliary order across the board: *why* – subject – auxiliary. The questions presented in Table 6.1 are from multiple speakers, but they also represent the variability within a child's use of auxiliaries in *wh*-questions. For instance, Akila produces, "Hello, what are you doing?" with an overt auxiliary and "What they number?" ('What is their number?') with a Ø auxiliary.

De Villiers (1991) argues that for children (developing MAE) who are younger than 4 years, questions introduced by adjunct question words such as *why* and *how* are basically formed by attaching the *wh*-word – *why*, for instance – to the beginning of the sentence. Put another way, extending de Villiers's observations to child AAE, for *why* questions such as those in Table 6.1, this would mean that a child (younger than 4 years, of course) would produce the question

Why he was doing that? by simply attaching *why* to the beginning of the declarative sentence *he was doing that.* The process would be something like the following:

30. *why* + _{declarative sentence} *he was doing that.*⇒ _{wh-question}*Why he was doing that?*

These children would be argued not to have acquired the rule of question inversion with *wh*-questions, the explanation for why children produce *Why he was doing that?* instead of *Why was he doing that?* The inversion process – which the child does not use in the question in (30) – is illustrated in (31):

31. (a) he was doing that why
    (b) _{left peripheral position for wh-words}why$_1$ [he was$_2$ doing that *why$_1$*]
    (c) why$_1$ was$_2$ [he *was$_2$* doing that *why$_1$*]

    Why was he doing that?

The type of syntactic analysis that is assumed here is one in which *why* is not simply attached to the beginning of the sentence. Instead it is moved to a special left peripheral position, which is distinguished from the position that immediately precedes the subject *he*. The two-step inversion process involves the leftward movement of *why* to the left peripheral position for *wh*-words, as shown in (31b), followed by the leftward movement of the auxiliary (*was*) to the position immediately following *why* (31c). The movement of the *wh*-word triggers the movement of the auxiliary. In this way, auxiliary inversion is related to the leftward movement of the *wh*-word in a way such that if the *wh*-word moves, then it can trigger movement of the auxiliary. The reasoning is that if the *wh*-word only attaches to the beginning of the sentences and does not go through the movement process, then it will not trigger movement of the auxiliary. De Villiers's account explains why the auxiliary in (30) is still in its initial position. However, once children acquire the rule of *wh*-movement, they can invert the auxiliary.

Plunkett (1991) also considers general English data in which children actually invert the auxiliary and data in which they do not. Given her analysis, children can have both question types in their grammars:

32.   (a) Where the mouse is?
      (b) What $\emptyset_{aux}$ that? (p. 126)

For Plunkett, (32a) is a clear case of non-inversion, in which the *wh*-word *where* is attached preceding the subject (*the mouse*), so the auxiliary *is* is not triggered to invert, but (32b) is also a true case of inversion, where *what* moves to the left peripheral position for *wh*-words and the $\emptyset$ (zero) auxiliary *is* ($\emptyset_{aux}$) does move to the position following it. The only difference between the sentence in (32b) and *What is that?* is that the latter sentence has an overt *is*, but (32b) does not; it has a covert auxiliary. Davis (1986) also notes such optionality in children's general English questions.

By now, it should be clear that there is a three-way split in the optionality in AAE-speaking children's *wh*-questions just as there was in yes–no questions where auxiliaries are concerned. *Wh*-questions may have overt auxiliaries, which may or may not be inverted, and they may have zero auxiliaries. These properties of developing AAE overlap with those observed in developmental stages of *wh*-questions in general English. However, there is no optionality with respect to the *wh*-word. It invariably occurs at the beginning of the sentence. The view that I will take here for *wh*-questions produced by developing child AAE speakers by age 4 is that, in all of the cases, the *wh*-word occurs in the left peripheral position, but the auxiliary does not always follow the *wh*-word to that position. In the auxiliary inversion case (e.g., *Where was SpongeBob book at?*), *where* is inverted to the left peripheral position, and the auxiliary *was* follows it, resulting in a case of overt auxiliary inversion. In the second case, non-inversion, the auxiliary is overt but not inverted, or it is not immediately following the *wh*-word (e.g., *What this is?*). In this case, *what* is inverted to the sentence left peripheral position, and the auxiliary remains in its base position following the subject. The assumption here is that in AAE it is sufficient for the *wh*-word to appear in the left peripheral position without the requirement of inversion of the auxiliary. That is, the auxiliary is free to follow the *wh*-word or stay in its base position. Perhaps the analysis for *wh*-questions in child mainstream American English that concludes that the auxiliary is only able to invert once the *wh*-word inverts can be extended to questions in child AAE *wh*-questions. As in developmental general English, in developing AAE children go through a stage in which the *wh*-word inverts to the left peripheral position and triggers inversion of the auxiliary. If AAE-speaking children also have the same kind of *wh*-inversion process as children developing general English, why the differences? That is, why do they continue to produce *wh*-questions with the *wh*-word at the beginning of the sentence but with non-inverted auxiliaries beyond age 4? The claim that I want to put forward here is that in AAE, even if the *wh*-word inverts, the auxiliary does not need to do so obligatorily. Of course the most obvious support for the claim that auxiliary inversion in AAE is not obligatory is the question in which the auxiliary (copula *BE*) (e.g., *are*) stays in the position following the subject of the sentence (e.g., *What color they are?*), although the *wh*-phrase (*what color*) inverts to the left peripheral position. The other type of question that supports the non-obligatory auxiliary inversion claim is the one in which the auxiliary is contracted onto the subject, as in the case of *What else I'ma do?* ('What else am I going to do?') and *Where I'm at?* ('Where am I?'). Certainly if *I'm* is construed as a whole in which it is impossible to separate the *'m* from *I*, then there is no way for the auxiliary to invert past *I*. In Chapter 3, it was shown that a few children still allow zero copula with the first person singular subject *I*, so it would be interesting to determine the extent to which *I* and *I'm* are variants in *wh*-questions, especially given the situation with zero auxiliaries (e.g., *Where I'm at?/Where I at?*). Another piece of data that supports the claim that auxiliaries in AAE do not have to invert with *wh*-words is the *wh*-question in which there is a zero auxiliary, such as *What time you gon meet me boy?* and *What else we gon do?* As has been discussed in Chapter 3, *gon* favors situations in which there is no overt auxiliary *BE*. For this reason, I take the position preceding *gon* in the corresponding declarative to be a Ø auxiliary position, although in some instances an auxiliary *BE* form can occur there. The corresponding declarative sentence for *What else we gon do?* is postulated to be *We Ø gon do what else*, and to form the *wh*-question, *what else* inverts to the position preceding *we*. Nothing else happens in the absence of an overt auxiliary, or the zero auxiliary ($\emptyset_{AUX}$) also inverts (although it cannot be pronounced), giving the options of (33a) and (33b):

33. We Ø gon do what else
    (a) What else$_1$ we $\emptyset_{AUX}$ gon do what else$_1$
    (b) What else$_1$ $\emptyset_{AUX2}$ we $\emptyset_{AUX2}$ gon do what else$_1$

Either option would work, but the one we choose would depend on some technical details. Then, obviously, there is no overt auxiliary that is available for inversion. Of course, it is possible to say that there is inversion of the Ø auxiliary for the sake of maintaining theoretical consistency (e.g., 33b) (cf. Plunkett 1991). However, the following question would still need to be answered: What makes it obligatory for a Ø auxiliary to invert and optional for an overt auxiliary to invert?

Questions with overt copula and auxiliary *BE* help to show that all auxiliaries do not behave identically, so they should be considered individually. For instance, the type of properties associated with forms of the copula and auxiliary *BE* are not associated with *do*, for instance, so *do* might surface in questions where forms of *BE* might not. Consider the two questions taken from Table 6.1:

34. (a) Why you *don't* like it?
        'Why don't you like it'
    (b) Why this $\emptyset_{AUX}$ *not* working?
        'Why isn't this working'

While *do* must occur with *not* (*do* + *not* = *don't*) in (34a), the auxiliary *BE* (i.e. *is*) does not have to occur with *not* in (34b). That is, the sentence in (34b) is fine in child AAE as well as in adult AAE, but the version of (34a) that would be *Why you not like it?* (without *do*) is certainly ungrammatical in adult AAE. In addition, that version of (34a) without *do* does not seem to be a type of sentence that children at this stage in the development of AAE produce either – although younger developing AAE-speaking children might produce it. The point is that different auxiliaries may have different restrictions on their occurrence in questions due to their other general properties, such as the nature of their occurrence in declarative sentences or whether they must occur with *not*, for example. It is very clear, however, that it is possible for an auxiliary *BE* form to precede *gon*, as in the *why* question (f) in Table 6.1 *Why you ain't gon give me a sticker?* Also, claims about late acquisition of auxiliary inversion in *why* questions in research such as de Villiers (1991) are not overlooked here. In previous research on general English child questions, it is consistently noted that auxiliary inversion occurs later with *wh*-questions such as *how* and *why* as compared to *what*. If there is a general trend in late development of inversion in *why* questions across dialects, due to the meaning of *why*, then the effects may also be seen in the *why* questions in child AAE. However, the fact still remains that (34a) and (34b) are produced well after developmental stages, so it will not suffice here to link non-inversion in (34a) just to development.

Auxiliaries occur in all of the questions except those beginning with *how*. It is not clear whether all of the *how* questions are formed with Ø auxiliary forms because of the nature of the questions, meaning of *how*, or whether the limited number of *how* questions in the data fail to represent accurately the range of variation in auxiliaries that occur with them. In all of the *how* questions, the Ø auxiliary is *do*, and nothing requires it to occur on the surface. The presentation here is largely descriptive in nature. A next step would be to take a more theoretical approach to the type of variation that is represented in the sample of questions and to extend the age group to older children to be certain about developmental patterns. One of the patterns that we see is non-inversion of auxiliaries even when the *wh*-word inverts. An issue to pursue in the theoretical approach relates to the following question: In AAE why is it sufficient for just the *wh*-word to invert without triggering auxiliary inversion?

In a study designed to determine the extent to which question inversion in (adult) AAE is more like inversion in English-based Creoles or reflects more patterns of inversion in Early Modern English, Van Herk (2000) notes that the connection between causativity and negation is one factor that is responsible for the high rate of non-inversion reported for adult AAE. He reports the following examples (p. 189):

35. (a) Why you don't like him? (Labov *et al.* 1968, p. 294)
    (b) Why I don't need no grease? (Labov *et al.* 1968, p. 294)
    (c) Why she ain' over here? (Dillard 1972, p. 63)

In considering that non-inversion in AAE might be due to the structure of the grammar or to general linguistic principles, Van Herk compares constraints on non-inversion in child language acquisition, second language acquisition, and Early AAE.[7] The point of the comparison is to get a picture of the extent to which non-inversion shares similar properties among these cases because similarities might strongly suggest that some common principles govern non-inversion in child language acquisition, second language acquisition, and Early AAE. As Van Herk points out, the non-inversion in AAE may not be due just to historical origin and relation to non-inversion in Creoles, but it may also be due to general linguistic principles. The variation with respect to auxiliaries that has been observed in the child AAE *wh*-questions (and yes/no questions) also includes Ø auxiliary questions, which are not consistently discussed in Van Herk's study. Non-inversion in questions such as those in (35) should be underscored, as they are in Van Herk's study, given the consistent behavior of auxiliaries in acquisition and in AAE *why* questions;

however, it would also be useful to bring Ø auxiliary questions into the discussion.

It has been shown that Ø auxiliary questions are found in (informal) registers of MAE, not just in AAE. As such, we would expect some overlap in the two varieties. As reported in Green (2007), reduced *wh*-questions have been discussed in Hendrick (1982), in which it is argued that they are produced by a phonological rule that deletes the auxiliary. In this study, Hendrick notes that the reduced *wh*-questions are prohibited by three restrictions: (a) the deleted auxiliary is *will* or *do*, (b) the subject is first or third person, and (c) the main verb *be* is deleted. In addition, he notes that where deletion of the auxiliary is possible, contraction is also possible. The following examples are taken from Hendrick's study, and the ungrammatical sentences are flagged with an asterisk (*) (p. 811):

36.　(a)　Why're you sitting here?
　　　(a')　Why you sitting here?
　　　(b)　Who've they been insulting tonight?
　　　(b')　Who they been insulting tonight?
　　　(c)　Why's she sitting here?
　　　(c')　*Why she sitting here?
　　　(d)　Who's he been insulting tonight?
　　　(d')　*Who he been insulting tonight?

Examples such as those in (36) show that there is also variation in the occurrence of auxiliaries in *wh*-questions in registers of MAE, but what is clear from Hendrick's view is that there is no variation in auxiliary inversion. The auxiliary always inverts, but it may not be visible due to the fact that it gets deleted in certain environments after inversion. While adult and child AAE *wh*-questions may be superficially identical to the derived Ø auxiliary questions in the register of MAE questions represented in (36), there is sufficient evidence to conclude that not all Ø auxiliary questions in AAE are derived from deleting the auxiliary after it inverts to the left peripheral position following the *wh*-word. At least in some cases, the auxiliary seems to have never occupied the left peripheral position following the *wh*-word. Green (2007) notes that all of the Ø auxiliary questions in (36), including those flagged with an asterisk (*), are grammatical in AAE and that there is no restriction on the type of pronouns that occur with them. Some evidence has already been given to support the claim that auxiliaries may not be in a position to invert in AAE, especially given properties associated with the occurrence of *be* forms.

The yes–no questions and *wh*-questions presented in this chapter give a clear indication of the range of variable structures that the children developing AAE use. The claim is that although some of the question structures may be identical to – at least superficially – sentences that are produced by children who have not yet developed inversion, explanations that appeal to development and acquisition of auxiliary inversion do not give a complete account of the children's questions. It is true that some of the children's *wh*-questions are introduced by *wh*-words with a contracted auxiliary *BE* that could be taken together as unanalyzed wholes, such as *what's* in *What's this?* That is to say that if *'s* is an inextricable part of *what*, then there is no separate auxiliary inversion process; children might simply understand that the unit *what's* goes at the beginning of the sentence. The case that the children in this study are actually performing inversion is a strong one, although some of the questions that are introduced by *what's* may not reflect actual inversion given that *what's* may be learned as a unit that occurs at the beginning in some questions. Given the results for *that's*, *it's*, and even *I'm*, that is forms that look like the contracted copula, it makes sense to reason that something similar is going on with *what's*. However, the presence of *what's* does not rule out inversion in *what* *wh*-questions because there are other clear cases of *what* + auxiliary that strongly suggest or indicate that inversion applies. Finally, the actual meaning of *wh*-words, such as *why* and *how*, might have an effect on auxiliary inversion, along the lines of de Villiers (1991) and Van Herk (2000). The effect might be that the meaning somehow "relaxes" the inversion requirement, not just delays acquisition of inversion.

A major piece of information that would provide more insight into the types of issues addressed in this chapter is the yes–no and *wh*-question input developing AAE-speaking children get, especially in considering variation with respect to auxiliary inversion and auxiliary occurrence.

6.2.2 *Wh*-question elicitation

Elicited *wh*-questions might provide additional data that can be used in the description of AAE-speaking children's process of question formation. Controlled experiments that go beyond the informal elicitation tasks used here have the potential to yield a set of data that could greatly supplement the spontaneous samples in Table 6.1. The problem with some of the informal elicitations is that they were not always carefully constructed, so in some cases they included *wh*-questions that the children could simply repeat. Along the lines of the tasks in the yes–no question section, in the informal *wh*-question tasks participants were directed to pretend to call an area store by using a toy cell phone and ask the clerk about various items in the store. Some examples from exchanges in that informal task follow:

37.   LJG: Yes, call 'em A__. Ask 'em what's in that store.
       Akila: What's in that store?
       LJG: Talk loud so we can hear you.
       Akila: What do they got in that store?

On the first attempt, Akila (5, F, AAE) repeated my words *what's in that store*, but in her second attempt, she uses a different *wh*-question which includes an inverted auxiliary *do*. In a *why* question Akila uses double auxiliaries, perhaps because she does not know exactly what question to ask about new bicycles:

38.   LJG: I wanna ask them one more thing. I wanna know about their uh new bicycles.

Akila: Why do your bicycles are there? *<PAUSE>* 'Cause you
gotta buy them.

One auxiliary *do* occupies the inverted auxiliary position and the
other (*are*) is in the base position, in which an auxiliary would occur
before inversion. It is not clear whether the auxiliaries are intended
to agree in number with *your* and/or *bicycles*, or whether their purpose is to signal a question. Akila's questions are variable: inversion,
non-inversion, and Ø auxiliary. (See Table 6.1.) Her other instance of
are also occurs with the second person singular pronoun: *What are
you doing*; however, she also uses *do* with the third person: *Hey, do
this spoon come down or go up?* The data on question formation also
brings to the forefront issues about tense and agreement marking in
developing AAE. Extending and formalizing these elicitation tasks
might also generate data that could go a long way in providing information about tense and agreement in questions.

In the following example, similarities between direct and
indirect questions are evident. Julius (4;4, M, AAE) repeats the questions he is instructed to ask:

39.   (a) LJG: Okay. Good. Uhm hmm. Alright J__. Ask her what
                kind of movies they have.
       (b) Julius: She said, "What kind of movies they have?" She
                said, uhm "Rugrats and" uhm "Batman and
                <unintelligible>."
       (c) LJG: Oh. Ask her how much?
       (d) Julius: She said, "How much?" She said, uhm.
       (e) LJG: How much are those?
       (f) Julius: She say, "How much are those?" She said, uhm,
                "Good."

Julius's direct *wh*-questions are introduced by "she said" (39b, d)
and "she say" (39f), given variable past marking. In both cases Julius
repeated my questions verbatim, so his first question (39b) does not
include inversion, but the second (39g) does. Given that AAE does

not require auxiliary inversion or an overt auxiliary in *wh*-ques-
tions, the indirect question in the first line (LJG) and Julius's direct
question "She said, 'What kind of movies they have?'" are identical
in syntax. Now his next request for information is in the form of an
indirect question, in which auxiliary inversion is applied:

40.   (a) LJG: Now what movies does she have?
     (b) Julius: She say what movies do you have.

Julius's question in (40) is a true indirect question put in his own
words, not a direct quote or repetition of my statement. One difference
between the two is in pronouns: LJG uses *she*, and Julius uses *you*, directly addressing the (make-believe) listener. According to de Villiers,
de Villiers, and Roeper (in press), auxiliary inversion in such indirect questions helps AAE-speaking children in the interpretation of
medial *wh*-questions. For instance, de Villiers *et al.* found that AAE-
speaking children were less likely to answer medial *wh*-questions
incorrectly than mainstream American English-speaking children,
who do not generally produce inversion in indirect questions. That is,
AAE-speaking children were less likely to make mistakes in answering questions that contain two *wh*-words, such as in the sentence *Who
did the boy ask what to bring?* than mainstream American English-
speaking children. The latter group incorrectly answered the *what*
(e.g., bologna) in such questions more often than the AAE-speaking
children, who correctly answered the *who* (e.g., the teacher).

6.3   NEGATION AND INVERSION

The final note in this chapter brings together negation (the topic
of Chapter 5) and inversion, which has been discussed throughout
this chapter. As indicated in Table 6.1, negative auxiliaries (e.g.,
don't) occur in *why* questions, and they are all non-inverted auxiliaries. There is no requirement that these negated auxiliaries
invert to occupy the position immediately following *why*. A construction in AAE in which negation and inversion interact and in
which auxiliaries are required to invert is referred to as Negative

Inversion (NI). The following two examples of NI are from Green (2002, p. 78):

41. (a) Can't nobody tell you it wasn't meant for you.
        'Not a single person can tell you it wasn't meant for you'
     (b) Don't nothing come to a sleeper but a dream.
        'Not a single thing comes to a sleeper but a dream'

These negative concord constructions (in which the negated auxiliary is the true negation and the indefinite noun agrees with it), which may have a kind of affective interpretation that can be paraphrased as "not a single" as a means of focusing negation, are referred to as NI because of the order of the negated auxiliary (e.g., *can't*, *don't*) and negative indefinite NP subject (e.g., *nobody*). Just as is the case in yes–no questions, the auxiliary is in the left most peripheral position in the sentence; it is inverted. The difference between a yes–no question and an NI construction is that in NI the auxiliary is necessarily negative and the sentence is declarative, not interrogative. In a yes–no question the auxiliary can be positive. NI constructions have been attested in varieties of American English, including AAE, Appalachian English, and other varieties spoken in the southern United States (Green 2007).

One description of how the negative auxiliaries in NI sentences come to be at the left periphery or edge or beginning of the sentences, as in (41), links these NI constructions to inversion of auxiliaries in yes–no questions. The step-by-step process of the negative inversion process can be stated as follows: the auxiliary starts off in a position to the right of the negative indefinite subject (42a) and then moves to the left peripheral position in the sentence preceding the subject (42b) (Green 2007):

42. (a) Nobody can't tell you it wasn't meant for you.
     (b) left periphery for negative auxiliary in NICan't nobody <u>can't</u> tell you it wasn't meant for you.

Before auxiliary inversion takes place, the auxiliary (*can't*) is in the position following *nobody*, as in (42a). As (42b) illustrates, the auxiliary shifts to the left peripheral position for negative auxiliaries. According to the representation in (42), the NI process is quite similar to auxiliary inversion in the yes–no question formation process. The difference is that the NI construction is strictly a negative declarative, not a question or interrogative.

Sobin (2003) addressed the occurrence of a type of auxiliary inversion in MAE, which occurs in the presence of an initial negative adverbial (e.g., *never again*). He was concerned with sentences such as the one in (43).

43.   Never again will I eat raw spaghetti. (p. 183)

Given the presence of an initial negative phrase, these sentences can also be taken to be negative inversion sentences. The sentence represents a kind of auxiliary inversion given the position of the auxiliary *will* to the immediate left of the subject (*I*) of the sentence. The sentence in (43) can be argued to be derived as a result of auxiliary inversion much like the process in questions and like the process of inversion in AAE NI. The claim is that alongside the sentence in (43), there is also the sentence in (44), which includes the non-inverted auxiliary that follows the subject (*I*):

44.   I will never again eat raw spaghetti.

To derive the corresponding sentence in (43), in which the negative adverbial material (*never again*) takes a position in the left peripheral position of the sentence and the auxiliary *will* subsequently inverts following the negative phrase, Steps 1 and 2, respectively, are given:

Step 1: never again₁ I will ₙₑᵥₑᵣ ₐ𝓰ₐᵢₙ₁ eat raw spaghetti.

Step 2: never again₁ will₂ I ᵥᵢₗₗ₂ ₙₑᵥₑᵣ ₐ𝓰ₐᵢₙ₁ eat raw spaghetti.

Never again will I eat raw spaghetti

Sobin (2003) is against the kind of analysis in which the auxiliary in (44) inverts to the position before the subject because such inversion is too much like the process we have seen with inversion in yes–no and *wh*-questions. One of the problems that Sobin sees with the inversion process for negative inversion in MAE sentences such as (43) is that it does not seem to be in line with child language data. That is, Sobin reasons that were the inversion process involved in generating sentences such as the one in (43), negative inversion should also occur in child English when children have already acquired processes generating *wh*-questions, which involve inversion, but such negative inversion does not occur in mainstream American child English. Specifically, he notes that children develop *wh*-questions relatively early, but they do not develop the negative inversion structures until later. His point is that the negative sentence in (43) is not an inversion structure, and the type of inversion illustrated in Steps 1 and 2 above to derive it should not be put forth to account for it. According to Sobin, the acquisition patterns suggest that there are differences between question inversion and negative inversion and that the latter is not an actual inversion construction. He offers a non-inversion explanation for how the auxiliary comes to be in the position to the left of the subject. (See Sobin (2003) for the full analysis.)

In considering NI in child AAE, a number of questions arise. If developing AAE-speaking children use negative concord, and they also have auxiliary inversion, do they show signs of producing NI constructions? If so, are there any parallels between the development of question inversion and the development of NI? Given the extensive spontaneous speech that I have collected, I have not found any instances of NI in developing AAE-speaking children's language, although they do have negative concord as well as inversion in yes–no and *wh*-questions. They do not appear to combine negative concord and inversion at this stage. However, the negative non-inverted declarative sentences are attested in the child data as shown in the preceding chapter on negation and repeated here.

45.   (a) Nobody can't get in this. (Zeke)
            (cf. Can't nobody get in this.)
        (b) And nobody ain't gon get me 'cause I be riding my bike.
            (Zeke)
                (cf. And ain't nobody gon get me 'cause I be riding my
                bike)

In her study of negation patterns in 3-, 4-, and 5-year-old AAE-speaking children, Stokes (1976) found three negative responses to her positive statements in her elicitation tasks that seemed to exhibit auxiliary inversion:

46.   (a) Ain't nobody gon eat my lunch. (p. 125)
        (b) Ain't nobody gon tell him something. (p. 128)
        (c) Don't nobody know him. (p. 122)

Interestingly, the auxiliary in the cases in (46a, b) is *ain't*, and the construction may be linked to expletive deletion, as in *(It) ain't nobody gon eat my lunch*, in which case the negated auxiliary *ain't* is in the initial position because the expletive, which was initially at the beginning of the sentence, has dropped out of the sentence. However, (46c) does indeed seem to be a "genuine" NI construction, in which the initial negated auxiliary *don't* is not linked to expletive drop. Even so, such constructions should be studied, and tasks designed to elicit NI should also be developed.

NI may develop later than inversion in questions in child AAE. Carefully designed elicitation tasks may also work in eliciting data that could provide insight into children's comprehension and maybe even production of NI in AAE. Also, it is necessary to consider children's data beyond the age of 5 in search of information about these constructions. I should add, too, that if child AAE speakers do acquire these NI constructions much later than they do inversion in questions, the reason might not be that the NI constructions are totally different and must not be a type of inversion. It may be that children acquire these NI constructions later due to the pragmatic and possibly other meaning associated with these constructions. Also, as discussed in Roeper and Green (2007), NI may make use of a syntactic node that is acquired later and that differs from the structure associated with auxiliaries in questions. The idea is that in the syntactic representation of NI, the negated auxiliary has negative features, and in the syntactic representation of yes–no questions, the auxiliary has question features. Because these two auxiliary types have different features, they have different syntactic representations.

As the theme of variation runs throughout the discussion in child AAE in these chapters, it is very interesting to consider NI in connection with variation. As we saw in the case of yes–no questions and *wh*-questions, child AAE speakers have variable ways of producing questions with respect to the position or even presence of the auxiliary. It would be interesting to determine the extent to which the NI and non-inverted structures (e.g., (41) vs. (45), respectively) seem to behave as variants – if they do at all. Or more specifically, once children get NI, do they use sentences such as *Nobody can't get in this* and *Can't nobody get in this* interchangeably or as variants? In pursuing research on this topic, it would be interesting to determine whether children continue to produce sentences such as (45a) after NI (e.g., (41)) enters their grammars.[8]

7 Variation: intra-dialectal/variable-shifting and inter-dialectal/code-shifting

> LJG: *If you gon be a mailman, you have to learn where everybody lives.*
> Dawn: *I know where everybody live.*

INTRODUCTION

Throughout the discussion of child AAE in this book I have tried to emphasize the importance of taking into consideration inherent variability of AAE and variation in language use in AAE speech communities in the study of patterns in the development of child AAE. It is important to understand that the linguistic variety and language use that have been the focus of the previous chapters should be considered from the angle of speech communities and to some extent networks of communication. The point is that children developing AAE as their native variety hear it consistently in their communities, so their situations are different from those who may be gaining passive knowledge of AAE and those who may have varying experiences with different speech communities and wider access to MAE. They are learning the rules of the linguistic variety, including rhetorical strategies, pragmatic contexts of particular constructions, and intonational patterns that convey particular meaning in association with certain sentence structures.

Communities of African American speakers are diverse, and the speakers' language experiences are also diverse. Invariably, groups of African Americans who have or have had contact with AAE-speaking communities on whatever level may report that they are familiar with the types of language patterns discussed in this book, but do or did not use them for one reason or another, ranging from parental reprimand condemning the language use to parental intervention with the goal of extinguishing the stigmatized features from their children's language and replacing them with MAE. Many of these speakers may also admit that they consider themselves capable of shifting from the variety(ies) that they may hear in the AAE-speaking communities to that which they know as part of MAE. Those who received the intervention may have been in diverse networks, and their parents may have had various linguistic experiences. Two crucial points: the first is that there is no doubt that the children from the AAE-speaking communities represented in this book will have diverse language experiences that will place them at different points on the language continuum with respect to the language use within and outside of their communities. Secondly, many of the children in the speech communities referenced here will not experience the kinds of linguistic reprimand and parental intervention as do other speakers who have more direct contact with MAE-speaking communities for the very obvious reason that they are speaking the linguistic variety that conforms to the language use of their mothers, fathers, siblings, relatives, and other persons they respect in their communities. These children are growing up with AAE as their native variety, and unlike those who received constant intervention and reprimand for using a few stigmatized features, the children in the AAE speech communities under discussion are not using a few stigmatized features periodically; they are developing a complete system of AAE and interact intimately with those who also actively use the system at home as well as outside of the home. Linguistic reprimand and parental intervention also take place in the households in these AAE speech communities, however. As it turns out, the intervention may target conventions of respect and politeness, as in the use of "politeness terms" such as "sir" and "mam" (e.g., *yes sir, yes mam*), and it might also target tone and other language characteristics that could be construed as expressing negative or untoward attitude, rather than a host of stigmatized grammatical patterns that are not accepted as part of MAE. It certainly is the case, however, that children may be called out for their use of *ain't*.

The many different issues involved in and associated with networks and linguistic experiences are complicated, and deserve a more sophisticated and systematic treatment than I am offering here, especially when we consider the type of parental and community input that help to shape children's language. Without a doubt, community networks and input from members impact the type of variation in forms and use of language children exhibit. The goal of this chapter is to take a closer look at variable forms and to raise questions about them regarding the extent to which they are part of the AAE grammar and what it means for some of the variable forms to be compatible with forms that are associated with MAE.

7.1 PAST VARIANTS AND INTRA-DIALECTAL SHIFTING

Looking back to Chapters 3 and 4, the discussions of tense–aspect marking, we note that 4- and 5-year-olds produce present tense sentences in which no overt form of the auxiliary *BE* or copula occurs (e.g., *They brown* 'They are brown'). Also, data show that 4- and 5-year-olds use *had* + VERB (*–ed*) in past contexts to highlight the accomplishment or achievement of an event. One common way in the literature of approaching AAE copula/auxiliary *BE* and preverbal *had* constructions is from the viewpoint of MAE and code-shifting. That is, the copula/auxiliary *BE* context is an "addition" case, in which an inflected *BE* form must be added to turn the AAE construction into a MAE-compatible construction (1b). On the other hand, the preverbal *had* construction is taken to be a case of subtraction, in which something must be left out, namely *had*, to make the construction comply with MAE (2a):

1. (a) What his number?
    (b) What is ('s) his number? (copula addition)
2. (a) I saved him. (preverbal *had* subtraction)
    (b) I had saved him.

Immediately, two issues come to mind. The first has to do with whether or not adding the copula/auxiliary *BE* to sentences in which it does not already occur and omitting the preverbal *had* in sentences in simple past contexts actually involve shifting from AAE to MAE, especially for AAE-speaking children for whom variation is a reality, a part of their linguistic system. In other words, if AAE-speaking children sometimes produce sentences with the overt copula (1b) and perfective sentences without the marker *had* (2a), in those instances, are they actually shifting when they choose the variant with the copula or the one without *had*? The data in Chapters 3 and 4 show unquestionably that developing AAE-speaking children have both the copula variants in (1a, b) and those in (2a, b), which occur in perfective and past contexts, in their grammars already. They do not have to acquire or learn, say, (1b) and (2a) at some later stage, in school perhaps. It may be that they just need to know that (1b) and (2a) also overlap with MAE, but (1a) and (2b) do not. In addition, for some children it may be necessary to point out explicitly that (1a, b) and (2a, b) are indeed variants. The claim that I want to make here is that there is a difference between types of shifting. Inter-dialectal is another way of referring to code-shifting or moving from one code to another. On the other hand, moving between (1a) and (1b) and between (2a) and (2b) are instances of intra-dialectal shifting, a shift between variants within one dialect, AAE. Given the claim about intra-dialectal shifting, one requirement is that both variants be part of the same grammar. It may be that one variant is preferred in certain linguistic environments or in certain contexts more frequently than in others. A number of factors conspire to influence one variant over another, but the variants do not have to be in different linguistic varieties.

The picture of the variable use of *had* V (–*ed*) is complicated indeed, given the tense and aspect interactions that must be taken into consideration. For instance, *had* V–*ed* is characterized as referencing a verb that indicates the achievement or accomplishment of an event, so technically the construction varies with V–*ed* (i.e. Verb–*ed*, without preverbal *had*) that also occurs in those contexts.

Furthermore, because V–*ed* and V-Ø$_{ed}$ may also occur as variants, then by reciprocity there is certainly a reading in which *had* V–*ed* (*had saved*), V–*ed* (e.g., *saved*), and V-Ø$_{ed}$ (e.g., *save*) are variants. If we consider the issue from the angle of variation and variants of the perfective/past marking variable, then what we have is a situation in which there are multiple options for talking about accomplishments and achievements in the past: *had* V(–*ed*), V–*ed*, and V–Ø$_{ed}$. These options are theoretically possible, and more systematic analysis of child language data that takes into consideration pragmatic and semantic contexts would be useful in establishing real patterns in language development and development of variation in past and tense–aspect marking. All of these variants are taken to be possible in AAE, and this means that it is possible to use all of them as part of the dialect. In other words, they may all occur in the same past environments of achievements and accomplishments, as illustrated by the following constructed examples:

3. (a) I <u>had started</u> the pinball machine.
    (b) I <u>had start-Ø$_{ed}$</u> the pinball machine.
4. I <u>started</u> the pinball machine.
5. I <u>start-Ø$_{ed}$</u> the pinball machine.

Although the set consisting of (3), (4), and (5) is somewhat artificial in that the examples are not the exact statements recorded from any one speaker to refer to the same event of having started the pinball machine, they are possible sentences. It is clear from child data, such as that presented in Chapter 4, that all instantiations of the past constructions occur. The point of the set in (3)–(5) is to show that preverbal *had* constructions (3a, b) can obviously indicate the same meaning or tense–aspect properties as non-preverbal *had* constructions (4) and (5). The examples actually reflect the morphological alternations that are possible in past tense contexts and the way that *had* interacts with these forms, or at least with the meaning they assign and the past contexts in which they occur.

The examples in the set help to illustrate two points about variation. The first point is related to variation in forms that directly relate to constructions that are compatible with MAE, and the second point concerns variation within AAE. Note that in the set, one variant is compatible with a construction in MAE (i.e. (4)). For some, the compatibility of (4) with MAE simple past and the incompatibility of the other variants with MAE past forms lead to the judgment that one form is grammatical, the one that is compatible with MAE, and the others are ungrammatical, the ones that are incompatible with MAE. Such an assessment is in line with a prescriptive view of grammar; only the variant that conforms to prescribed rules of standard English is acceptable and grammatical. Another way of viewing the compatibility of the variants with one variety or the other is not really linked to prescriptive grammar: One (or more) variant is associated with AAE and the other(s) with MAE. In this second way of considering the variants, MAE-compatible variants are seen as cases in which the speaker who uses them has engaged in inter-dialectal shifting by moving from AAE to MAE. It is not difficult to see how attitudes about language and standards help to shape the way we think about the variants: under one view, a variant is grammatical (the "standard" option) and the other is not, and under the other view, one variant belongs to MAE (the "standard" option) but the other one does not. Both ways of construing the variants are quite viable and realistic assessments; however, they are not the only way to characterize variants, and what is paramount is that they are not always the most accurate description of the linguistic situation. Putting aside the language attitudes and refraining from inserting the notion of standard where it is not relevant, there is another way of understanding the variation, which does not involve separating the variable paradigm to associate one variant with one variety and the other with the other variety, or to label one variant as grammatical and the other as ungrammatical. It is logical and natural, also, to picture the variants as all being part of the same system. That is to say that all of the variants are part of AAE, so speakers can use

Table 7.1 *Preverbal* had *and perfective/ past variable: inter-dialectal variation*

Variants	Variety
Variant 1: *had* started	AAE
Variant 2: *had start*	AAE
Variant 3: *started*	MAE
Variant 4: *start*	AAE

either (3a, b), (4), or (5), and still be speaking AAE, or put another way, speakers can use any of the variants and still be "in AAE mode."

What these three ways of understanding the variants have in common is that they all make a distinction between the variants. The distinction can be between the variants along the lines of one being grammatical and the other being ungrammatical and one belonging to MAE (i.e. standard) and the other to AAE (i.e. non-standard). Finally, in the case in which all variants are associated with AAE, they can be distinguished according to their featural specifications. For instance, the variants in (3), (4), and (5) can be characterized according to whether they take preverbal *had* or *–ed*. I am going to dispense with the prescriptive grammar view here under which variants are grammatical/ungrammatical because it is irrelevant; all of the preverbal *had* (perfective/past) variants are grammatical given that the target language is AAE. It is true that if the target is MAE, then only the V–*ed* variant (4) is grammatical, but that is not the topic under discussion. The variants are presented from an inter-dialectal perspective in Table 7.1 and from an intra-dialectal perspective in Table 7.2.

The major difference between the organization of the variants in Table 7.1 and Table 7.2 is that in the former, one variant is associated with MAE and the remaining three with AAE, and in the latter, all variants are within the AAE system. Both tables show that there is a range of variation within AAE. Here I have used a set of undefined

Table 7.2 *Preverbal* had *and perfective/past variable: intra-dialectal variation*

Variants	Features: X (*had*), Y (past morphology)	AAE
Variant 1: *had started*	[X, Y]	✓
Variant 2: *had start*	[X, Y$_{\emptyset\text{ed}}$]	✓
Variant 3: *started*	[X$_{\emptyset\text{HAD}}$, Y]	✓
Variant 4: *start*	[X$_{\emptyset\text{HAD}}$, Y$_{\emptyset\text{ed}}$]	✓

features that are specified as being overt or covert as one way of expressing the difference among variants. The feature [X] refers to overt preverbal *had*, and the feature [Y] refers to overt *–ed* verbal morphology. Certainly the properties of [X, Y] should be further specified, so that it would be possible to state precisely what both *had* and *–ed* contribute to the meaning of the construction. For instance, presumably *had* will be defined in terms of its aspectual properties, which are compatible with the endpoint of an event or with marking the achievement or accomplishment of an event. In addition, its property of being a preverbal element will also have to be specified. Another type of feature that is relevant for preverbal *had* is tense. While the marker does occur in past contexts, it is not clear whether the marker should be marked as past tense or whether it just has aspectual functions. These questions should be addressed further in specifying the features associated with preverbal *had* because, once answered, they will give further insight into specifically what kinds of linguistic features and properties of events children are paying attention to when they acquire the preverbal *had* construction.

The features [Y] that are associated with *–ed* in this context must also be specified. So far I have assumed that *–ed* marks past, but it should also be determined what relationship, such as agreement, it has with preverbal *had*. Another important property that the features must be able to express has to do with whether the morphemes are actually pronounced or not. In Variant 1 both *had* and *–ed* are pronounced, and neither is pronounced in Variant 4. In Variant 2 *had* is overt and *–ed* is not, and in Variant 3 *–ed* is overt and *had* is not. I am not making any claims about whether some type of phonological deletion has taken place in the cases in which a morpheme is not overt. As these are all variants, the claim is that even in cases in which the morphemes remain unexpressed, the construction still carries the meaning that can be expressed by Variant 1, in which both morphemes are overt. These features should also be discussed in broader contexts that might throw light on different factors that correlate with their occurrence. Although the features [X, Y] take the discussion to a relatively abstract level, it really is important to talk about them. It might be that description on this abstract level is necessary to give an accurate description of AAE developmental patterns that are manifest in child speech. Even in its crude form, the information in Tables 7.1 and 7.2 underscore some important factors. One noteworthy point is that even in the absence of overt morphological marking in AAE, information about time and events gets conveyed. Also, another practical point that comes out of the view of AAE to MAE inter-dialectal variation, as depicted in Table 7.1, is that it is not always accurate to equate forms in MAE and AAE; they may look the same but may be used in different contexts. This is obvious with a form such as Variant 4 *start*, which may look like a non-past, but it occurs in past contexts (as well as in the same contexts as preverbal *had* constructions). Less obvious examples are Variant 1, which resembles the past perfect in MAE, and Variant 3, which resembles the simple past in MAE. Both forms occur in other contexts in AAE. The overlap in MAE and AAE in form has consequences for education as well as for communication, a point that I will discuss in Chapter 8.

7.2 INTER-DIALECTAL SHIFTING: PRE-NOMINAL POSSESSIVES AND VERBAL *–S*

The goal here is to bring to the forefront issues and raise questions about dialectal variation, not to make all of the distinctions between inter- and intra-dialectal variation, but the property of variation that relates to the overlap of features or variants that occur in both varieties is worth noting. So far, we have seen that due to the morphological properties such that suffixes or tense markers optionally occur on verbs, from one angle, verb forms conveying a particular meaning can appear to be identical in MAE and AAE. For instance, *saved* (with overt –*ed*) can be said to be both in AAE as well as in MAE. From yet another angle, the overlap is superficial in that the forms simply look alike but have different meanings or can occur in different contexts. A simple case in point is the preverbal *had* constructions and the past perfect, which have very similar structures. However, not all variation in AAE has the same type of overlap in properties, such that the variants are identical in form to constructions associated with MAE. Exploring variation that involves different types of data and data sets leads to more information about AAE, and it also helps to view the linguistic system in its own light – not just in relation to MAE. In this light, I would like to consider two additional constructions with unique variants. One is the pre-nominal possessive construction and the other is the third singular verbal –*s* construction.

7.2.1 Pre-nominal possessives

In the case of the possessive or genitive, the major focus will be on pre-nominal forms, in which the possessor precedes the possessed. In most varieties of English, in these constructions, the first noun in the sequence of two nouns is the possessor and it is marked with an –*'s*, as in *the dog's bone*; the second noun (*bone*) is the entity that is possessed or that is in some type of relationship with the entity expressed by the preceding noun. Such constructions may be referred to as adnominal possessives. The data to be considered here are limited to possessive constructions in four children's *Good Dog, Carl* narratives. As noted in Chapter 3, children were read a novel story written to accompany the pictures in the *Good Dog, Carl* picture book and asked to retell the story while looking at the pictures. The story is given in Appendix B. The genitive –'s constructions (adnominal) that occurred in the story read to the children are *Carl's back*, *mom's bedroom*, *mom's mirror*, *Carl's nose*, *baby's cup*, and *baby's crib*. All of the children's pre-nominal possessors were expressed as common nouns (e.g., *dog*) except *Carl*, a proper noun. What the children's productions show is that the preferred or default form of the constructions is a double noun sequence, with the first being the non-morphologically marked possessor and then the possessed following. The possessor is always marked by virtue of being the first noun in the sequence, but it is seldom morphologically marked with –'s. Consider the following examples:

6.   Dawn (5; 9, F, AAE)
    (a) Then he was trying to dry the <u>baby hair</u>.
       ('baby's hair')
    (b) And then, where the <u>dog head</u>?
       ('dog's head')

7.   Terry (5;11, M, AAE)
    (a) The baby got out of his crib and got on <u>Carl's back</u>.
    (b) They went through the door and went to mama went to <u>mama bedroom</u>.
       ('mama's bedroom')
    (c) and the baby put makeup on the <u>dog's nose</u>
    (d) and the baby ride on <u>Carl's back</u>
    (e) Carl poured chocolate milk into <u>baby cup</u>.
       ('baby's cup')
    (f) and then Carl pour um milk in <u>baby's cup</u>
    (g) and then bubbles came out of <u>Carl's mouth</u>
    (h) and then Carl took a good rest in in in by the <u>baby crib</u>
       ('baby's crib')

8.   Kerry (5;11, M, AAE)
    (a) and then the dog had put some chocolate in the <u>baby cup</u>.
       ('baby's cup')

(b) and then the dog had pick up the soap with <u>his mouth</u> and his <*unintelligible*> and then he had rub the soap on his on the rag, and then he had wipe the <u>baby face</u> off.

('baby's face')

9. Nia (5;9, F, AAE)

(a) Then they went in they ... mom <u>they mama room</u> and the baby dump the powder on <u>Carl's head</u>.

('their mama's room')

(b) Carl pus pour some umm [*LJG: chocolate*] in the <u>baby cup</u>.

('baby's cup')

(c) And then Carl pour some milk in the <u>baby cup</u>.

('baby's cup')

(d) They went in in back in the they went in <u>his mom room</u>.

('his mom's room')

The possessive constructions in the data sets range from those in which common nouns are not morphologically marked for possessive to a sample in which Terry (7) uses –'s variably (e.g., *baby's cup*, *baby cup*). (Some children, including Terry, used "baby" as a name.) In the sample (7) Terry produces *dog's nose* and *baby's cup* with overt morphological marking, on the one hand, and *mama bedroom*, *baby cup*, and *baby crib*, on the other, without overt morphological possessive marking. Without a doubt, some of the non-morphologically marked double noun constructions in the examples above can be construed as compounds much like *toy box* or *baby bed*, but given that some constructions were presented in the story with genitive markers and some of them are actually produced by a child with –'s morphological marking, it is conceivable and almost certain that even the non-morphologically marked double noun constructions are genitive or possessive forms. In addition, the crib and cup were portrayed in the story as belonging to the baby, so the unmarked genitives do not seem to have been construed as compounds. Both Terry and Nia use overt possessive marking with the proper name *Carl* (i.e. *Carl's*, in (7a, d, g) and (9a)), respectively, but that is the only noun in Nia's entire narrative that reflects overt possessive marking. One question is whether children consistently overtly marked the possessive on *Carl* (i.e. *Carl's*) because they took –'s to be part of the dog's name, not a separate marker, or whether they paid more attention to genitive marking on the proper name than on the common nouns. It does not seem to be that –'s was taken to be part of the dog's name given the use of *Carl* (without –'s) in subject position in Terry's narrative (7e, f, h) and in Nia's narrative (9b, c). A version of the proper name (*Carly*) in (10a) below occurs in one other narrative, which is not represented in the data set above, and even that form gets the genitive morphological marking (*Carly's*):

10. (a) Carly and the baby went to the room. (Xavier, 5;9, M, AAE)
    (b) The baby climbed on the Carly's back.
    (c) powder on the um Carly's nose.

There was no attempt to get all of the children to produce the proper name *Carl* in possessive contexts, so the actual examples in which children produced the name are limited; however, it would be useful to determine whether the children treat proper names differently with respect to genitive marking or whether they paid particular attention to *Carl* as a novel name and produced it the way it was presented in the story. Both *Carl's back* and *Carl's nose* occur in the story that the children heard, but further data are needed to determine whether the children consistently mark possessive on proper nouns or names, thus treating them differently than they treat common nouns. Nia used *Carl's head*, which did not occur in the original story, so she did not just produce the possessive constructions that she heard. As an aside, it should be noted that there are no clues in the spontaneous speech samples or in the conversations that accompanied the elicitation tasks that lead to the conclusion that across the board children are inclined to use morphological –'s marking with proper names. The children produced sentences such as the following, for instance:

11.   (a) He broke Kynosha phone. (Rashanna, 3;4, F, AAE)
            'He broke Kynosha's phone'
    (b) Now I'm in Miss Sayvoie class.
            'Now I'm in Miss Sayvoie's class'
    (c) They in John car. (Deon, 3;10, M, AAE)[1]
            'They're in John's car'

No child used all of the pre-nominal –'s morphemes in the way they were presented in the *Good Dog, Carl* story, but almost all of the cases of the –'s constructions that the children used were identical to those in the original story. One novel possessive was *dog's nose* (Terry); only *Carl's nose* was used in the original story. *Baby face* was used by Kenny, and the corresponding possessive construction (*baby's face*) was not used in the story presented to the children. The sketchy genitive marking with common nouns stands out alongside the default non-marked possessive, and the consistent possessive morphological marking of the proper name *Carl/Carly* also stands out. The observations lead to the question about whether the children show variability in the –'s marking on common nouns because the noun–noun construction can be taken as compounds, which do not require possessive marking, as in *the doll house* vs. *the doll's house*, which can have slightly different readings, and whether, consequently, proper names occur with possessive marking because the construction in which the proper noun is the possessor cannot be construed as a compound, *Carl's room* but not *the Carl room*. Finally, it is also necessary to ask the question about whether the variable possessive marking reflects a developmental trend in AAE, or whether such variation indicates that the genitive –'s is not really an intrinsic part of AAE grammar. More directed study involving production and comprehension tests would help to answer these questions.

In addition to using proper names and common nouns as the pre-nominal possessor in the noun–noun constructions, some children used the pronouns *his, they,* and *her* (e.g., *her gloves*), as illustrated in the examples in (12–15):

12.   (a) And the baby got on his back. (Dawn)
       (b) The dog was seeing if his mama was coming.
       (c) Mom was rubbing his head.
13.   (a) The baby got out of his crib and got on Carl's back. (Terry)
       (b) And then Carl put baby back in in his crib.
14.   (a) And then the dog had put some milk in his cup. (Kerry)
       (b) And then the dog had pick up the soap with his mouth and his <*unintelligible*> and then he had rub the soap on his on the rag, and then he had wipe the baby face off.
15.   (a) The baby climb on his back. (Nia)
       (b) They went in in back in the they went in his mom room.
              'his mom's room'
       (c) He lookin at the window. Seeing his momma come back.

There is no variation in the examples in (12–15) in the case of *his*, so it is invariable when used in third person singular masculine pre-nominal possessive (or adjectival) constructions; it always occurs in the same form and it appears to be obligatory. Compare *his* to the occurrence of non-overt morphological possessive marking on *mom* in (15b), a potential recursive possessive construction. The construction is taken to be a potential recursive possessive construction because in two potential sites for possessive marking, on *his* and *mom*, only the former gets the marking. Here again, one question is whether the marking on the pronoun, but not on the following noun, is developmental or whether the marking follows the pattern set in adult AAE. These are the types of recursive possessive constructions that will have to be elicited in production tasks to determine what the actual possessive marking strategies are. As an aside, I note that there are also a few cases of *him* in possessive constructions in the narratives (e.g., *Then the mama was rubbing him on him head*) and in spontaneous speech, which seem to be a reflection of development.

Another pronoun that is used as a pre-nominal possessor is the third person plural pronominal form *they*, as in (16a, b), examples from *Good Dog, Carl* retells. It also occurs in the reflexive, in which it combines with –*self* (*theyself*) in (16c):

16.   (a) They going in they mama room. (Jeffrey, 5;7, M, AAE)
        'They're going in their mama's room'
  (b) Then they hurry up and be quiet and get in they bed.
        '... get in their bed'
  (c) And then they look in the mirror and make theyself pretty. (Terry)
        '... and make themselves pretty'

These pre-nominal pronouns do occur in children's spontaneous speech, too, for instance, in (17):

17.   (a) They put it on they head. (Deon)
        'They put it on their heads'
  (b) Girls always don't like they boyfriends. (Rashanna)
        'Girls always don't like their boyfriends' (literally: 'Girls
          don't ever like their boyfriends')

They is used as the third person plural pre-nominal (adjectival) possessive and as pronominal in the third person plural reflexive.

A small tangential point that I will make here – but which certainly deserves further attention – is that in developing and adult AAE, when used as a third person plural pre-nominal possessive pronoun, *they* does not seem to be a form of *their* with "r"-deletion. Were possessive *they* a variable pronunciation of *their* without the "r," then we would have reason to expect the same pronunciation for *there*, which is certainly produced without the "r" in the regional variety of AAE that is being discussed. That is, we would expect pre-nominal *they* to sound like *their/there* without the "r" (or *their/there* with r-vocalization). However, *they* [ðe]/[de] and the pronunciation of *their/there* [ðɛ]/[dɛ] are vastly different with respect to the vowels, although they both reflect "r"-deletion. The phonetic symbols are intended to show the different pronunciations of the two words. Especially in child AAE, but also in adult AAE, the initial sound of *they* is pronounced (*d*), as in the initial sound in *day*. The phonetic symbol [ð] in the representations refers to the *th* pronunciation, and the symbol [d] refers to the *d* pronunciation, in which case *they* sounds just like *day*. Also, when *they* is used in subject position (e.g. *They read four books*), it has the same pronunciation as the form that is used in third person pre-nominal possessive pronoun contexts. The pronunciation of the vowel sound in *there*, on the other hand, is like the pronunciation of the vowel sound in *bet*. Based on the pronunciation of the vowel sound in they, which is close to the vowel sound in *day*, I conclude that the form *they* is third person pronominal possessive, *not* a variable pronunciation of *their* without "r."

A partial overview of the third person pre-nominal possessive system that is based on the structures in the *Good Dog, Carl* story retells is given in Table 7.3. In the case of the third person singular pre-nominal constructions, there is no variability; genitive pronouns are used. Some variability with respect to morphological possessive –'s marking is evident in the context of common nouns, in which zero marking occurs most often, but there are instances of –'s. Genitive –'s was used more or less consistently with the name *Carl*.

Considering the type of possessive constructions that have been highlighted in the children's spontaneous and directed speech samples and in the absence of more proper noun tokens, I would like to present a possible picture of variation and possessive marking in child AAE or in the AAE grammar.

The picture Table 7.4 presents is one in which zero possessive –'s marking is part of the AAE grammar and overt possessive –'s marking is part of MAE. The claim is that the overt possessive –'s is an MAE morphological property, so when it occurs in the speech

Table 7.3 *Partial summary of third person pre-nominal (adjectival) possessive marking*

Pre-nominal possessive forms	Sample constructions
third person singular feminine and masculine: *his, her*	*his head, her gloves*
third person plural pronoun: *they*	*they mama room*
common nouns (zero morphological possessive marking and variable possessive –'s)	*dog head, baby cup, baby's cup*
proper nouns/names (morphological possessive marking was used specifically in context of the name Carl)	*Carl's nose, Carly's back*

Table 7.4 *Possessive –'s variable: inter-dialectal variation*

Variants	Variety
Possessive –'s variant 1: *the baby cup*	AAE
Possessive –'s variant 2: *the baby's cup*	MAE

of an AAE speaker, that speaker is using a form that is part of the grammar of MAE and other varieties of English, but not intrinsic to the AAE grammar.

In the case of pre-nominal pronouns in possessive constructions, the inter-dialectal variation is drawn along the lines of specific lexical items within the third person. The third person plural form is not the same one that occurs in MAE; the third person singular is (including masculine and feminine). This is shown in Table 7.5.

Given the limited data, it appears that recursive possessive marking does not occur in AAE grammar, so corresponding variants in which an overtly marked noun follows the possessive pronoun are part of MAE as in Table 7.6.

Table 7.5 *Pre-nominal possessive pronoun variable: inter-dialectal variation*

Variants	Variety
Pre-nominal third person plural possessive pronoun variant:	
they mama	AAE
their mama	MAE
Pre-nominal third person singular possessive pronoun variant:	
his mouth	MAE
	AAE

Table 7.6 *Recursive possessive constructions*

Variant	Variety
Recursive possessive: *his mom room*	AAE
Recursive possessive: *his mom's room*	MAE

There are some clear differences between what might be claimed to be part of the AAE grammar and what is MAE, so it is worth pursuing the question about intra-dialectal variation. Are there possessive variants within AAE? That is, can AAE speakers choose to use one variant over another within AAE, or is one variant strictly part of AAE and the other part of MAE? I will offer the following summary in response to that question.

Table 7.7 takes a very conservative view as to the possessive forms that are intrinsically part of the AAE grammar (indicated by the symbol "✓") and those that are not (indicated by the symbol "✗"). For instance, $\emptyset_{-'s}$ is presented as part of AAE and overt possessive –'s as part of MAE. The claim, however, is not that overt possessive –'s, third person possessive plural pronoun (*their*), and recursive possessive constructions are never used by AAE speakers. The claim is that AAE speakers have access to these variants through general English, which has consequences for issues relating to

Table 7.7 *Possessive variables: intra-dialectal variation*

−'s Variants	Descriptive property	AAE
Variant 1: *the baby cup*	$\emptyset_{-'s}$	✓
Variant 2: *the baby's cup*	−'s	✗
Singular pre-nominal possessive		
Variant (singular): *his, her*	Possessive pronoun	✓
Plural pre-nominal possessive variants		
Variant 1 (plural): *they*	Default pronoun	✓
Variant 2 (plural): *their*	Possessive pronoun	✗
Possessive recursion		
Variant 1: *his mom room*	Possessive pronoun – $\emptyset_{-'s}$	✓
Variant 2: *his mom's room*	Possessive pronoun – −'s	✗

inter-dialectal shifting or code-shifting. Table 7.7 only presents part of the possessive system in AAE given that it does not address what happens in first and second person pre-nominal or adjectival possessive pronouns (e.g., *my hat, your hat*). Other possessive forms that have not been addressed are absolute possessive pronouns, which can stand alone, and post-genitives, such as *a cousin of Lucy's*, in which *of* is followed by a post-genitive noun marked by −'s. There have been some informal claims suggesting that overt −'s occurs in post-genitive contexts in AAE; however, I had no evidence to support that claim earlier, and I do not find the evidence here. Post-genitives are not prevalent in the child data here, but the following example reported in Chapter 2 gives an idea about the kinds of constructions to consider further:

18.   LJG: Have you ever gone to a birthday party?
      Dawn: Yes mam, a girl birthday to my cousin.

Literally, Dawn's response is in reference to a girl's birthday party that was at her cousin's (house).

The examples in (19) and (20) are representative of the absolute or stand-alone possessive pronouns in the data set; however, I did not come across any post-genitive constructions in the spontaneous or elicited speech.

19. (a) Troy: <u>Mines</u> go fast. (3;7, M, AAE)
     (b) LJG: <u>Yours</u> goes fast, T__.
     (c) Deon: <u>Mines</u> go fast. (3;6, M, AAE)
20. Put <u>mines</u> right here. (Troy)

It is not easy to tell whether *mines* is a reflection of children's over-generalization of *'s* on *his*, *hers*, and *yours*, which are productive, or whether the children are actually producing the adult AAE form, which may be linked to a generalization across all absolute posses-sive forms. *Mine* and *mines*, which appear to be variants, are both produced by speakers of AAE. It would need to be determined at this stage to what extent they are also variants in child AAE. The fun-damental question here is about the "form" that is used to express a possessive or genitive relation, not about the concept of possession. The concept of possession is part of AAE-speaking children's gram-mars although it is not always expressed by an overt morphological form (e.g., *–'s*).

7.2.2 Verbal –s

The final construction to be considered in the context of inter-dialec-tal shifting between AAE and MAE is the verbal –s form that occurs with non-past verbs with third person singular subjects. Speakers of MAE readily identify unmarked verbs that occur with third per-son singular subjects as ungrammatical, but it is not clear to what extent speakers of AAE pay attention to the markers to get infor-mation about the person (third person) and number (singular) of the subject. That is, for AAE speakers the third person singular subject *Bruce* in the sentence *Bruce write fast* does not require the verb form *writes* with third person singular –s marking, given the form of the verb *write*. Verbs in third person singular non-past contexts occur in children's spontaneous speech and elicited speech samples in preceding chapters in this book, but I will focus on a small data set here. A sample of verbs used in third person singular non-past contexts by the same children whose *Good Dog, Carl* possessives were highlighted in the preceding section are presented below. Because the *Good Dog, Carl* story retells were often presented in the past context, the third person singular non-past tokens are taken from the children's free speech sessions that occurred right before and after they engaged in the story retells:

21. (a) <u>A one go</u> with seven. (Dawn)
    (b) Then <u>a zero go</u> with seven.
    (c) That's so funny. <u>It go</u> like that?
    (d) <u>My cousin</u> always <u>beat</u> me up.
    (e) LJG: If you gon be a mailman, you have to learn where everybody lives.
        Dawn: I know where <u>everybody live</u>.
    (f) <u>M__</u> don't live by us no more.
    (g) You know <u>pa pa sell</u> crackling?[2]
22. (a) LJG: Now what did you say about rest? It gets you what?
        Terry: <u>Rest get</u> you energy.
    (b) Terry: I defeated Ock Doc, Green Goblin, and Scorpion, but I never get to Sandman.[3]
        LJG: ... But you might get to Sandman soon.
        Terry: Well um it got to be all day so I can get to um Sandman because Sandman got that big fist with sand made of it.
        LJG: Oh, that's what he is?
        Terry: And to make that big hand with the fist full of sand he don't even have to get close to you. He can get far if he want because ...
23. T__ is the biggest and K__ is almost big. Even K__ <u>give</u> T__ piggy back rides. (Kerry)
24. LJG: Let's go back to the feet ... What kind of thing did you do there?

> Nia: <u>She run</u> some water some warm water in the tub. Then
> <u>she get</u> a soap.
> <u>She dip</u> the um soap in the um thing. Then <u>she rub</u> my
> feet with some soap. And then after we do um our finger-
> nails and our toenails she got a massage hand thing. <u>She</u>
> <u>put</u> you put your hand in it and you put it on the lil hump,
> then you gotta rub it.
>
> LJG: ... How does it feel when you finish?
>
> Nia: It feel it tickle you.

The non-past verbal constructions represented in (21–24) reflect a pattern of zero third person singular verbal –s marking (Ø$_{-s}$) and are consistent with the property of third person singular verbal marking that is listed as a feature of AAE. For instance, see #14 on the feature list in Chapter 2: subject–verb agreement variations.

The type of ambiguity that arises in parts of Nia's narrative (24) is what is predicted given the absence of overt morphological verbal past marking (e.g. –ed) and overt third person singular non-past verbal –s marking. That is, the first three sentences given in (24) could be construed as events in the past or non-past events given that there is no morphological marking (e.g., –ed, –s) on the verbs. However, the last sentence in that section has a second person singular subject (you), and the event is clearly non-past, a type of generic reading or a description of what happens in the process. At least at the stage of development represented here, third person singular verbal –s does not seem to be part of the children's grammar. The remaining examples also feature verbs that are not overtly marked with third person verbal –s; however, they are less ambiguous in their reference to non-past events, which may be due to other cues such as verb forms and context. For instance, in (21) verbs such as go and sell, which have irregular past tense forms (i.e. went, sold), are used. Given children's production of irregular past tense forms, we would expect different forms for go and sell were the reference past. Note Terry's use of the modal can in (22), and the following verb

Table 7.8 *Third person singular verbal –s variables: inter-dialectal variation*

Variants	Variety	AAE
Variant 1: –Ø–$_s$	AAE	✓
Variant 2: –s	MAE	✗

want is certainly referring to the non-past. From my perspective, in thinking back to the discussion of the non-past copula contexts in Chapter 3, I find that it is accurate to say that although it is variable in its occurrence, singular non-past copula has a better chance of occurring in its overt form in some contexts than third person singular verbal –s. At least from the examples provided, it does not seem that any of the contexts, with respect to meaning, induce the occurrence of verbal –s in child AAE. If we want to claim that the –s is associated with events that are general or that usually happen, then it might be possible that it would occur at least in those third singular environments that lean toward habitual meaning. Take, for instance, Kerry's line in (23) when he refers to K__'s giving T__ piggy back rides. Given the reference to plural rides, we might expect the event to take place from time to time, to be a general or habitual event that occurs on different occasions. Nevertheless, he uses the unmarked *give*, not the morphologically marked *gives*. The marker occurs rarely in the data; however, I am not claiming that children will not use it. I do contend that if they do use it, they may be relying more on a pattern in MAE rather than on a marker that is intrinsically part of AAE. This point is summarized in Table 7.8.

More focus is being placed on third singular verbal –s in early AAE and in its use by school-age children. For instance, de Villiers and Johnson (2007) report that based on comprehension tasks, AAE-speaking children in the 4- to 7-year-old age range did not use the third person verbal –s to determine whether an event attributed to a third person singular subject was generic rather than past (e.g. *cuts/cut*), nor did they use it to determine whether the construction was a verb or part of a noun compound (e.g. *The penguin dresses/The penguin dress*, respectively) (p. 133). In the appropriate context, that means that the *penguin dress* could be construed as a type of dress decorated with penguin pictures, but if the verbal –*s* is construed as a non-past marker in third person singular contexts in which *penguin* is the subject, then *dress* should be taken to be a verb in which the meaning would be that the penguin dresses or puts on clothes. The AAE-speaking children had no problem associating *cut* with a generic event, which generally happens, or a non-past event. Children could take the question *Who cut the bread?* to mean 'Who cuts/has the job of cutting the bread in general?' instead of 'Who cut the bread in the past?' The strong suggestion is that the children did not use the –*s* on *cuts* to distinguish the past and non-past meanings. In a study conducted on data from African American second-graders, Terry, Evangelou, Smith, Roberts, and Zeisel (in press) note that there is a correlation between third person singular marking in word problems and performance on the Woodcock-Johnson-R Test of Applied Mathematics. Specifically, their finding is that verbal –*s* influenced AAE-speaking children's scores negatively more so than other MAE-related features that are used in academic writing, such as that in standardized tests. There was a correlation between test scores and the presence of third singular –*s* in the word problems.

The virtually across-the-board absence of third person singular verbal –*s* morphological marking in the child AAE data in this book, reports in de Villiers and Johnson (2007) of the lack of comprehension of third person singular verbal –*s* as a generic or non-past marker, and the findings in Terry *et al.* (in press) strongly suggesting that word problems including verbs with third singular –*s* marking negatively influence test scores of AAE-speaking school-age children, support the claim that the morphological marker may not be part of the AAE grammar. Third person singular verbal –*s* is an excellent entry into research on developmental AAE and variation, especially given the way its meanings relate to the tense–aspect system and generic and habitual marking, which are prominent in AAE. In addition, research on the topic can provide more insight into the distinction between types of intra-dialectal shifting and inter-dialectal shifting that I introduced in the preceding discussions of morphological past and possessive.

This chapter raises questions about variation, especially in constructions in which some preverbal element (e.g., preverbal *had*) or word final morphological marker (e.g., verbal past *–ed*, possessive *–'s*, and third person singular verbal *–s*,) may or may not occur in certain contexts in the speech of AAE speakers. This morphosyntactic variation and other types of variation are directly related to questions about AAE shifting intra-dialectally or using variants that are intrinsic to the AAE grammar on the one hand, and shifting from one dialect to another or inter-dialectal shifting, in this study the case of shifting from AAE to use a variant that is part of the mainstream English repertoire but not so closely associated with AAE grammar. The general claim is that not all variation is equal, so to speak, which leads to the conclusion that some variants may be more closely associated with one variety over the other, and yet other variants may be associated with just one of the varieties. It stands to reason that if variants are found within one variety and not the other, speakers may be able to shift between the two varieties and use the variant that is not in the native variety, but shifting will depend on linguistic as well as extra-linguistic contexts and the speaker's knowledge that two forms are variants. However, because variants may be available in a single variety, not all shifts involve moving from one code to another or from one dialect to another. A shift can occur between variants, all of which are within a single dialect. For a concrete example, take the picture of the past tense marking in Table 7.2, in which all variants (e.g., *–ed*, $\emptyset_{-ed}$) are intrinsically part of the grammar of AAE. My contention is that some type of shifting is involved in using one form or the other or moving from one form to the other, but it is the type of shifting that occurs within AAE. This type of intra-dialectal shifting is what I will refer to as variable-shifting. Variable-shifting certainly may require moving from one type of morphological or phonological representation to another, but it does not involve moving from one code or dialect to another. Simply put, when AAE speakers move from say a morphologically unmarked verb (e.g., *start*) to express an event in the past to the morphologically marked verb (e.g., *started*) to express an event in the past, they are not necessarily shifting to another American English code or dialect, such as MAE; they may very well be operating within AAE because both variants are available in AAE.

It is reasonable to assume that not all shifts fall under the category of intra-dialectal or variable-shifting. Those shifts that do not fall within this category may be candidates for inter-dialectal or code-shifting, shifts that actually involve moving from one code to another. Third person singular non-past verbal −*s* and overt possessive −'*s* might count as morphological variants that involve code-shifting, such that when AAE speakers move from zero marked forms $\emptyset_{-s}$ and $\emptyset_{-'s}$ to overtly marked forms verbal −*s* and possessive −'*s*, respectively, for example, from *papa sell crackling* to *papa sells crackling* and from *the baby nose* to *the baby's nose*, they can be said to be shifting from one code to another, in this case from AAE to another variety of American English, such as MAE.

A significant amount of research on the topic of shifting lies ahead, and many questions are raised here and many more need to be formulated. Empirical data based on spontaneous samples, elicitation tasks, and comprehension exercises are needed to provide more insight into the questions about the status of variants and variation within a dialect and between dialects. It is also the case that many areas of AAE grammar need to be considered in the discussion of variation and the status of variants, especially given the claim that AAE is inherently variable. If we consider a broader range of patterns in the AAE system, how would the variation be characterized or what might be considered intra-dialectal variation/variable-shifting on the one hand and inter-dialectal variation/code-shifting on the other?

The information in Table 7.9, along with that in Tables 7.2, 7.7, and 7.8, presents a summary of variables discussed in AAE and

Table 7.9 *Variants and the child AAE grammar*

Variables	AAE Grammar
Habitual marking	
1. be_{asp}	✓
2. $V_{\emptyset-s}$	✓
3. V–s	non-applicable (developmental)
Generic marking	
1. be_{asp}	non-applicable (developmental)
2. $V_{\emptyset-s}$	✓
3. V–s	✗
Remote past	
1. BIN	✓
2. 'for a long time'	✓
3. 'a long time ago'	✓
Copula (non-past contexts)	
1. $\emptyset_{BE}$	✓
2. BE (singular)	✓
3. BE (plural)	? (more data)
Negation (agreement)	
1. negative concord	✓
2. single negation	✓
Negation (auxiliary)	
1. negative inversion	non-applicable (developmental)
2. non-negative inversion	✓
Yes–no questions (auxiliary inversion)	
1. inversion	✓
2. non-inversion	✓
Yes–no questions (intonation)	
1. level	✓
2. falling	✓
3. final rise	? (more data)
Wh-questions (auxiliary inversion)	
1. inversion	✓
2. non-inversion	✓

indicates the variants of the variables that may be taken to be part of the AAE grammar.

The type and level of complexity of information that can be conveyed in tables and charts are limited, and all of the empirical data required to make decisions about what may or may not be part of the AAE grammar are not available, so for these two reasons the information in Tables 7.2, 7.7, 7.8, and 7.9 is far from conclusive, but it does provide a beginning point from which to raise questions about variation in certain areas of the grammar of AAE. Some variants are assumed to be part of AAE grammar but are not reflected in the data discussed here due to developmental stages. For instance, the data from the 3-, 4-, and 5-year-olds do not provide any evidence that children have acquired negative inversion constructions (e.g., *Can't nobody get in this* – see Chapters 5 and 6.) Also, there is clear evidence that verbal –s is used as a habitual marker in adult AAE, but data supporting such use in child AAE have not been reported. Sentences such as the following are attested in adult AAE:

25. (a) 'Cause I keeps him in the house. (75 years, F, AAE)
          'Because I generally keep him [dog] in the house'
     (b) Sometimes I buys the jell kind.
          'Sometimes I buy the jell kind'
     (c) When I do keep somebody, I wants to get paid.
          'Indeed when I keep (i.e. babysit) somebody, I want to get paid on those occasions'

Verbal –s that occurs (possibly) with all persons, but certainly with first person singular in habitual contexts, is taken to be part of the adult AAE grammar, although it is not reflected in child AAE. Verbal –s used specifically in third person singular generic contexts is not taken to be part of the adult or developing AAE grammar. Also, according to Table 7.9, verbs without overt –s (e.g., *Lisa drink tea*) marking and aspectual *be* constructions are used in this context, although there is no evidence that children use aspectual *be* in generic contexts or to express general states of affairs, as in

Wal-Marts be on the outskirts of town to indicate that it is generally the case that Wal-Marts are located on the outskirts of town. As noted in Table 7.9, in some cases due to limited data, there is a question about whether a particular variant is part of AAE grammar. For example, there is sufficient data to support the claim that final falling and level tones in questions are part of AAE grammar, but it is not clear what the empirical data would tell us about the extent of question intonation with a final rise, which also occurs in AAE.

In the discussion here, variation has been approached from the angle of the grammar of AAE; however, some of the questions that are raised with respect to intra-and inter-dialectal variation will also have to be taken into consideration from the perspective of the individual due to a number of extra-linguistic factors that bear on speakers' language competence, language use, and experiences. Obviously, some of these issues should also be taken up from the perspective of (regional) variation in different varieties of AAE. The data here are from southwest Louisiana and, no doubt, patterns of use are shared with other varieties of AAE, but there are certainly sustainable differences that should be addressed. Finally, there is a significant amount of work to be done in lining up models and theories of variation with intuitions and empirical data, such as the type of parametric approach discussed in Snyder (2007) and the multiple grammars view in Roeper (2006).

8 The D.I.R.E.C.T. Model: linking linguistic description and education

Terry: You just gotta practice, practice, practice ... and don't give up.

INTRODUCTION

I would like to end this book with a discussion that considers child AAE developmental patterns in light of practical application. I am well aware that those engaged in practical application, such as educators and speech pathologists, are always concerned about the level of feasibility of new methods of instruction, approaches, and assessments and the extent to which the methods will lead to academic gains. I hope that the type of description that has been presented in the preceding chapters and the accompanying data will be useful first in helping to discern patterns in developing AAE and will also encourage more research that will answer the many questions sparked by the data. First and foremost, I want to make clear that, on the whole, the data presented throughout the chapters represent systematic language development, not language disorders and not imperfect MAE acquisition. That point has to be reinforced; we cannot give up.

The tradition of linking AAE language use to education, and more specifically to the achievement gap between some African American students and their school-age peers from other American English backgrounds is long-standing, although there may have been some change in the themes of discussion along the way. For instance, in the linguistics-based reading program advocated in Labov (2006), emphasis is placed on the restrictions on word final sounds on the basis that the differences between the acceptable final consonant combinations in AAE and MAE may need to be underscored in phonics and reading-related lessons for AAE-speaking children. Beyond the claim that the subtle differences in sound patterns in different positions in words in AAE and MAE influence the development of decoding and phonics-related skills that are paramount to learning to read, there have not been any research-related projects that have reported findings on concrete AAE developmental linguistic patterns that present challenges for school-age children acquiring the necessary skills for mastering the academic curriculum in areas such as reading and math, although there is more recent speculation about verbal –s in third person singular contexts. The low achievement level reported for some African American children is likely to be due to multiple and complex combinations of factors, including students' challenges in the use of academic language, a genuine misinterpretation of children's classroom behavior on the part of educators, and students' lack of understanding of what is expected in educational realms and the kinds of skills required for academic success. However, even in the presence of the complex factors that are barriers to children's academic success, some researchers still maintain that while the use of AAE as a native variety may not be the sole factor serving as a barrier to academic success, it does play a role. In the limited body of current work with an AAE academic success and achievement gap thrust, the focus is on children's ability to apply academic English in school settings. A common thread that runs through current work in this area is the advantage of code-shifting in mitigating the achievement gaps that might be linked to language. That is, according to more current studies, such as those conducted by Charity, Scarborough, and Griffin (2004) and Craig and Washington (2006), an important factor in doing well in school settings is the ability to use academic language or to shift from AAE to MAE "when necessary." Keeping such research in mind, as the chapter progresses, I want to raise some issues in relation to the adoption of code- and variable-shifting as a strategy that bridges the gap between the native use of AAE and school language and helps to compensate for language barriers that might interfere with the processing, comprehension, and writing that are necessary for successful performance in school.

8.1 THE D.I.R.E.C.T. MODEL: INSTRUCTION AND AAE TENSE–ASPECT MARKING

Some classroom instruction is specifically designed to teach school-age children to recognize the difference between certain features that are associated with AAE and corresponding words and phrases in classroom English (mainstream American English). Some of these models will be mentioned later, but in this section I will present a model that underscores the fact that children acquire systems of language use. In the preceding chapters, we have seen some patterns in the development of tense–aspect marking with grammatical-ized markers or free morphemes and bound morphemes (e.g., suf-fixes –ed, –ing). The message that I have tried to convey is that we get a better understanding of AAE once we begin to look at systems of language use rather than isolated features. As a pictorial represen-tation of types of information children must piece together in talk-ing about events, consider the model in Figure 8.1.

Information that children acquire to talk about events refers to tense–aspect grammaticalized markers (or words such as aspectual *be*, preverbal *had*, and remote past *BIN*) that have come to be associ-ated with some notion of how an event takes place, bound morph-ology (or verb endings) that gives meaning about when the event occurred or whether it is ongoing, and type of situation (ways of pre-senting or talking about an event). In some cases only part of an event is presented, as in *running*, which can refer to part of the situation of the running event that is in progress. In other cases the entire situ-ation can be presented, as in *opened the box*, in which reference is to a complete opening the box situation. As indicated in the diagram in Figure 8.1, there is still space for other types of information.

The tense–aspect grammaticalized markers all add some meaning to verb sequences in which they occur, and the verbs may take a bound morpheme, such as, –ing and –ed. One interesting

Figure 8.1 Information about events

comparison that can be made between the grammaticalized markers and the bound morphemes is that there seems to be a general
trend; that is, the data suggest that the children are in tune with
the grammaticalized markers, but they do not always pay so much
attention to the bound morphemes. That is to say that children have
a propensity toward the use of some preverbal tense–aspect markers
(e.g., preverbal *had*, remote past *BIN*, aspectual *be*), while they neg-
lect bound morphemes (e.g., *–ed*, verbal *–s*) in different contexts. As
has been shown in Chapter 4, the bound morpheme past *–ed* is variable; it can be omitted possibly because past meaning can be derived
from the contexts in some cases. On the other hand, while it is relatively easy to reconstruct the past meaning of the past progressive
from the context, we still see very few instances of cases in which
a free morpheme or word *was* is omitted. For instance, in the following example the past context can be inferred from *saw*; however,
sentences are seldom produced without *was*, although, as shown in
Chapter 4, *was* seems to have been omitted in some narratives. As it
stands, sentences such as that in (1) are preferred to the one in (2), in
which *was* is not expressed:

1. I saw my cousin yesterday. She <u>was</u> riding her bike.
2. I saw my cousin yesterday. She Ø$_{was}$ riding her bike. (unlikely
   to occur)

What is found consistently in child AAE as well as in adult AAE is the presence of the bound morpheme –*ing* both in present progressive and past progressive contexts (*He running, He was running*, respectively) and in aspectual *be* contexts (*He be running*). As discussed in Green (2007), it might very well be the case that –*ing* is indispensable in that it indicates information about events, that they are in progress in progressive contexts and that they have a recurrence or other related property in the case of be_{asp} contexts (e.g., *be running*). For this reason, –*ing*, unlike other suffixes (e.g., –*ed*, verbal –*s*, possessive –'*s*), must be expressed to provide crucial information about events. Also, perhaps preverbal tense–aspect markers are more salient and distinctive in that they mark or indicate meaning that cannot be so easily retrieved from context. As such, children pay attention to this property of AAE.

While the picture here of the verbal markers, suffixes, and general interpretation of events that can be associated with developing AAE is not complete, the diagram in Figure 8.1 gives a broad description of some information that children have to master. The way the descriptions might be used in addressing linguistic-related questions about the development of tense–aspect patterns in AAE and comparison to developing patterns in other languages is obvious. What is generally not discussed in the context of linguistic descriptions of AAE are ways in which the information can be systematically linked to classroom instruction that is related to the direct teaching of MAE patterns that are compatible with AAE constructions to native AAE speakers. By direct teaching or simply placing emphasis on MAE constructions, I mean using strategies and instruction in which children are made aware of systematic AAE patterns and constructions, given corresponding MAE patterns, and taught to identify distinctions independently. The instruction may be supported on the basis that some AAE constructions differ from the academic or classroom language in subtle ways, and these subtleties must be made explicit for some speakers. Also, the impetus for such instruction may be that there is evidence that children who can use a variety of language patterns, including those that are compatible with class-room English, make gains in education.

It is true that in some cases the instruction may focus on a certain construction, such as preverbal *had* + VERB, so quick tips may be more desirable than detailed lessons. For instance, the tip may be formatted such that it underscores the similarity in mean-ing between preverbal *had* constructions and simplex V–*ed* forms, both of which are likely to be in the child's grammar to express an event that took place before now. The "tip" has to be tailored to the student's grade level, because, depending on level, it may also be appropriate to talk about past perfect in relation to preverbal *had*. Different instructors may approach the information from dif-ferent angles, but some level of explanation beyond the judgment that preverbal *had* is wrong would be more useful – and, in fact, accurate – in pointing out a marked difference between AAE and classroom English. Some developing AAE speakers produce prever-bal *had* sequences quite productively at age 4; however, the type of instruction that I have in mind here is not appropriate for children in developing stages of AAE. From my vantage point, the goal is not to "wipe out" AAE; it is to offer a linguistic alternative that hap-pens to be acceptable in academic settings. As I have found, given the many hours I have spent with the developing AAE-speaking children, opportunities for children to talk and engage in literacy-related activities that they enjoy, find challenging, and can play a role in directing are beneficial. They help to bring out children's rich language and linguistic skill in creative ways and contribute to the children's confidence in using language. Such activities are not useful just at the level of sentence structure and elements of mechanics of language use, but also on semantic, pragmatic, and rhetorical levels. From my position, I did not see those sessions as time to give children MAE correspondences to AAE constructions, which I also used along with some version of academic language and "teacher talk", so I always find it interesting when I get feedback and questions that suggest that I am attempting to model the "right" language for the participants. I used the time to engage naturally, actively, and encouragingly with the children while they were still developing and working out their native language. To be sure, many of the children in the group will become proficient in AAE and in MAE without coaching and extra instruction. For others, depending on their schools and experiences, some classroom English lessons will be useful in extending children's language repertoire. In general, in order to move between AAE and MAE, some children will need specific instruction that may sometimes include reference to notions in traditional grammar, such as "agreement," "tense," and "inflection." Other students may make natural transitions due to exposure to MAE and individual language skills, but a good deal may also depend on other factors, such a child's level of AAE use, views about language and identity, and the attitudes toward his/her language that he/she will encounter.

An alternative to quick tips is an instructional plan dedicated to explicit MAE instruction in the context of students' systematic use of AAE patterns. The methodological approach that I will review is framed within the context of the theme of systems of development of AAE. I refer to it as the D.I.R.E.C.T. Model, which has the major goal of teaching students to use the American English variety of the classroom and marketplace, that is MAE, alongside their own native variety by capturing the nuances in the mainstream dialect that they are accustomed to expressing in their native variety. The D.I.R.E.C.T. Model does not use labels such as formal and informal to refer to MAE and AAE respectively. They are characterized as being two different language varieties. One is the language of the marketplace, mainstream, and academia; the other is not. The D.I.R.E.C.T. Model is illustrated in Figure 8.2.

The model is one in which AAE is consistently viewed as a systematic variety, and it can be tailored to instruction involving a single pattern or multiple patterns within the system of the grammar of AAE. It can be taken as a (sketch of a) guide that can be used as part of instructional materials.

D.I.R.E.C.T. — **Roadmap to Understanding AAE and Teaching Students to Use the Language of the Marketplace**

D — **Define African American English (AAE)**

I — **Identify systems, patterns, and use of AAE**

R — **Recognize and respect AAE as rule-governed**

E — **Educate by presenting classroom English correspondences to AAE**

C — **Create an environment that supports the difference**

T — **Transition to awareness of two varieties and additional use of classroom English**

Figure 8.2 The D.I.R.E.C.T. Model

In Figure 8.3 the D.I.R.E.C.T. Model is elaborated to include a specific example of the type of information and data that might be expressed in its component parts.

At the outset, AAE is defined as a variable system with patterns of use of tense–aspect markers. The definition sets up a context in which to address the use of the verbal marker aspectual *be* with consideration of the fact that in AAE, in general, verbal markers are used to indicate information about events and that aspectual *be* falls squarely within that system, and is not haphazard use of *be*. This marker is the one in the system that gives information about the frequency or regularity of an event. It is important to note that although aspectual *be* shares similarities with the copula and auxiliary *BE*, it differs from them in systematic ways.[1] Some of the differences that are reflected in the use of aspectual *be* in child language are underscored in Chapter 3. The final two components, "Create" and "Transition," are directed toward making the connection between the two varieties, AAE and mainstream or classroom English. Within the "Create" component, the point about child

AAE system of time and events in the D.I.R.E.C.T. model with variation awareness

D > Define		AAE is an inherently variable variety that has set patterns of use of temporal markers.
I > Identity		AAE uses verbal markers to indicate information about the way events progress.
R > Recognize		AAE is not haphazard language use; it is not mainstream English "unconjugated" *be* use with mistakes.
E > Educate		AAE *be* marker (within tense/aspect system) indicates meaning about how often an event occurs (e.g., *usually, always*).
C > Create		AAE is the native variety of child speakers, so they should be comfortable using verbal markers where adverbials may occur in mainstream English.
T > Transition		AAE and mainstream English express the same concepts by using different strategies of marking information about events; AAE is variable.

Figure 8.3 AAE tense–aspect in the D.I.R.E.C.T. Model with variation awareness

speakers' being comfortable using verbal markers refers to the children's native use of AAE, in which grammaticalized markers convey information about events. The children will have acquired the system of tense–aspect marking in AAE, so they use the markers naturally and with ease in certain environments. In the "Transition" component, the two varieties are acknowledged, noting that both can express the same concepts, although they may use different types of constructions and sequences of words in doing so. In effect they may use the same inventory of words but with different meanings and functions, and in different combinations.

The "R" component is intended to communicate that negative attitudes toward the variety might be rooted in one's own personal views and preferences, but they cannot be based on the erroneous and uninformed claim that the variety is not systematic. R: "Recognize and respect AAE as rule-governed. AAE is not haphazard language use; it is not mainstream English 'unconjugated' *be* use with mistakes." For some, it is very difficult to move to the point of seeing an unconjugated or uninflected *be* in a sentence without another auxiliary (such as in *They be thinking hard*. 'They usually/generally think hard') as grammatical. In response to such sentences, even some of those who have good intentions make comments such as the following: "The sentence includes an incorrect form which shows that the speakers who use such a sentence do not know how to use conjugated *BE*, or they do not know that it must be conjugated in certain contexts." Also, they may say, "Such sentences should not be used because they cannot convey complex thoughts." Both statements are unconditionally false simply because the sentences are based on a grammar in which a non-conjugated *be* has principled uses. By now, it should be clear that children who use sentences such as the one above, including aspectual *be*, also use conjugated *BE* forms (e.g., *I'm, was*) in sentences where notions of present and past tense are expressed, as is obvious from the data presented earlier. Secondly, it is possible to use such sentences in AAE to express complex thoughts and form complex sentences. Consider how much a 5-year-old has to know in order to be able to distinguish and use the following sentences in appropriate contexts:

> Which box is in the garage?
> Which box be in the garage?

A 5-year-old also has to know that the sentence *Which box in the garage?* is compatible with the first sentence but not with the second, and results presented in Chapter 3 show that children growing up in the AAE-speaking community do distinguish the two. The fact is that people are not trained to teach students to use AAE in writing as they are trained in the use of academic English because of attitudes toward it and views about language standards, but people are trained to discern deviations from MAE as mistakes. I am not advocating for courses that teach writing and analytical skills in AAE. I am just pointing out that AAE has no inherent limitations as a linguistic variety, in the same way that MAE has no inherent advantages as a linguistic variety. In both cases people are trained or conditioned to accept certain views. AAE simply is not the chosen variety of academia, so standards for it have not been established. Of course, there is no incentive for "the academy" to learn about its nuances, so it may be easier to see it as an incorrect or inappropriate use of MAE than it is to see it as a separate variety that could serve the purposes of MAE had it been chosen or had the people who speak it been those in power. The language situation is what it is, and I do not write naively or futilely to effect change. What I hope to communicate is that respecting and recognizing AAE as rule-governed does not suggest that the variety should be thought of as supplanting MAE. It does, however, require acknowledgment that it is a separate system, and that it is illogical to see children who speak it as breaking rules of MAE when their target is AAE. On the other hand, when the target of speech *is* MAE, then the appropriate instructive route should be taken. It is true that if listeners are only familiar with one dialect of English as being governed by rules, then it is easy for them to judge everything they hear by that variety, and if what they hear deviates from their notion of the standard, then the "different" variety must be wrong. Judgment about AAE speakers' use of MAE should be reserved for situations in which speakers are actually using or attempting to use MAE, not when they are speaking another variety. It is a person's prerogative to view AAE negatively, but such views are due to attitudes, and they are not based on evidence or informed investigation. However, no matter how strong negative attitudes are toward AAE, the fact is that AAE is rule-governed as is MAE – in some cases by the same rules and in other cases by different rules.

8.2   OTHER APPROACHES TO MAE

The D.I.R.E.C.T. Model avoids statements that polarize AAE and MAE, in terms of informal vs. formal for example, but such characterizations can be worked into different components of the model, such as in the "Define" and "Transition" components. However, it is important to note that any such descriptors will not be a characterization of the grammatical or inherent patterns of AAE or provide any information about its linguistic structure. The descriptors, on the other hand, will focus specifically on social types of information and standards and norms set by society, such as that having to do with (un)acceptability of the varieties in certain environments.

As Wolfram and Schilling-Estes (1998) explain, labels such as standard and non-standard are also tied to the groups of people who use these registers and to attitudes about what should be accepted as mainstream or standard. Formal and informal are related to the use of certain linguistic features that may mark the register as more formal, where formal may be tied to academic or corporate settings, or informal. In addition, if such labels are used in reference to AAE, it should be made clear that they are ways of characterizing the social status of the variety in comparison or contrast to standard English. For instance, if the label "informal" is chosen as a descriptor for AAE, the nature of "informal" should be explained in terms of whether it means that AAE is used basically in informal or non-academic contexts, what such contexts are taken to be, or whether the variety is assumed to be an informal register of standard English. Such labels may be very useful in terms of the type of message that they are intended to communicate about the social environments in which AAE may be acceptable and when MAE must be used. In this way, the syntactic, phonological, morphological, and semantic patterns are de-emphasized and certain commonly discussed features of AAE are highlighted to show how they differ from the standard features of MAE. In thinking of AAE in these terms, it is easy to take a kind of features-per-utterance approach in which the evaluation is that the child is speaking AAE if he or she uses a feature that is commonly associated with the variety (e.g., absence of morphological third singular verbal –s), or if there are no common AAE features in the utterance, the child has switched to MAE. In actuality, the features-per-utterance approach that determines whether a child has shifted from one variety to the other is an oversimplified way of looking at the language situation mainly because of the inherent variation in AAE, as I have tried to show in Chapter 7. Due to the overlap in features in all varieties of English, AAE will share features with MAE, Appalachian English, and so on. Also, AAE is inherently variable such that speakers may be speaking it, and, in doing so, still use a "feature" that is heard as part of MAE, not because of shifting from AAE to MAE, but because the "feature" is also part of the inventory of AAE as well as other varieties of American English. Some who take this labeling approach are certainly aware of the issues I have mentioned, but they may believe that the advantages of the characterization outweigh any subtleties, generalizations, and explanations that are missed by the descriptors.

A type of labeling related to informal/formal and features-per-utterance approach is assumed in some code-shifting programs that have been put into place in schools. In the instructional approach outlined in Wheeler and Swords's (2006) *Code-Switching: Teaching Standard English in Urban Classrooms*, the authors discuss strategies for teaching standard English to children who use what they refer to as urban language. They do not think that AAE is an appropriate term for the variety they are addressing, so I do not want to equate their variety with the AAE that is the subject of this book, especially because I do not have firsthand data from urban contexts; however, I do want to comment on the labels they use in distinguishing the urban language from standard English. For them, the formal/informal contrast works because the labels meet their criteria of being "simple, positive, and intuitive." Moreover, they report: "First, focusing on the target language, Standard English, we realized that children and vernacular speakers *experience* speaking Standard as a kind of dress-up" (p. 21). They go on to explain their choice of "informal": "We then wanted to make a clear, parallel contrast, to name the child's more natural, comfortable, unmonitored way of using language. That led us to *informal*. These (obviously) are not technical linguistic terms. Instead, with *formal* versus *informal English*, we seek to reach our diverse audience intuitively" (p. 22).

Using my best judgment about what the Wheeler and Swords labels were intended to convey, I suggest that it is easy for the authors to characterize the urban variety as informal because there is little to no emphasis on the variety as a system that children acquire in developmental stages, a system that itself must have ranges from formal to informal. Children who grow up in AAE-speaking communities must also engage in formal activities in those communities, so their language must also have a way of "presenting" in those formal situations. It is important for the authors to be able to make broad appeal, noting that in many classrooms children may use a variety or combination of different forms that may be representative of non-standard English, and teachers may very easily apply the "informal" label to these forms. Also, the "informal" label avoids denigration of the urban language because it carries with it the assumption that the urban language is a viable means of communication, although it is not compatible with classroom English on the formal spectrum.

There is no reason to get bogged down in the business of critiquing labels, but it is very important to be up front about what labels actually suggest and the kind of views that they can perpetuate. To be sure, it is definitely the case that Wheeler and Swords use the labels "formal" and "informal" in the most general sense without any technical or political underpinnings, and others who adopt the terms probably have the same intentions. From my position, it is necessary to talk about the type of (mis)understanding that the formal/informal labels may lead to when the full range of their meanings is not taken into consideration. I say from my position because one of my goals is to show that children may acquire a non-standard English variety as their native language system. When considering that children acquire and use the variety as their day-to-day mode of communication, it is crucial to see it as a complete system that children use for communication in a range of situations. In this way, "informal" must be put into its proper context. The fact is that as a native variety, Wheeler and Swords's urban language, as well as AAE, can span the continuum to be used in the informal and formal contexts the speakers encounter, as native speakers who rely on it must use it. Native speakers of urban language and AAE may styleshift from one end of the urban language and AAE spectrum, respectively, to the other, and the shifts may be characterized by a number of properties, including shifts in intonational patterns as well as shifts in grammatical patterns, although these patterns may not measure up to standard English or to the standards of formal language as people understand it. And, as I hope, Chapter 7 should have reinforced the claim that variable-shifting within the native variety can also take place, leading to the use of compatible MAE constructions. Along these same lines, a similar continuum should be applied to mainstream or classroom English, that ranges from formal, in which "the norms are prescribed for language by recognized sources of authority, such as grammar and usage books, dictionaries, and institutions like language academies" to informal (Wolfram and Schilling-Estes 1998, p. 9). Pronominal case is a clear example of an area in which informal and formal registers in mainstream English can be distinguished. It is possible to use *Who did you see?* and *Between you and I, this is a secret* and still be thought by some to be speaking MAE (or something close enough to it to escape the stigmatized language label), even if the language is taken to be part of an informal register – especially among people who may have grown up in MAE environments but have not paid much attention to "rules." *Whom did you see?* and *Between you and me, this is a secret*, respectively, are corresponding forms that are expected in writing.

On the face of it, the standard or formal and non-standard or informal correlations seem to be intuitive and advantageous; however, they oversimplify the linguistic situations such that it is easy to lose sight of formal to informal, as far as language patterns of non-standard varieties are concerned. Any formal that is associated with the non-standard is not the norm that has been dubbed acceptable in academic contexts. For the approach that I aim to take in this book, labeling the system of AAE as informal has to be qualified with an explanation for a number of reasons. One, as I have noted, is that children developing the variety as their native system can use it in a range of situations for which it is adequate. For many, there has been a tradition of giving "speeches" in churches, and a certain language register – formal in its own right and not standard English – is used. The bottom line is that AAE is used in churches, which is a formal context, and its speakers are not perceived as using an informal register in that environment.

The Los Angeles Unified School District's Academic English Mastery Program (AEMP), directed by Noma Le Moine for twenty years, takes into consideration the native linguistic varieties of children who acquire languages other than MAE as their native variety, so it is necessary to address these languages and language varieties as total systems and not simply as informal varieties. Beyond that step, it is necessary for such a program to take into consideration the fact that these non-native mainstream English speakers have gone through a full acquisition process in developing their native varieties, and certain steps must be taken for them to learn MAE patterns, although their native varieties share many patterns with general English. The AEMP emphasis is beyond the focus on a few contrasts between what may be taken as formal English and the children's varieties of English to the point of moving children to the acquisition of the mainstream variety. In fact, one of the AEMP critical instructional approaches specifically mentions second language acquisition: "Utilize second-language acquisition methodologies to support the acquisition of school language and literacy." Given the growing attention to the link between linguistics and education, more and more research is being conducted in this area, which has relevance for practice in educational contexts (e.g., Charity Hudley and Mallinson 2010).

Different methodological approaches can be used in classrooms in which one of the goals is to provide an alternative classroom language for non-native MAE speakers. A common link that connects some of these different approaches is the attention to code-shifting. That is, there is a growing desire to make code-shifting a part of the academic experience for native AAE-speaking children, especially given the claim that children who can use MAE on different levels fare better in academic settings. However, what is not always clear is the extent to which different approaches actually foster code-shifting, whether they eventually have a replacive effect, such that non-MAE patterns are replaced with MAE patterns or to what extent differences are manifested in the speaker's linguistic output.

Given the prominence of code-shifting in discussions about language use of school-age AAE-speaking children, a number of serious questions should be raised first about what is actually meant by code-shifting in schools and then next about ways to achieve the code-shifting goals. At this point, it is well established that AAE is inherently variable, and it is not always clear when and what variation is part of the AAE system on the one hand or a conscious effort to use MAE on the other, or at least the reports in the literature do not always make the difference. (See the discussion of code-shifting and styleshifting in Baugh (1983).) The answer is not always obvious, especially without some type of recourse to descriptions of AAE. It may be easier to make a code-shifting judgment for some constructions than for others. For instance, consider the two aspectual *be* constructions in (3) and (5) and their corresponding simple tense constructions in (4) and (6), respectively, which can have the same meanings as the aspectual sentences:

3.   I be sleeping all the time.
4.   I sleep all the time.
5.   I be too tired to talk when they call.
6.   I'm too tired to talk when they call.

Clearly (3) and (5) are associated with AAE, but should an AAE speaker who uses (4) and (6) be said to have code-shifted from AAE into MAE when she uses (4) and (6)? It is not automatic that AAE speakers are out of AAE mode when they produce sentences such as (4) and (6).

That is, it is possible for both (3) and (4) and/or (5) and (6) to be part of the AAE grammar, and, in some contexts, they can be used as variants, as I explained in the distinction between intra-dialectal and inter-dialectal shifting in Chapter 7. While (3) and (4) have the same meaning, they might not have the same status with respect to occurrence in AAE for all speakers, so the use of (4) might signal a move to MAE for some speakers but certainly not others. As exemplified in (3), (4) and (5), (6) there are constructions in the AAE grammar that are identical to constructions in MAE (and in other varieties of English); this is the overlap or intertwining in the patterns- and systems-based approach introduced in Chapter 2. When speakers use them, they are not automatically and necessarily making a switch from AAE to MAE. By the same token, some constructions that occur in MAE may not be variants for AAE constructions, so when such MAE constructions are used, that does indeed constitute a shift. These levels of shifting – intra-dialectal and inter-dialectal – must be taken into consideration in descriptive analysis of AAE patterns, and they are clearly important in the context of educational practice.

Research in the area of syntactic variation, how features and patterns of the sentence vary, would definitely be useful in addressing various issues related to code-shifting. One point – among many – that can be made in relation to the examples in (3–6) is that the bottom line is that native AAE-speaking children can still use the AAE code and produce structures that are also in MAE; they do not have to engage in code-shifting to produce MAE-acceptable constructions because of the overlap in AAE and general English variants and the inherent variability of AAE. The simple conclusion is that AAE speakers do not always need to (be taught to) code-shift to produce MAE-acceptable constructions because some of them already exist in their own native grammar. What can be taken away from the conclusion is that it is useful for speakers to know which types of constructions or patterns also pass as MAE and which do not.

8.3   CODE-SHIFTING, VARIABLE-SHIFTING, AND PRE-SCHOOL CHILDREN

AAE is the most widely discussed English variety; however, not as much progress has been made in some areas of research on its linguistic system as in other varieties. The body of research on AAE child language from theoretical, empirical, and practical perspectives continues to grow. For quite some time the focus in discussions about academic success and AAE has been on the school-age group. Now with the growing number of child development centers that service AAE-speaking populations (and other non-native-MAE speakers) and the advantages of building reading and other academic skills into early learning programs, there will be greater efforts to develop materials and instructional strategies for pre-school age groups. From the very early research on AAE, there have always been appeals for educators to take the children's language variety into consideration in instruction to prevent barriers to language of academia that might interfere with students' success (e.g., Baratz and Shuy (1969) and research emanating from the 1979 Ann Arbor Case). In addition the role of phonics and reading instruction for dialect speakers has always been addressed, and it continues to be a theme in discussions about AAE and reading (e.g., Labov 1995, 2006).

In more recent considerations in the area of broadening the language experience of AAE speakers, it is suggested that code-shifting or awareness of the differences between academic language and AAE is very useful in early reading achievement. For instance, Charity, Scarborough, and Griffin (2004) found that in their cohort of African American children from 5 to 8 years, more familiarity with standard English was associated with better reading achievement. If educational programs act on findings such as that in Charity *et al.* (2004), and, as a result, put into place instructional materials and curricula that will broaden language experiences and contribute to intra-dialectal and inter-dialectal shifting abilities and MAE awareness, what would be starting points or target age groups, and what would such materials and curricula entail? I am not in any position to lay out a language curriculum or an instructional plan. However, I would like to note that it is important to move beyond feature lists and to consider descriptions of developmental patterns in making decisions about strategies for broadening children's language experiences or designing literacy-related instructional materials. In future research it will be necessary to take seriously questions about the types of language behavior that code-shifting entails for developing AAE-speaking children. I assume that a goal would be to make AAE-speaking children cognizant of the fact that there is a difference between their native variety and classroom English in some of the ways they natively and intuitively put words together as well as differences in the choices about which words and morphemes can be left out of sentences.

Academic achievement and educational success are topics that seem to loom larger than life in discussions about language and school-age, and now to some extent pre-school-age, AAE-speaking children. When code-shifting is offered as a partial answer to language-related underachievement in education, it is hard to ignore suggestions about incorporating it into educational programs, or at least considering what it might mean to help children become proficient in using MAE-compatible constructions. However, alongside the predictions that skill in code-shifting – and now variable-shifting also needs to be considered – will make a significant difference in non-native-MAE speakers' performance in school, there should also be specific guidelines for code-shifting and variable-shifting instruction and discussions about what it means for pre-school-age children to code-shift, that is, how it interacts with or influences language development. Given the limited research on the acquisition of AAE, basic questions about development of particular patterns are still being raised, and they must be researched, especially given that children develop variation patterns of the community and engage in variable-shifting or intra-dialectal shifting. It is hoped that what we learn about developing AAE will be useful in our thinking about educational opportunities for pre-school-age children in this population. One of the issues with respect to outcomes that should be addressed is the type of changes that are expected in a developing AAE speaker's language as a result of code-shifting and variable-shifting instruction during a time when he or she is still acquiring AAE. Would the code-shifting instruction result in replacing the child's variety with MAE or have other linguistic or non-linguistic effects and consequences, desirable or undesirable? Another related question is the following: What effect, if any, would code-shifting and variable-shifting instruction have on the variation that developing AAE speakers obviously acquire in early developmental stages? Some strong points have been made in the arguments in support of code-shifting instruction for elementary school-age children; however, it is not clear that enough research has been conducted on developmental stages of AAE and code-shifting to call for a plan of code-shifting action and instruction in pre-kindergarten classes.

In many discussions of AAE we revisit the topic of education and academic achievement, often rehashing issues and approaches that have been pursued and addressed in the past. The major reason for the continued focus on some of these issues is that parts of the research simply have not addressed head on the persistent questions and problems, and the proof is in the reports about academic achievement gaps. I have not made any attempts to raise or address the question about whether or the extent to which the use of AAE as a native variety inhibits academic achievement because the questions seem to have already been stated and restated adequately in the literature. My goal has been to lay out some of the patterns of language use in developing AAE-speaking children. My view is that more information about patterns of language use will help to shed light on the systems that children are developing and the subtle as well as ostentatious differences between their native variety and other varieties of American English, including the language of schools. The descriptive analyses of the language samples (from spontaneous speech and elicitation tasks) highlight patterns in the way units are put together to form phrases and sentences, the meaning they convey, and their pragmatic uses. Such information can be used in the D.I.R.E.C.T. model and other types of approaches designed for language-related instruction. Some generalizations about these developmental patterns that might be useful in working through linguistic descriptions of systems of language use in developing AAE speakers and that could be pursued in further research are highlighted below.

8.4 GENERALIZATIONS ABOUT AAE AND PATTERNS OF DEVELOPMENT

1. 3-, 4-, and 5-year-old developing AAE-speaking children show consistent patterns of development of AAE, not imperfect MAE acquisition.

2. Developing AAE-speaking children show signs of development of variation, but it is not always easy to distinguish general developmental patterns from patterns of variation that resemble language use in their communities.

3. Morphological properties of AAE, such as optionality or across-the-board absence of suffixes, may lead to ambiguity, so it is necessary to use context in deriving meaning of AAE constructions.

4. Lack of overt morphological marking for concepts such as past and possessive, for instance, does not mean that children do not comprehend such concepts; they comprehend them, but just do not mark them overtly.

5. Developing AAE-speaking children have a preference for preverbal markers as opposed to morphological endings (e.g., suffixes indicating tense).

6. In addition to developing semantics or meaning of the preverbal markers, children also develop rhetorical and pragmatic uses of the markers.

7. Children also show signs of developing intonational patterns that have been identified in adult AAE, especially in yes–no questions. In the absence of syntactic markers such as subject and auxiliary inversion, the intonation signals "true" question meaning.

8.   Feature lists are useful tools but are limited in the information
      they can provide about developmental trends and systematic
      language use. The lists can promote myths about code-shift-
      ing or inter-dialectal shifting because they present AAE as a
      variety that incorporates only the features on the list, which
      are maximally different from MAE. They do not incorporate
      patterns of overlap between AAE and MAE. This view leads
      to the erroneous assumption that when speakers do not use
      the "marked" features that occur on lists, then they are code-
      shifting into MAE.

9.   Data suggest that some forms are inherently intrinsic to AAE
      grammar and others may not be. The extent to which these
      forms are used have implications for levels of intra- and inter-
      dialectal shifting, or variable- and code-shifting, respectively.

10.   While the tradition has been to focus on features of AAE that
      are maximally different from MAE, there is considerable over-
      lap between the two varieties, which should be taken into con-
      sideration in descriptions of the AAE system. Consequently,
      when children use forms that are compatible with MAE, they
      are not necessarily moving from AAE to MAE or engaging in
      inter-dialectal shifting.

11.   Emphasis seems to be placed on code-shifting or inter-dialectal
      shifting for gains in educational contexts, and some children
      may learn to do it naturally. More research is needed to address
      questions about what it means to introduce code-shifting les-
      sons in pre-kindergarten contexts, especially because there is
      clear evidence showing that at that stage children have not
      acquired AAE fully.

Appendix A: List of participants

Participant	Age	Sex	Speech Community
Akila	5	F	AAE
Alisa	5;3	F	AAE
Alya	3;4	F	AAE
Angelle	5;9	F	AAE
Barry	5	M	AAE
Bethany	3	F	AAE
Bobby	4;1	M	SwLVE
Darnell	5;3	M	AAE
Dawn	5;9	F	AAE
Deon	3;6,3;10	M	AAE
Dina	4;11	F	AAE
Donovan	5	M	AAE
Jabari	4;9	M	AAE
Jamal	4;8	M	AAE
James	5;2	M	AAE
Jamilla	3;6	F	AAE
Jasmine	4;4	F	AAE
Jeffrey	5;7	M	AAE
Joya	5;3,5;7	F	AAE
Julius	4	M	AAE
Kara	4;11	F	AAE
Kendra	4	F	AAE
Kerry	5;11	M	AAE
Lela	3	F	AAE
Lenny	5	M	AAE
Marcus	5;1	M	AAE
Mitchell	5	M	AAE
Myron	5;6	M	AAE
Nia	5;9	F	AAE
Omar	5	M	AAE

Participant	Age	Sex	Speech Community
Rashandra	5	F	AAE
Rashanna	4	F	AAE
Raven	5;1	F	AAE
Ray	5;0	M	AAE
Rayna	4;8,4;11,5;3	F	AAE
Ryan	4	M	SwLVE
Sami	4;7	F	SwLVE
Talia	4;2	F	AAE
Terrell	4;11	M	AAE
Terry	5;11	M	AAE
Thomas	4;6	M	AAE
Tiffini	5;5	F	AAE
Troy	3;7	M	AAE
Tyra	5;3	F	AAE
Tyron	4	M	AAE
Valencia	5;6	F	AAE
Xavier	5;9	M	AAE
Zeke	4;5,4;8, 4;11	M	AAE
Zyrion	5;2	M	AAE

Appendix B

Page 1: The mom went for a walk. She said, "Look after the baby, Carl. I'll be back shortly."

Page 2: Carl looked out the window and watched the mom leave. The baby woke up.

Page 3: The baby climbed out of his crib and onto Carl's back.

Page 4: The baby rode Carl through the hallway and into a room.

Page 5: It was mom's bedroom. Carl jumped on the bed and the baby jumped on the bed. They bounced and bounced.

Page 6: They went to the mom's mirror. The baby put powder on Carl's nose.

Page 7: They played with the makeup and made themselves look pretty. Then they looked in the mirror.

Page 8: Then Carl and the baby went to the laundry chute. A laundry chute is like a slide that takes clothes to the basement to be washed. The baby went down the slide.

Page 9: Carl ran down the stairs to the basement.

Page 10: Carl found the baby in the basement, sitting on a pile of laundry. That was fun!

Page 11: The baby hopped on Carl's back and Carl ran back up the stairs. They went to find more fun things to do.

Page 12: They ran into the living room and slid on the rug. Then they went to look at the fish tank.

Page 13: Carl helped the baby swim in the fish tank. The baby swam around and around.

Page 14: Then Carl went to the stereo. He turned on some music. The baby sat on the floor and watched.

Page 15: Carl danced to the music. The baby watched as he danced and danced.

Page 16: Then they went into the kitchen. The baby was on Carl's back again. Carl opened the refrigerator/ice box.[1]

Page 17: Carl opened the bag of bread. The baby opened a stick of butter.

Page 18: Carl held the grapes and the baby took some. Carl poured chocolate into the baby's cup.

Page 19: Carl poured milk into the baby's cup. The baby got chocolate milk, yum! Then Carl helped the baby get some cookies out of the cookie jar.

Page 20: Ooh. Look at the mess they made. The baby was really dirty.

Page 21: Carl carried the dirty baby upstairs.

Page 22: He turned on the bathwater and put the baby in the tub.

Page 23: He used his mouth to rub soap on the washcloth. And then bubbles came out of his mouth! He used the washcloth to wash the dirty baby.

Page 24: Carl used the hair dryer to dry the baby off. Then he put the baby back in his crib.

Page 25: Carl went back to the kitchen and picked up the bread crust. He put the garbage in the trash and he cleaned up the milk.

Page 26: Carl looked out the window to see if the mom was coming home.

Page 27: Then Carl made the bed and he cleaned up the makeup.

Page 28: Carl saw the mom coming in the gate.

Page 29: He went and lay down by the baby's crib.

Page 30: When the mom came in, Carl was lying quietly.

Page 31: She patted his head and said, "Good dog, Carl."

Notes

I   CHILD AAE: AN INTRODUCTORY OVERVIEW OF THE
      DATA AND CONTEXT

1 The data show that both groups of speakers use expletive *it* followed by *have*, although the type of agreement patterns used by the two groups differs. That is, the AAE-speaking children use *have* as a default verb with first, second, and third person subjects; however, the SwLVE-speaking children also mark third person singular agreement. Also, expletive *it* has been associated with other varieties of AAE in the United States, although it may not be reported as commonly occurring with *have* in those varieties.

2 Instead of using phonetic transcription, I use general orthography to try to capture the relevant part of the pronunciation. The general English spellings of words are given in square brackets [ ], where necessary.

2   CHARACTERIZING AAE: FEATURE LISTS, DUAL
      COMPONENTS, AND PATTERNS AND SYSTEMS

1 The zero form of auxiliary *BE* in the context preceding *finna* is discussed in Chapter 3.

3   SYSTEM OF TENSE–ASPECT MARKING I: NON-PAST
      AND HABITUAL

1 *Good Dog, Carl* is a picture book by Alexandra Day, which features the adventures of a dog (Carl) and baby who spent part of a day together.

2 I have chosen to locate the $\emptyset_{\text{COP}}$ after the subject *he*, so if *be* were pronounced, this would be *He's a boy?* and not *Is he a boy?* My motivations are based on theoretical and empirical notions, which will not be discussed here.

3 The *SpongeBob* pictures were designed to illustrate scenarios that would be used to elicit responses that would provide insight into children's comprehension of certain *be* constructions.

4 Some of the children, such as Rayna, were tested several times at different ages.

5 This example, (14c) in Data Set 5, and (20) in Data Set 6 are similar to (6a) in Data Set 1. I have chosen to indicate the auxiliary and copula positions after the subject and not preceding it. It is also possible to have the following representation: *Why $\emptyset_{\text{AUX}}$ they driving?*

6 In the discussion of narratives in Chapter 4, I will consider contexts that can be interpreted as past, yet *was* is not overt.

7 Montgomery and Mishoe (1999) discuss an uninflected *be* that is used in the Carolinas and shares some similarities with AAE aspectual *be*, but differs from it in systematic ways.

8 The character's name is "Mr. Krab."

4   SYSTEM OF TENSE–ASPECT MARKING 2: PAST TIME

1 Rickford and Théberge-Rafal (1999) is a slightly revised version of Rickford and Rafal (1996), which is published in Rickford (1999).

2 See Wolfram (1991) and Wolfram and Schilling-Estes (1998) for a discussion of *a*-prefix in Appalachian English.

3 Note that in general *have* may not occur in perfect contexts in AAE, as in *She been running* 'She has been running.'

4 *BIN having* may also be used or preferred in AAE speech communities in other regional areas in the United States, but I know of no other reports on this topic of regional variation and the marker.

5 The goal is not to give a detailed analysis of the prosodic properties (e.g., stress, pitch, duration, and intonation) of *BIN*. Here it is just to provide some evidence that the developing child speakers also pay attention to the prosodic and other phonological properties of *BIN* and produce the marker with (some feature-related) stress.

6 A full discussion of the experiment appears in Green and Roeper (2007).

7 Two points should be noted about this question. The first is that it is not written in the form of a *wh*-question (i.e. "Which shoes Bruce BIN had?"). Given a number of factors, I decided to use the non-inverted order for some questions. The second point is that *BIN had* was used instead of *BIN having*, as a means of getting some information about the comprehension of *BIN having/BIN had* in this context.

5   NEGATION: FOCUS ON NEGATIVE CONCORD

1 J. Michael Terry (1999) addresses just this issue in an unpublished manuscript on negative concord in AAE-speaking children.

2 The data in Bellugi's (1967) thesis are from the developmental language of "Adam," "Eve," and "Sarah," who were described as having "heard only standard English and no other language" (p. 3).

6   ASKING QUESTIONS: SEEKING CLARIFICATION AND REQUESTING ELABORATION

1 After listening to the recording several times, judges were not able to hear *to* after *how* in this line.

2 There are cases of *that* occurring without *'s* even in adult AAE where we might expect an overt form, as in the following attested example: *Here you got something that gonna lead you astray.* 'Here you have something that's going to lead you astray.'

3 Also, see references cited in Gunlogson (2008) for more research on the topic.

4 The discussion programs from which the questions were taken were the *McLaughlin Group* and *Washington Week*.

5 For instance, formal theories of intonation and systems for labeling the intonational contours are in Pierrehumbert (1980); Silverman, Beckman, Pitrelli, Ostendorf, Wightman, Price, Pierrehumbert, and Hirschberg (1992); and Pitrelli, Beckman, and Hirschberg (1994).

6 There is no audible *to* between *duck* and *talk*.

7 Early AAE refers to language argued to be spoken in areas settled by free African Americans who migrated from the United States to places such as enclaves in Canada and Samaná, Dominican Republic.

8 Sentences such as (45a) are allowed by some adult speakers; however, others claim that they prefer the NI counterparts (41a) (i.e. *Can't nobody get in this*).

7 VARIATION: INTRA-DIALECTAL/VARIABLE-SHIFTING AND INTER-DIALECTAL/CODE-SHIFTING

1 The names in (11a, b, c) are not the actual names the children produced; however, the pseudonyms are close to the actual names. The examples make the point that the names did not bear genitive marking.

2 Crackling refers to a type of fried pork rind, which is still made in the homes of some people in the South – in this case, Louisiana.

3 When Terry uses "Ock Doc," he almost certainly has the Hasbro character Doc Ock in mind.

8 THE D.I.R.E.C.T. MODEL: LINKING LINGUISTIC DESCRIPTION AND EDUCATION

1 See Green (2000, 2002) for a discussion of aspectual *be*.

APPENDIX B

1 If it was determined before I presented the story description to the child whether he or she used "refrigerator" or "icebox," I used the label the child chose when I read the description.

References

Ambridge, Ben, Caroline Rowland, Anna L. Theakson, and Michael Tomasello 2006. 'Comparing different accounts of inversion errors in children's non-subject wh-questions: what experimental data can tell us?', *Journal of Child Language* 33: 519–557.

Antinucci, F. and R. Miller 1976. 'How children talk about what happened', *Journal of Child Language* 3: 169–189.

Baratz, John and Roger Shuy 1969. *Teaching Black Children to Read*. Washington, DC: Center for Applied Linguistics.

Baugh, John 1980. 'A re-examination of the black English copula', in William Labov (ed.), *Locating Language in Time and Space*. New York: Academic Press, pp. 83–106.

Baugh, John 1983. *Black Street Speech*. Austin: University of Texas Press.

Becker, Misha 2000. 'The acquisition of the English copula', in S. C. Howell, S. A. Fish, and T. Keith-Lucas (eds.), *Proceedings of the 24th Annual Boston University Conference on Language Development, vol. 1*. Somerville, MA: Cascadilla Press, pp. 104–115.

Behrens, Heike 2001. 'Cognitive-conceptual development and the acquisition of grammatical morphemes: the development of time concepts and verb tense', in Melissa Bowerman and Stephen C. Levinson (eds.), *Language Acquisition and Conceptual Development*. Cambridge University Press, pp. 450–474.

Bellugi, Ursula Herzberger 1967. 'The acquisition of the system of negation in children's speech'. Ph.D. diss., Harvard University.

Benedicto, Elena, Lamiya Abdulkarim, Debra Garrett, Valerie Johnson, and Harry N. Seymour 1998. 'Overt copulas in African American English Speaking Children', in A. Greenhill, M. Hughes, H. Littlefield, and H. Walsh (eds.), *Proceedings of the 22nd Annual Boston University Conference on Language Development, vol. 1*. Somerville, MA: Cascadilla Press, pp. 50–57.

Blake, Renée 1997. 'Defining the envelope of linguistic variation: the case of "don't count" forms in the copula analysis of African American vernacular English', *Language Variation and Change* 9: 57–80.

Bohnemeyer, Jurgen and Mary Swift 2004. 'Event realization and default aspect', *Linguistics and Philosophy* 27: 262–296.

Bolinger, Dwight 1957. *Interrogative Structures of American English*. Tuscaloosa: University of Alabama Press (The American Dialect Association)

Bronckart, Jean-Paul and Hermina Sinclair 1973. 'Time, tense, and aspect', *Cognition* 2: 107–130.

Charity, Anne H., Hollis S. Scarborough, and Darion M. Griffin 2004. 'Familiarity with school English in African American children and its relation to early reading achievement', *Child Development* 75: 1340–1356.

Charity Hudley, Anne and Christine Mallinson 2010. *Valuable Voices: Understanding English Language Variation in American Schools*. New York: Teachers College Press.

Cole, Lorraine Theresa 1980. 'Developmental analysis of social dialect features in the spontaneous language of preschool black children', Ph.D. diss., Northwestern University.

Coles, D' Jaris R. 1998. 'Barrier constraints on negative concord in African American English'. Ph.D. diss, University of Massachusetts, Amherst.

Coles-White, D' Jaris 2004. 'Negative concord in child African American English: Implications for specific language impairment', *Journal of Speech, Language, and Hearing Research* 47: 212–222.

Coles-White, D' Jaris, Jill de Villiers, and Tom Roeper 2004. 'The emergence of barriers to wh-movement, negative concord, and quantification', in Alejna Brugos, Linnea Micciulla, and Christine E. Smith (eds.), *Proceedings of the 28th Annual Boston University Conference on Language Development*, pp. 98–107.

Connor, Carol McDonald and Holly Craig 2006. 'African American preschoolers' language, emergent literacy skills, and use of African American English: A complex relation', *Journal of Speech, Language, and Hearing Research* 49: 771–792.

Craig, Holly K. and Julie A. Washington 2004 'Grade-related changes in the production of African American English', *Journal of Speech, Language, and Hearing Research* 47: 450–463.

Craig, Holly and Julie Washington 2006. *Malik Goes to School: Examining the Language Skills of African American Students from Preschool-5th Grade*. Mahwah, NJ: Lawrence Erlbaum Associates, Inc.

Craig, Holly, Julie Washington, and C. Thompson-Porter 1998. 'Performance of young African American children on two comprehension tasks', *Journal of Speech, Language, and Hearing Research* 41: 445–457.

Cukor-Avila, Patrica and Guy Bailey 1995. 'Grammaticalization in AAVE', in J. Ahlers, L. Bilmes, J. Guenter, B. Kaiser, and J. Namkung (eds.), *Proceedings of the Twenty-First Annual Meeting of the Berkeley Linguistics Society*. Berkeley: Department of Linguistics, University of California.

Davis, Henry 1986. 'Syntactic undergeneration in the acquisition of English: wh-questions and the ECP', in S. Berman, J-W. Choe and J. McDonough (eds.), *Proceedings of the Northeast Linguistics Society* 16, McGill University.

Day, Alexandra 1985. *Good Dog, Carl*. New York: Simon and Schuster.

DeBose, Charles and Nicholas Faraclas 1993. 'An Africanist approach to the linguistic study of black English: getting to the roots of the tense-aspect-modality and copula systems in Afro-American', in Salikoko S. Mufwene (ed.), *Africanisms in Afro-American Language Varieties*. Athens, GA: University of Georgia Press, pp. 364–387.

Demuth, Katherine 1998. 'Collecting spontaneous production data', in Dana McDaniel, Cecile McKee, and Helen Smith Cairns (eds.), *Methods for Assessing Children's Syntax*. Cambridge, MA: MIT Press, pp. 3–22.

de Villiers, Jill 1991. 'Why questions', in Thomas L. Maxfield and Bernadette Plunkett (eds.), *Papers in the Acquisition of WH: Proceedings of the UMass Roundtable, May 1990*. Amherst: University of Massachusetts, pp. 155–173.

de Villiers, Jill and Tom Roeper 1996. 'Questions after stories: on supplying context and eliminating it as a variable', in Dana McDaniel, Cecile McKee, and Helen Smith Cairns (eds.), *Methods for Assessing Children's Syntax*. Cambridge, MA: MIT Press, pp. 163–187.

de Villiers, Jill and Valerie Johnson 2007. 'The information in third-person /s/: acquisition across dialects of American English', *Journal of Child Language* 34: 133–158.

de Villiers, Jill, Tom Roeper, and Anne Vainikka 1990. 'The acquisition of long-distance rules', in Lyn Frazier and Jill G. de Villiers (eds.), *Language Processing and Language Acquisition*. Dordrecht: Kluwer, pp. 257–297.

de Villiers, Jill, Peter de Villiers, and Tom Roeper (in press). 'Wh-questions: moving beyond the first phase', *Lingua*.

Dillard, J. L. 1972. *Black English: Its History and Usage in the United States*. New York: Vintage Books.

Estigarribia, Bruno 2007. 'Asking questions: language variation and language acquisition'. Ph.D. diss, Stanford University.

Green, Lisa 1998. 'Remote past and states in African American English', *American Speech* 73: 115–138.

Green, Lisa 1990. 'Intonational patterns of questions in black English: some observations', mimeo, University of Massachusetts.

Green, Lisa 2000. 'Aspectual be-type constructions and coercion in African American English', *Natural Language Semantics* 8: 1–25.

Green, Lisa 2002. *African American English: A Linguistic Introduction*. Cambridge University Press.

Green, Lisa 2004. 'Syntactic and semantic patterns in child African American English', in Fong Chiang, Elaine Chun, Laura Mahalingappa, and Siri Mehus (eds.), *Texas Linguistic Forum vol. 47*: Austin: University of Texas, pp. 55–69.

Green, Lisa 2007. 'Syntactic variation', in Robert Bayley and Ceil Lucas (eds.), *Sociolinguistic Variation: Theories, Methods, and Applications*. Cambridge University Press, pp. 24–44.

Green, Lisa and Tom Roeper 2007. 'The acquisition path for tense-aspect: Remote past and habitual in child African American English', *Language Acquisition* 14: 269–313.

Green, Lisa, Toya Wyatt, and Qiuana Lopez 2007. 'Event arguments and "be" in child African American English', in Toni Cook and Keelan Evanini (eds.), *Penn Working Papers in Linguistics, Papers from NWAV 35*, Vol. 13.2. Philadelphia: University of Pennsylvania, pp. 95–108.

Gunlogson, Christine 2008. 'A question of commitment', in Philippe De Brabanter and Patrick Dendale (eds.), *Commitment*. Amsterdam: John Benjamins, pp. 101–136.

Hedberg, Nancy and Juan Sosa 2002. 'The prosody of questions in natural discourse', *Proceedings of Speech Prosody*. Aix-en Provence, France.

Hedberg, Nancy, Juan M. Sosa, and Lorna Fadden 2006. 'Tonal constituents and meanings of yes-no questions in American English', *Proceedings of Speech Prosody*. Dresden, Germany.

Hendrick, Randall 1982. 'Reduced questions and their theoretical implications', *Language* 58: 800–819.

Henry, Alison 2002. 'Variation and syntactic theory', in J. K. Chambers, Peter Trudgill, and Natalie Schilling-Estes (eds.), *The Handbook of Language Variation and Change*. Oxford: Blackwell, pp. 267–282.

Henry, Alison, Rose Maclaren, John Wilson, and Cathy Finlay 1997. 'The acquisition of negative concord in non-standard English', in E. Hughes, M. Hughes, and A. Green (eds.), *Proceedings of the 21st Annual Boston University Conference on Language Development, vol. 1*. Somerville, MA: Cascadilla Press, pp. 269–280.

Honda, Maya and Wayne O'Neil 2007. *Thinking Linguistically: A Scientific Approach to Language*. Malden, MA: Blackwell.

Horton-Ikard, RaMonda and Susan Weismar 2005. 'Distinguishing African American English from developmental errors in language production of toddlers', *Applied Psycholinguistics* 26: 597–620.

Horton-Ikard, RaMonda and Susan Weismar 2007. 'A preliminary examination of vocabulary and word learning in African American toddlers from middle and low socioeconomic status homes', *American Journal of Speech-Language Pathology* 16: 381–392.

Jackson, Janice 1998. 'Linguistic aspect in African American speaking children: an investigation of aspectual *be'*. Ph.D. diss, University of Massachusetts, Amherst.

Jackson, Janice and Lisa Green 2005. 'Tense and aspectual *be* in child African American English', in Henk Verkuyl, Henriette de Swart and Angeliek van Hout (eds.), *Perspectives on Aspect*. Dordrecht: Springer, pp. 233–250.

Jun, Sun-Ah and Christina Foreman 1996. 'Boundary tones and focus realization in African-American English intonation', talk presented at the third joint meeting of ASA and ASJ.

Kovac, Ceil 1980. 'Children's acquisition of variable features'. Ph.D. diss, Georgetown University.

Labov, William 1969. 'Contraction, deletion, and inherent variability in the English copula', *Language* 45: 715–776.

Labov, William 1972. *Language in the Inner City: Studies in the Black English Vernacular*. Philadelphia: University of Pennsylvania Press.

Labov, William 1995. 'Can reading failure be reversed: a linguistic approach to the question', in Vivian Gadsden and Daniel A. Wagner (eds.), *Literacy Among African-American Youth: Issues in Learning, Teaching, and Schooling*. Cresskill, NJ: Hampton Press, Inc., pp. 39–68.

Labov, William 1998. 'Coexistent systems in African-American vernacular English', in Salikoko S. Mufwene, John R. Rickford, Guy Bailey, and John Baugh (eds.), *African-American Vernacular English: Structure, History and Use*. New York: Routledge, pp. 110–153.

Labov, William 2006. 'Reducing the achievement gap for African American children', a PowerPoint presentation to the Fourth Annual Reading First Superintendents Summit Meeting in San Francisco, CA.

Labov, William and Joshua Waletzky 1967. 'Narrative analysis', in J. Helm (ed.), *Essays on the Verbal and Visual Arts*. Seattle: University of Washington Press, pp. 12–44.

Labov, William, Paul Cohen, Clarence Robbins, and John Lewis 1968. *A Study of the Non-standard English of Negro and Puerto-Rican Speakers in New York City*, 2 volumes. Philadelphia: US Regional Survey.

Montgomery, Michael and Margaret Mishoe 1999. 'He bes took up with a Yankee girl and moved up there to New York: the verb bes in the Carolinas and its history', *American Speech* 74: 240–281.

Oetting, Janna and Janet McDonald 2001. 'Nonmainstream dialect use and specific language impairment', *Journal of Speech, Language, and Hearing Research* 44: 207–223.

Oetting, Janna B. and April Wimberly Garrity 2006. 'Variation within dialects: a case of Cajun/Creole influence within child SAAE and SWE', *Journal of Speech, Language and Hearing Research* 44: 207–233.

Oetting, Janna, B., Julie P. Cantrelle, and Janice E. Horohov 1999. 'A study of specific language impairment (SLI) in the context of non-standard dialect', *Clinical Linguistics and Phonetics*, 13: 25–44.

Ogiela, D. A., M. W. Casby, and C. Schmitt 2005. 'Event realization and default aspect: evidence from children with specific language impairment', in A. Brujos, M. R. Clark-Cotton, and S. Ha (eds.), *Proceedings of the 29th Annual Boston University Conference on Language Development.* Somerville, MA: Cascadilla Press, pp. 425–435.

Olsen, Mari and Amy Weinberg 1999. 'Innateness and the acquisition of grammatical aspect via lexical aspect', in A. Greenhill, H. Littlefield, and C. Tano (eds.), *Proceedings of the 23rd Annual Boston University Conference on Language Development.* Somerville, MA: Cascadilla Press, pp. 529–540.

Pierrehumbert, Janet Breckenridge 1980. 'The phonology and phonetics of English intonation'. Ph.D. diss, MIT.

Pitrelli, John F., Mary E. Beckman, and Julia Hirschberg 1994. 'Evaluation of Prosodic Transcription Labeling Reliability in The Tobi Framework', in *Third International Conference on Spoken Language Processing (ICSLP 94)*, pp. 123–126.

Plunkett, Bernadette 1991. 'Inversion in early wh questions', in Thomas L. Maxfield and Bernadette Plunkett (eds.), *Papers in the Acquisition of WH: Proceedings of the UMass Roundtable, May 1990.* Amherst: University of Massachusetts, pp. 125–153.

Pruitt, Sonja and Janna Oetting 2009. 'Past tense marking by African American English-speaking children reared in poverty', *Journal of Speech, Language, and Hearing Research* 52: 2–15.

Rickford, John R. 1975. 'Carrying the new wave into syntax: the case of black English *been*', in Ralph W. Fasold (ed.), *Variation in the Form and Use of Language.* Washington, DC: Georgetown University Press, pp. 98–119.

Rickford, John R. 1998. 'The creole origin of African American vernacular English: evidence from copula absence', in Salikoko S. Mufwene, John R. Rickford, Guy Bailey, and John Baugh (eds.), *African-American Vernacular English: Structure, History and Use.* New York: Routledge, pp. 154–200.

Rickford, John R. 1999 *African American Vernacular English: Features, Evolution, Educational Implications.* Malden, MA: Blackwell Publishers.

Rickford, John R. and Christine Théberge-Rafal 1996. 'Preterit *had* + V-*ed* in the narratives of African-American preadolescents', *American Speech* 71: 227–254.

Rickford, John R. (with Christine Théberge-Rafal) 1999. 'Preterite *had* + Verb *-ed* in the narratives of African American preadolescents', in John R. Rickford, *African American Vernacular English: Features, Evolution, Educational Implications*. Malden, MA: Blackwell, pp. 34–60.

Roeper, T. 2006. Nodes and features: How the multiple grammar perspective predicts stable and unstable dialects and the order of acquisition. Unpublished ms., University of Massachusetts.

Roeper, Tom 2007. *The Prism of Grammar: How Child Language Illuminates Humanism*. Cambridge, MA: MIT Press.

Roeper, Thomas and Lisa Green, 2007. 'Node labels and features: stable and unstable dialects and variation in acquisition', *Linguistic Variation Yearbook* 7: 1–26.

Ross, Sarah H., Janna B. Oetting, and Beth Stapleton 2004. 'Preterite *had* + V-*ed*: a developmental narrative structure of African American English', *American Speech* 79: 167–193.

Santelmann, Lynn, S. Berk, J. Austin, S. Somashekar, and Barbara Lust 2002. 'Continuity and development in the acquisition of inversion in yes/no questions: dissociating movement and inflection', *Journal of Child Language* 29: 813–842.

Seymour, Harry N. 2004. 'The challenge of language assessment for African-American English-speaking children: a historical perspective', *Seminars in Speech and Language* 25: 1–12.

Seymour, Harry N., Linda Bland-Stewart, and Lisa Green 1998. 'Difference versus deficit in child African American English', *Language, Speech, and Hearing Services in Schools* 29: 96–108.

Seymour, Harry, Tom Roeper, and Jill de Villiers 2000. Dialect Sensitive Language Test. The Psychological Corporation.

Seymour, Harry N., Thomas W. Roeper, and Jill de Villiers, with contributions by Peter A. de Villiers 2003. *Diagnostic Evaluation of Language Variation*™ – Screening Test (DELV™ – Screening Test), Harcourt Assessments.

Seymour, Harry N., Thomas W. Roeper, and Jill de Villiers, with contributions by Peter A. de Villiers 2005. 'Final report 3/1/1998–8/29/2005 NIH contract N01-DC8–2104 – Development and validation of a language test for children speaking non-standard English: a study of children who speak African American English'.

Shirai, Yasuhiro and Roger W. Andersen 1995. 'The acquisition of tense-aspect morphology: a prototype account', *Language* 71: 743–762.

Silverman, Kim, Mary Beckman, John Pitrelli, Mori Ostendorf, Colin Wightman, Patti Price, Janet Pierrehumbert, and Julia Hirschberg 1992. 'TOBI: A standard for labeling English prosody', in Second International Conference on Spoken Language Processing (ICSLP'92), pp. 867–870.

Smith, Carlota 1997. *The Parameter of Aspect*. Dordrecht: Kluwer.

Smith, Carlota 2005. *Modes of Discourse: The Local Structure of Text*. Cambridge University Press.

Smitherman, Geneva 1977. *Talkin and Testifyin: The Language of Black America*. Detroit: Wayne State University Press.

Snyder, William 2007. *Child Language: The Parametric Approach*. Oxford University Press.

Sobin, Nicholas 2003. 'Negative inversion as non-movement', *Syntax* 6: 183–212.

Steffensen, Margaret S. 1974. 'The acquisition of black English'. Ph.D. diss., University of Illinois at Urbana-Champagne.

Stockman, Ida J. 2007. 'Social-political influence on research practices: examining language acquisition by African American children', in Robert Bayley and Ceil Lucas (eds.), *Sociolinguistic Variation: Theories, Methods, and Applications*. Cambridge University Press, pp. 297–317.

Stockman, Ida 2010. 'A review of developmental and applied language research on African American children: From deficit to difference perspectives on dialect difference', *Language Speech and Hearing Services in Schools* 41: 23–38.

Stockman, Ida and Fay Vaughn-Cooke 1982. 'Re–examination of research on the language of working class Black children: The need for a new framework', *Journal of Education* 164: 157–172.

Stockman, Ida and Fay Vaughn-Cooke 1986. 'Implications of semantic category research for the language assessment of nonstandard speakers', *Topics in Language and Language Disorders* 6: 15 25.

Stockman, Ida and Fay Vaughn-Cooke 1992. 'Lexical elaboration in children's locative action constructions', *Child Development* 63: 1104–1125.

Stokes, Nona H. 1976. 'A cross-sectional study of negation structures in black children'. Ph.D. diss., Georgetown University.

Stromswold, Karin J. 1990. 'Learnability and the acquisition of auxiliaries'. Ph.D. diss, MIT.

Stromswold, Karin 1995. 'The acquisition of subject and non-subject wh-questions', *Language Acquisition* 4: 5–48.

Stromswold, Karin 1998. 'Analyzing children's spontaneous speech', in Dana McDaniel, Cecile McKee, and Helen Smith Cairns (eds.), *Methods for Assessing Children's Syntax*. Cambridge, MA: MIT Press, pp. 23–53.

Tarone, Elaine 1972. 'Aspects of intonation in vernacular white and black English speech'. Ph.D. diss., University of Washington.

Terry, J. Michael 1999. 'Interaction between a, the, prosody and negative concord in African American English speaking children 4.4–6.8 years old', mimeo, University of Massachusetts.

Terry, J. Michael 2005. 'The past perfective and present perfect in African American English', in Henk Verkuyl, Henriette de Swart, and Angeliek van Hout (eds.) *Perspectives on Aspect*. Dordrecht: Springer, pp. 217–232.

Terry, J. Michael, E. Evangelou, R. L. Smith, J. E. Roberts and S. A. Zeisel (in press). 'Dialect switching and mathematical reasoning tests: implications for early educational achievement', *Lingua*.

Thomas, Erik 2007. 'Phonological and phonetic characteristics of African American Vernacular English', *Language and Linguistics Compass* 1/5: 450–475.

Van Herk, Gerard 2000. 'The question question: Auxiliary inversion in early African American English', in Shana Poplack (ed.), *The English History of African American English*. Oxford: Blackwell, pp. 175–197.

Van Valin, Robert 2002. 'The development of subject-auxiliary inversion in English wh-questions: an alternative analysis', *Journal of Child Language* 19: 161–175.

Vaughn-Cooke, A. Fay 2007. 'Lessons learned from the Ebonics controversy: implications for language assessment', in Robert Bayley and Ceil Lucas (eds.), *Sociolinguistic Variation: Theories, Methods, and Applications*. Cambridge University Press, pp. 254–275.

Wagner, Laura 2001. 'Aspectual influences on tense', *Journal of Child Language* 28: 661–681.

Walker, James A. 2000. 'Rephrasing the copula: Contraction and zero in early African American English', in Shana Poplack (ed.), *The English History of African American English*. Oxford: Blackwell, pp. 35–72.

Wheeler, Rebecca S. and Rachel Swords 2006. *Code-Switching: Teaching Standard English in Urban Classrooms*. Urbana, IL: National Council of Teachers of English.

Wolfram, Walt 1969. *A Sociolinguistic Description of Detroit Negro Speech*. Washington, DC: Center for Applied Linguistics.

Wolfram, Walt 1974. 'The relationship of southern speech to vernacular black English', *Language* 50: 498–527.

Wolfram, Walt 1991. *Dialects and American English*. Englewood Cliffs, NJ: Prentice-Hall.

Wolfram, Walt 2007. 'Sociolinguistic folklore in the study of African American English', *Language and Linguistics Compass* 1: 1–22.

Wolfram, Walt and Ralph Fasold 1974. *Social Dialects in American English*. Englewood Cliffs, NJ: Prentice-Hall.

Wolfram, Walt and Natalie Schilling-Estes 1998. *American English: Dialects and Variation*. Malden, MA: Blackwell.

Wyatt, Toya 1991. 'Linguistic constraints on copula production in black English child Speech'. Ph.D. diss., University of Massachusetts, Amherst.

Wyatt, Toya 1995. 'Language development in African American child speech', *Linguistics and Education* 7: 7–22.

Wyatt, Toya 1996. 'Acquisition of the African American English Copula', in Alan G. Kamhi, Karen E. Pollock, and Joyce L. Harris (eds.), *Communication Development and Disorders in African American Children: Research, Assessment, and Intervention*. Baltimore: Paul H. Brookes Publishing Co., pp. 95–115.

Yang, Charles 2006. *The Infinite Gift: How Children Learn and Unlearn the Languages of the World*. New York: Scribner.

Index